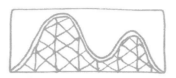

AMUSEMENT PARKS
of New York

JIM FUTRELL

STACKPOLE BOOKS

Published by
STACKPOLE BOOKS
5067 Ritter Road
Mechanicsburg, PA 17055
www.stackpolebooks.com

Printed in the United States of America

10 9 8 7 6 5 4 3 2 1

First Edition

Cover design by Wendy Reynolds

Photographs by the author and other illustrations from the author's collection unless otherwise noted

Library of Congress Cataloging-in-Publication Data

Futrell, Jim.
    Amusement parks of New York / Jim Futrell.
        p.   cm.
    Includes bibliographical references and index.
    ISBN-13: 978-0-8117-3262-8 (pb)
    ISBN-10: 0-8117-3262-2 (pb)
        1. Amusement parks–New York (State)–History.   2. Amusement parks–New York (State)–Guidebooks.   I. Title.

GV1853.3.N7A68   2006
791.'06'809747–dc22

2005020548

CONTENTS

FOREWORD

NEW YORK STATE IS HOME TO AN EXTENSIVE COLLECTION OF AMUSEMENT parks and attractions. Whatever direction you go, from the Big Apple to the Niagara Frontier, from the Adirondacks to the Finger Lakes, you will have no trouble finding a park that suits your particular style and taste. With family-owned and -operated parks, corporate theme parks, and everything in between, New York has it all.

From a historical perspective, the state can point with pride to Coney Island as the birthplace of the American amusement park industry. Coney Island began operation in the early 1800s and continues to entertain guests today with such nationally known landmarks as the Wonder Wheel and the Cyclone. The modern-day theme park also owes a debt to the trend-setting work done at places like Santa's Workshop and the Great Escape, where whole parks were built up around a single theme. New York parks have an outstanding legacy of longevity, with places like Seabreeze in operation since 1879 and the Enchanted Forest since 1956.

The state's amusement parks offer an incredible variety of entertainment options for families. You can go camping, stay in a hotel, take in a concert, or enjoy the attractions at Six Flags Darien Lake. Enjoy some cotton candy or ice cream and stop to play some skill games as you walk down the midway at Nellie Bly Park, or Sylvan Beach. If you enjoy water parks, Long Island's Splish Splash is consistently rated one of the best in the country. For coaster fans, New York has its share of memory makers, such as the Comet, the Jack Rabbit, and Superman.

Every year, parks across the state are proud to open their doors and entertain you. From state-of-the-art coasters to classic carousels, at traditional and theme parks alike, New York's parks truly have something to offer everyone. I encourage you to get out and discover that for yourself.

Rob Norris
President, Seabreeze Park
Chairman, International Association
   of Amusement Parks and Attractions, 2006

ACKNOWLEDGMENTS

NO BOOK IS POSSIBLE WITHOUT THE SUPPORT OF NUMEROUS INDIVIDUALS. This one is no different. From the amusement parks themselves to their employees to the support and encouragement provided by family, friends, and coworkers, this book was the result of more than my efforts. Were it not for the generosity of the following people, this book would not have been possible.

Thanks would have to start with Kyle Weaver of Stackpole Books, who came up with the idea of a series of books profiling America's amusement parks. Thanks also have to go to his assistant, Amy Cooper, for all her hard work.

The owners and staff of New York's amusement parks were very cooperative, and I am certainly grateful for all their assistance: John Norris, Rob Norris, Jeff Bailey, and Matthew Caulfield of Seabreeze; Pat Goodenow of Sylvan Beach Amusement Park; Janice and Michael Walsh of Midway Park; Peter Tartaglia, Sally Reilly, and Pat Vinci of Playland; Bob Reiss and Stephanie Gates of Santa's Workshop; David Hoffman of Hoffman's Playland; Jennifer Mance of the Great Escape & Splashwater Kingdom; Katie and Tim Noonan of Enchanted Forest/Water Safari; Mike McGwire and Martin DiPietro of Martin's Fantasy Island; Steve Gentile of Adventureland; Jen Gapay, Carol Hill-Albert, and Mark Blumenthal of Astroland; Jack Gillette of Magic Forest; Gena and Antoinette Romano of Nellie Bly Amusement Park; Lauren Spallone and Linda Taylor of Six Flags Darien Lake; Dennis Vourderis of Deno's Wonder Wheel Park; Kathryn Schultz of Catskill Game Farm; Jay Goodwin of Harris Hill Park;

Diane and Melinda Novak of Long Island Game Farm; Glen Taus of Fun Zone; Rosemary Sansone of Olcott Carousel Park; and Frank Dillon of Victorian Gardens.

I also thank Tom and Bobbie Wages for sharing their memories of the Great Escape and Martin's Fantasy Island; Scott Merrill for reminiscing about Harris Hill Park; Charlie Denson for his memories of Coney Island; and Jim Abbate and George LaCross for their knowledge of New York amusement park history.

Thanks are due as well to my family and friends for all their support during the two-year process of making this book a reality. In particular, I would like to recognize my sister Mary for her editing expertise, and Dave, Terry, and David Hahner for their help in choosing the pictures.

Four people deserve my special gratitude for making this book a reality: my wife and best friend, Marlowe, and our sons, Jimmy, Christopher, and Matthew. They share and appreciate my passion for amusement parks, and I hope they will always remember the good times we had exploring the delightful variety in New York

Finally, I would like to give a special thank-you to my parents, Jim and Jo Anne Futrell. When I was a young kid, just starting to discover my amusement park passion, they never dismissed my interest and went out of their way to encourage and support it. They will always have a special place in my heart for that.

INTRODUCTION

NO STATE WAS MORE CRITICAL TO THE DEVELOPMENT OF THE AMERICAN amusement park industry than New York. The industry was born at Coney Island. At its peak in the late 1800s and early 1900s, this park inspired operators all over the world, who looked to it for the latest ideas, while entrepreneurs flocked there to test their mettle. Though Coney Island's size and stature have greatly diminished over the past fifty years, it remains a must-see for its remaining historic attractions and oceanfront atmosphere.

But New York's contribution to history does not stop at Coney Island. Seabreeze Amusement Park, Sylvan Beach Amusement Park, and Midway Park are all thriving after more than a century of operation, creating memories for new generations with their nostalgic atmospheres. New York even played a critical role in the development of today's theme park industry. Playland, now a national historic landmark with its Art Deco architecture and vintage rides, was the first totally planned amusement park, foreshadowing the carefully planned theme parks by three decades. Places like Santa's Workshop and the Great Escape helped build the industry by breaking new ground in postwar America, introducing themed environments and attractions that are now taken for granted.

New York today offers a tremendous variety of amusement parks, ranging from Six Flags Darien Lake, a large corporate-owned theme park, to Hoffman's Playland and Harris Hill Amusement Park, two of the last of the 1950s kiddielands. Through a trip around the state, you can almost trace the development of the American amusement park.

But what also sets the New York amusement industry apart is the abundance of family-owned facilities. Though the huge corporate-owned theme parks dominate the industry, family-owned parks continue to flourish in New York. Of the twenty-two parks profiled in this book, only seven are not owned by a family, and two of those passed into corporate ownership only after being established as successful family-owned operations. They are not just businesses, they are cherished family heirlooms, each with its own personality.

Each of New York's amusement parks, large or small, family- or corporate-owned, has a special story behind it, representing the dreams and hard work of generations of individuals. I have tried to convey those stories so that you can truly appreciate each park's personality when you visit.

Before you venture out, here are a few general tips to make your day more enjoyable:

- *Check the website.* Most parks have websites that provide up-to-date information. Always confirm hours and prices right before your visit. You can also check for special events and promotions; many offer discount coupons or reduced-price tickets.

- *Dress comfortably.* Make sure you wear comfortable shoes that are broken in. Wear cool, loose-fitting clothes, but not too loose, as they might get caught on something. Take along a jacket and a rain poncho, just in case.

- *Pack lightly.* You're going to be walking around all day, so don't weigh yourself down with a lot of stuff. Many parks have lockers where you can store things you might need during the day.

- *Eat a good breakfast.* Arriving at the park hungry means that you might waste time that could otherwise be spent riding. Don't stuff yourself with greasy food, however, which doesn't mix well with rides.

- *Arrive early.* Typically the best time of day at an amusement park is the first hour it's open, before the bulk of the people show up. This is often the best time to ride some of the big rides.

- *Hit the big rides first.* While most visitors tend to rush to the big rides first, the lines will only increase as the day wears on, although they usually grow shorter in the evening, when the roller coasters tend to be running faster. Try to avoid the big rides between noon and 5 P.M.

- *Follow the rules.* All parks have certain rules and regulations and set height limits for certain rides and attractions. A great deal of thought has gone into developing these limits, and they are there to protect you. Please respect them. Also note that in the state of New York, a rider responsibility act requires customers to follow posted rules and regulations.

One of the great things about amusement parks is that they are constantly evolving and changing. Though every effort had been made to ensure the accuracy of this book, some changes may have occurred.

A History of the Amusement Park Industry

HUMAN BEINGS ARE, BY NATURE, SOCIAL CREATURES. SINCE THE BEGIN-
ning of time, people have sought ways to come together and escape the
pressures of everyday life. As humankind started to settle in villages,
festivals and celebrations became popular ways for the community to
relax. As villages grew into cities, parcels of land were set aside as sort
of a permanent festival. In medieval Europe, these places were known
as pleasure gardens.

In the 1500s and 1600s, pleasure gardens sprang up on the outskirts of
major cities. At a time when Europe's cities were crowded, dirty, disease-
ridden places, these pleasure gardens provided a welcome respite. In
many ways, they were similar to today's amusement parks, offering landscaped gardens, live entertainment, fireworks, dancing, games, and even
primitive amusement rides, including the forerunners of today's merry-
go-rounds, Ferris wheels, and roller coasters.

Pleasure gardens remained extremely popular until the late 1700s,
when political unrest and urban sprawl caused a decline that lasted
until the mid-1800s. While most of the pleasure gardens are now faded
memories, two still exist. Dyrehavs Bakken, which opened in 1583 outside Copenhagen, Denmark, is the world's oldest operating amusement
park, and the Prater in Vienna, Austria, got its start in 1766 when the
emperor turned a portion of his private hunting preserve over to public amusement.

Coming to America

As the pleasure garden was dying out in Europe, a new nation, the United States, was growing into a world power. Immigrants flocking to cities such as New York, Philadelphia, and Boston clamored for recreation. Entrepreneurs responded by developing picnic groves and beer gardens throughout America.

Jones Woods, widely accepted as America's first large amusement resort, opened along the East River in New York in the early 1800s. Jones Woods' popularity was short-lived, however, as the rapid growth of Manhattan soon overtook the resort.

The continuing demand for amusement was soon answered in the outlying boroughs of New York—in particular, on a peninsula in Brooklyn known as Coney Island. The seaside location provided a cool getaway in the hot summer months, and in 1829, a hotel catering to visitors appeared on the sands. By the early 1850s, pavilions offering bathing, dining, and dancing were being constructed. In 1875, a railroad to the resort was completed, and the destination's popularity quickly increased. Entrepreneurs responded by opening cabarets, vaudeville theaters, fortune-telling booths, games, and rides such as small carousels. Throughout its history, however, Coney Island was never an amusement park. Rather, it was a neighborhood in Brooklyn that featured a collection of amusements.

Early amusement resort growth was not confined to New York. In 1846, large crowds gathered at a family farm in Bristol, Connecticut, to

Manila Park in Lansdale, PA, was typical of the early low-key trolley parks.

view a failed science experiment. The size of the crowd convinced the farm's owner, Gad Norton, that there was a big need for a recreational gathering place in central Connecticut. Norton converted his farm into an amusement resort called Lake Compounce, where people could enjoy picnicking, boating in the lake, listening to band concerts, and dancing. Today Lake Compounce continues as the oldest operating amusement park in the United States. Another early amusement resort, called Rocky Point Park, opened in nearby Warwick, Rhode Island, in 1847. This seaside resort continued to operate until 1995.

In the years following the Civil War, the personality of the country changed as America's cities became increasingly congested and industrialized. Farmers flocked to the cities to find jobs in the new factories. The growing congestion encouraged many to seek out recreation away from the cities. Many amusement resorts opened along the ocean shore or by a lake, where people could find a cool getaway in the hot summer. But the primary engine for the development of the amusement park in America was the trolley company.

In the wake of the opening of the first practical electric-powered street rail line in Richmond, Virginia, in 1888, hundreds of trolley lines popped up around the country almost overnight. At that time, utility companies charged the trolley companies a flat fee for the use of their electricity. The transportation companies looked for a way to stimulate weekend ridership to make the most of their investment. Opening an amusement resort provided the ideal solution. Typically built at the end of the trolley line, these resorts initially were simple operations consisting of picnic facilities, dance halls, restaurants, games, and a few amusement rides. These parks were immediately successful and soon opened across America.

Becoming an American Institution

The amusement park became an institution in the wake of the 1893 World's Columbian Exposition in Chicago. This world's fair introduced the Ferris wheel and the amusement midway to the world. The midway, essentially a wide walkway lined with a variety of rides, shows, and concessions, was such a financial success that America's burgeoning amusement park industry started adding more action-packed attractions. It would dictate amusement park design for the next sixty years.

The following year, Capt. Paul Boyton borrowed the midway concept and opened the world's first modern amusement park, Paul Boyton's Water Chutes, on Chicago's South Side. Boyton was a colorful figure who served in the Union navy during the Civil War and fought in the Franco-Prussian War. In 1874, he stowed away on an ocean liner with the intent of jumping overboard 200 miles out to sea to test an "unsinkable" rubber lifesaving suit. He was apprehended but was eventually permitted by the captain to jump overboard 30 miles off the coast of Ireland. Boyton made it safely to land and achieved international fame. He followed that accomplishment by becoming the first person to swim the English Channel. In 1888, he settled in Chicago, where he started an aquatic circus and raised sea lions in Lake Michigan. Soon he came across a Shoot the Chutes water ride in Rock Island, Illinois, where it had been invented in 1889. Boyton was intrigued by the simple ride, in which a boat traveled down an inclined plane into a body of water. This was the first major water-based amusement ride and the forerunner of today's log flumes and splash-down rides. Boyton purchased the rights to Shoot the Chutes and tested it in London in 1893 before setting it up in Chicago as the centerpiece of his new park.

Unlike the primitive trolley parks, which were just starting to come into their own, Boyton's Water Chutes was the first amusement park to charge admission and use rides as its main draw, rather than picnic facilities or a natural feature such as a beach or lake. Patrons from all over Chicago flocked to Captain Boyton's operation to ride the 60-foot-tall Water Chutes. More than five hundred thousand people showed up in that first season alone. Boyton's park relocated to a larger site in 1896, but it closed in 1908, eclipsed by larger and more modern facilities. However, the success of his Chicago park inspired him to try his luck at the burgeoning center of the amusement universe—Coney Island. There he opened a similar facility, Sea Lion Park, in 1895, the first of Coney Island's great amusement parks. The park featured not only a water chute ride, but also the Flip Flap, one of the first looping roller coasters, and a sea lion show that foreshadowed those at today's theme parks.

With the opening of Sea Lion Park, Coney Island entered its glory era. This was followed by the 1897 opening of Steeplechase Park, with its well-manicured gardens and signature Steeplechase ride, which allowed patrons to experience the thrills of a horse race by riding wooden horses along eight parallel, undulating tracks. Following the 1902 season, Boyton sold his now-struggling operation to businessmen Frederick Thompson and Elmer Dundy, who had parlayed a successful run at the Pan American Exposition in Buffalo, New York, in 1901, into a stint at Steeplechase, where they operated their Trip to the Moon, one of the first simulator attractions. The pair sought to transform Sea Lion Park into an amusement park the likes of which had never been seen before, renaming it Luna Park. The new park was characterized by its fanciful "Arabian Nights" style of architecture outlined by 250,000 electric lights.

When it opened in May 1903, Luna Park represented a new genre of amusement park known as the exposition park, which looked to the

THE "CHUTES"—Jackson Blvd. and Kedzie Ave.—CHICAGO.

Paul Boyton's Water Chutes in Chicago was the first amusement park to feature rides as its main draw when it opened in 1894.

Chicago World's Fair for inspiration. These parks featured elaborate buildings with fanciful designs outlined by thousands of electric lights. They offered attractions that were considered very complex for their time, such as re-creations of famous disasters, scaled-down replicas of distant lands, and displays of prematurely born infants being cared for with technology so advanced that even hospitals had yet to install it. Unlike the more pastoral trolley parks, exposition parks tended to be raucous, packed with attractions and located close to urban centers. Among the more famous exposition parks were White City in Chicago (opened in 1905); Luna Park in Pittsburgh (1905); Luna Park in Cleveland (1905); and Wonderland near Boston (1906). While most larger cities featured an exposition park, the phenomenon was largely short-lived because of high overhead and the cost of the elaborate new attractions they continually added. However, one remains in operation: Lakeside Park in Denver, which opened as White City in 1908 and still features its elaborate Tower of Jewels.

Perhaps the grandest exposition park of them all was Dreamland, which opened across the street from Coney Island's Luna Park in 1904. Dreamland tried to top Luna Park in every respect. A 375-foot-tall tower stood at the center of the park, the buildings were outlined with a million electric lights, and the entire place was adorned with elaborate facades, fountains, pools, and floral displays. With the opening of Dream-

392. General View of the White City taken from Chutes, Denver, Colo.

Denver's White City, now known as Lakeside Park, is the last exposition park still in operation.

land, Coney Island was at its zenith, with three immense amusement parks and dozens of individual concessions catering to the millions that flocked there.

Unfortunately, this glory was not to last. In 1911, a huge fire completely destroyed Dreamland. Soon Luna Park was bankrupt, and the city of New York started replacing amusements with housing complexes and infrastructure upgrades such as wider streets and the boardwalk. Luna Park was lost to fire in 1944, and Steeplechase closed in 1964. By then many of the independent amusements, bathhouses, and concessions in the neighborhood were falling victim to arson and decay. But these problems failed to completely destroy the storied resort, and over the past twenty years, it has slowly rebounded. Although a fraction of its original size, Coney Island is now enjoying a renewed appreciation with its surviving vintage attractions, such as the 1920 Wonder Wheel and the 1927 vintage Cyclone roller coaster, both now listed as national landmarks.

The success of Coney Island during the early part of the twentieth century helped spread the amusement park industry throughout the country. Trolley companies, breweries, and entrepreneurs opened parks by the hundreds. The number of operating parks grew from approximately 250 in 1899 to nearly 700 in 1905. By 1919, more than 1,500 amusement parks were in operation in the United States. In 1913, *World's Work* magazine described the growth as "a hysteria of parks followed by a panic."

Billboard magazine sounded a cautionary message in 1909: "The great profits made by some of the park men produce a mania for park building, which can well be compared to some of the booms in mining camps. Men from almost all professions of life flocked to this endeavor, and without knowledge or particular ability in this line endeavored to build parks." Soon every major city had at least one major park.

Amusement parks during this time had a much different personality than they do today. A review of the industry by *Billboard* in 1905 summed up the keys to a successful attraction as "plenty of shade, attractive landscaping, sufficient transportation, first class attractions (live entertainment) and a variety of good up to date privileges," as rides and concessions were then known. Rides were almost an afterthought in the article, mentioned only after an in-depth discussion of the importance of a summer theater, presenting summer stock, vaudeville, and concerts, which it considered to be the heart of the park. But that personality would soon change.

The Golden Age

With amusement parks opening at such a rapid pace in the early twentieth century, patrons were looking for more thrilling attractions, and soon a whole new industry sprang up to fulfill this need. The William F. Mangels Company was founded at Coney Island in 1890 and in 1914 introduced the whip, one of the first mass-produced rides. The Eli Bridge Company started operations in 1900 and to this day continues to manufacture the Ferris wheels that are a midway staple. Other companies founded during this period include the Philadelphia Toboggan Company, one of the largest manufacturers of roller coasters and carousels, which started making rides in 1904. In 1912, the Dayton Fun House Company was formed. This company was the forerunner to National Amusement Devices and, later, International Amusement Devices, one of the largest and most prolific builders of amusement rides before folding in the mid-1980s. The Dodgem Corporation opened in 1919 in Salisbury Beach, Massachusetts, introducing bumper cars to amusement parks.

In the competition to sell the most rides, innovation was the watchword of the era. Riverview Park in Chicago built a roller coaster called the Potsdam Railway in 1908, with the cars suspended beneath the track rather than riding above it. In 1912, John Miller, the most prolific ride builder of his era, patented a system of holding a roller coaster to the track that remains in use to this day. This new system, called underfriction, made it impossible for roller coasters to leave the tracks, forever changing the nature of roller coasters from mild-mannered scenic railways to true thrillers.

New technology such as the wide-scale rollout of underfriction roller coasters converged with the booming economy and the newfound popularity of the automobile in the 1920s to drive the amusement park industry into its golden age. As most trolley companies had long since divested their amusement park operations, a whole new generation of entrepreneurs flocked to the industry, building amusement parks that catered to the automobile trade. The automobile led to the closing of dozens of smaller amusement parks throughout the country that were unable to provide large parking lots, the surviving parks boomed, and thrill rides were the primary draw. America was in a mood to play, and there was an insatiable demand for thrills and entertainment at America's amusement parks.

Business continued booming through the 1920s, and amusement parks were constantly looking for new ways to thrill patrons. Roller coasters became larger and more thrilling, and every year a new ride was introduced to the masses. The Tumble Bug, a large ride featuring cars traveling along a circular undulating track, immediately became a favorite upon its invention in 1925. In 1926, Leon Cassidy constructed the first rail-guided dark ride at Tumbling Run Park in Bridgewater, New Jersey, leading to the formation of the Pretzel Amusement Company, a major manufacturer of dark rides. The Tilt-A-Whirl was also introduced to the midway that year. In 1929, inspired by the Winter Olympic bobsled tracks, Norman Bartlett introduced the Flying Turns, a roller coaster whose trains traveled down a trough rather than on tracks, at Lakeside Park in Dayton, Ohio.

Enterprising businessmen were not the only ones getting involved in the industry. In 1928, Westchester County, New York, recognizing the value of having a recreational community gathering place, acquired a collection of ramshackle amusements along the shores of Long Island Sound and replaced them with Playland. Unlike most amusement parks of the era, which had gradually evolved over several decades, Westchester County carefully laid out Playland to provide the optimal mix of rides and attractions. This precise planning was a predecessor to the design of the large corporate theme parks that would open three decades later. The basic design of Playland has changed little to this day, although many of the rides and attractions have been updated to appeal to new generations.

Hard Times

As Playland was setting new design standards for the amusement park industry, the stock market crash of 1929 drove America into the Great Depression. With unemployment peaking at 33 percent, consumers had little money to spend on entertainment, let alone a day at an amusement park. The Depression took a horrible toll on the industry, and hundreds of parks closed across the country. By 1935, only four hundred amusement parks remained open. With capital virtually nonexistent, parks did whatever it took to hang on. Popular strategies to attract crowds included food giveaways and live entertainment, or "flesh shows," as they were known. Not all was bleak, as this became the golden age of big bands, which toured amusement parks from coast to coast. The crowds that big bands attracted were credited with saving dozens of amusement parks during the 1930s.

Fortunately, things did improve, and amusement parks slowly started to get back on track by the late 1930s. Long-deferred maintenance was performed, and new attractions were added. But dark clouds were looming on the horizon once again. In late 1941, America entered World War II, and soon the resources of the nation were focused on the war effort.

The war was a mixed blessing for the amusement park industry. On one hand, with the economy booming in support of the war effort, patrons flocked to amusement parks located near industrial centers and military installations, providing a much-needed cash infusion for the parks. At the same time, gasoline rationing severely hindered operation at parks not easily reached by using public transportation. In fact, many parks closed for the duration of the war and in some cases never reopened. Also, with the nation's industrial output fully focused on wartime production, amusement parks could not add new rides, and material shortages made maintenance of existing rides difficult.

When World War II finally ended, America and the amusement park industry enjoyed a period of postwar prosperity. Attendance and revenues grew to record levels, and new parks opened across the country. But the world was a rapidly changing place. Veterans sought to capture their portion of the American dream and start families. Many flocked to the suburbs. Entrepreneurs reacted by developing a new concept that soon became as much of a fixture in suburbia as the tract home—the kiddieland, a special amusement park featuring rides just for kids. The concept had actually been developed in 1925, when C. C. Macdonald opened the Kiddie Park in San Antonio, Texas, which remains in operation. Kiddielands grew from fewer than two dozen in 1950 to more than 150 operating throughout the country by 1960. They were located mainly in large cities such as New York, Chicago, and Los Angeles. Even the primary monument to suburbia, the shopping center, got into the act as several constructed their own kiddielands, with the first opening at Northgate Mall in Seattle in 1950. The kiddieland boom was short-lived. Rising property values and an aging target market shut most of them down by the late 1960s. Though some grew into full-fledged amusement

San Antonio's Kiddie Park was the original kiddieland when it opened in 1925.

parks, fewer than a dozen kiddielands from this era remain in operation today, including Pixie Playland, Concord, California; Funland, Idaho Falls, Idaho; Hoffman's Playland, Latham, New York; and Memphis Kiddie Park, outside Cleveland.

As Americans were flocking to the suburbs, the core of the industry, the large urban amusement park, was being left behind in the face of aging infrastructure, television, urban decay, and desegregation. Coming off the capital constraints of the Depression and World War II, many parks were struggling to update and stay competitive. It seemed that these parks were becoming increasingly irrelevant as the public turned elsewhere for entertainment. What was needed was a new concept to reignite the industry, and that new concept was Disneyland.

The Theme Park Era

By the 1950s, Walt Disney was an internationally renowned filmmaker. He often spent Sunday afternoons with his kids at a local amusement park, lamenting the fact that there was nothing that the family could enjoy together. Disney initially considered building a small entertainment facility at his movie studio, featuring a train, boat and stagecoach rides, a Wild West town, and a circus. But as his dream grew, so did the size of the project.

When Disneyland first opened in 1955 on a former orange grove in Anaheim, California, many people were skeptical that an amusement park without any of the traditional attractions would succeed. There were no roller coasters, no swimming pool or beach, and no midway games. Instead of a midway, Disneyland offered five distinct themed areas—Main Street, Adventureland, Frontierland, Fantasyland, and Tomorrowland—providing guests with the fantasy of travel to different lands and times. Disneyland was an immediate success, attracting nearly 4 million people in its first year of operation. The theme park era was born.

Says Robert Ott, former chairman of Dorney Park in Allentown, Pennsylvania: "Disney changed so many things—the way parks are organized, cleanliness, the use of lights and colors. He catered to the customer, made them happy. His magic flowed into amusement parks. We all benefited from it." Carl Hughes, chairman emeritus of Kennywood, one of America's best remaining traditional parks, concurs: "The standards changed. You couldn't get away with dirty midways and surly employees." It was a whole new era of the amusement park industry.

Though Disneyland is often given credit for being the first theme park, the concept had actually been evolving for more than a decade before Disneyland, as several smaller attractions opened that embraced a single theme. Many of these attractions, which helped inspire Disney, are still in operation today. These include Knott's Berry Farm in Buena Park, California, which started building its Ghost Town in 1940; Holiday World (originally Santa Claus Land), which opened in 1946 in Santa Claus, Indiana; Santa's Workshop, North Pole, New York, which started in 1949; and Great Escape (formerly Storytown USA) in Lake George, New York, which first welcomed visitors in 1954.

As important as the opening of Disneyland was, another event was also critical in changing the face of the industry in the 1950s. In 1958, the industry trade association, then known as the National Association of Amusement Parks, Pools and Beaches, took a tour of Europe. Since the European industry was largely wiped out during World War II, it had been rebuilding with a level of sophistication not yet found in American parks—intricate flowerbeds, elaborate landscaping, and flashy new rides adorned with thousands of electric lights. "That trip changed the industry," Ott recalls. "We brought back new and more sophisticated ideas." While these new ideas created an even more complex industry in America, implementing them was quite expensive. For parks struggling to come back from the Depression and World War II, it was too much.

The excitement created by Disneyland and the ideas from Europe opened a new era for American amusement parks, but the industry suffered some growing pains. A variety of parks attempted to cash in on Disney's concept, but many lacked the appeal of Disney or simply did not have the financial resources. In 1958, Magic Mountain opened west of

Denver when it was only partially completed, and it closed almost immediately. It later reopened and now exists as a shopping village with a few rides. Pacific Ocean Park, widely credited with making the pay-one-price admission an industry standard, opened in Ocean Park, California, in 1958 with the backing of CBS, but collapsed under high maintenance bills in 1968. Pleasure Island debuted near Boston in 1959, but it could never get its main attraction, a giant robotic replica of Moby Dick that was supposed to rear out of a body of water, to work properly. It closed in 1969, never achieving its hoped-for popularity. But the most spectacular failure was Freedomland in the Bronx. Built in the shape of the United States, the park opened in 1960, incomplete and over budget. It was plagued by problems from the beginning, finally collapsing in 1964 under a mountain of debt.

It wasn't until 1961, when Six Flags Over Texas opened between Dallas and Fort Worth, that another major theme park was finally successful. Backed by the land development firm Great Southwest Corporation, the park was the first in what today is the largest theme park chain in the world. Six Flags adapted traditional amusement park rides to a theme park, introducing the log flume to the industry in 1963 and building the first Runaway Mine Train roller coaster in 1966.

Following on the success of Six Flags, which proved that the theme park was a viable concept apart from Disney, theme park development took off. Between 1964 and early 1965, fifteen theme parks opened, and

Pleasure Island, outside Boston, was one of the many failed attempts to capitalize on the success of Disneyland.

The Racer at Kings Island, outside Cincinnati, introduced the wooden roller coaster to the theme park.

Amusement Business magazine reported that twenty additional projects were in the works. While these tended to be smaller, short-lived road-side attractions, the success of Six Flags had caught the attention of major corporations such as Clairol, Penn Central, ABC, Marriott, Taft Broadcasting, and Mattel, which were soon planning their own parks. Even Bob Hope considered opening a theme park in Los Angeles in the 1960s. Among the major parks opening during this time were the first Sea World theme park, which debuted in San Diego in 1964; Six Flags Over Georgia in Atlanta in 1967; Astroworld in Houston in 1968; Magic Mountain near Los Angeles, Six Flags Over Mid-America outside St. Louis, and the immense Walt Disney World in Florida, all in 1971; and Opryland in Nashville in 1972. What these parks had in common was a location close to interstate highways on the outskirts of town, high standards of design and operation, and disdain for traditional amusement park attractions such as wooden roller coasters and midway games.

That disdain, however, changed in 1972, when Taft Broadcasting opened Kings Island near Cincinnati. Kings Island was different from most theme parks. Its roots were found in a very successful traditional amusement park—Coney Island in Cincinnati—which had been regarded as one of the most successful and best-run amusement parks in the country. Walt Disney even visited Coney Island to observe its operations while planning for Disneyland. Its popularity was a double-edged sword, however, because it became increasingly difficult to accommodate growing crowds in its cramped location on the Ohio River. In addition, flooding was a constant nuisance. As a result, in 1969 it was decided to relocate the park to a larger site in the suburbs, where it would become a major theme park. Given Coney Island's success as a traditional park, its owners had no reservations about including traditional amusement park attractions, even persuading the renowned roller coaster designer John Allen to come out of retirement and build two wooden roller coasters— the twin-track Racer and the smaller Scooby Doo (now the Beastie). The new park was called Kings Island.

People flocked to Kings Island and lined up for hours to ride the Racer, proving that they still longed for traditional thrills. The industry responded by opening more theme parks. In 1973, Carowinds opened near Charlotte, North Carolina, followed by Great Adventure in New Jersey and Kings Dominion in Richmond in 1974; Busch Gardens Williamsburg in Virginia in 1975; and Minneapolis's Valleyfair and the two Great America parks in California and Illinois in 1976. While these parks continued to embrace many of the design standards of their earlier cousins, their resistance to more traditional amusement park rides was not as strong as had been the case with their predecessors.

For every theme park that opened, however, several were proposed that never got off the ground, as the dreams of the developers were larger than the funds available. In the frenzy, other parks became reality, but their developers did not recognize the amount of capital and management expertise needed to successfully compete. Some failed, such as Pirates World in Dania, Florida (1966 to 1977); Marco Polo Park in Daytona Beach, Florida (1970 to 1975); and Old Chicago in Bolingbrook, Illinois (1975 to 1980), but most ended up being snatched up by the more successful operators at a fraction of their book value. Six Flags complemented its original base of three parks in Dallas, Atlanta, and St. Louis by acquiring Houston's Astroworld in 1975, Great Adventure in New Jersey in 1977, and Magic Mountain near Los Angeles in 1979. Taft Broadcasting picked up Carowinds in Charlotte in 1975 and the now closed Marineland, near Los Angeles, in 1977.

Trying to Compete

While theme parks increasingly dominated the industry in the 1960s and 1970s, the old traditional parks were facing hard times. Several factors made it difficult for many parks to compete in this new climate. Aging rides and buildings were in need of upgrades, and the increasing sophistication of attractions at the theme parks made new attractions increasingly expensive to purchase and maintain. The congested urban location of many older parks made expansion difficult, and urban decay often caused the loss of family business. Finally, increasing land values prompted many park operators to sell their facilities to developers. As a result, the industry saw the sad closing of many large urban traditional parks—parks that used to be the cornerstones of the industry.

Not all was bleak, however. Many traditional amusement parks learned from theme parks and revitalized their operations. One of the most dramatic examples was Cedar Point, located halfway between Cleveland and Toledo, in Sandusky, Ohio. Once known as the "Queen of American Watering Places," by the late 1950s the park was a shell of what it had been earlier in the century. In 1957, investors purchased the attraction with the intention of redeveloping the location. A local outcry persuaded them to retain the amusement park and rebuild it, using flashy new theme-park-style rides and adding themed areas. By the 1970s, Cedar Point was widely recognized as one of the most successful amusement parks. Building on this success, the owners purchased a theme park, Minnesota's Valleyfair, in 1978. Today the company owns five amusement and theme parks.

Cedar Point was not the only example of a traditional park successfully adapting to a theme park environment. Hersheypark in Pennsylva-

Riverview in Chicago was one of the greatest of the urban traditional parks to close in the 1960s.

Cedar Point, in Sandusky, Ohio, is a traditional amusement park that has thrived.

nia revived its business by adding a series of themed areas. Other parks, such as Kennywood in West Mifflin, Pennsylvania; Geauga Lake in Aurora, Ohio; Riverside in Agawam, Massachusetts; and Lagoon in Farmington, Utah, maintained their traditional atmosphere but incorporated ideas pioneered by theme parks, including uniformed employees, live entertainment, costumed characters, and theme-park-style rides such as log flumes, observation towers, and monorails.

Competition and New Concepts

Theme park development had slowed dramatically by the late 1970s, simply because most of the markets large enough to support such a facility now had a park. As a result, most theme park operators concentrated on expanding and improving existing facilities. Most attention was focused on topping one another with record-breaking roller coasters. Sparked by the interest generated by Kings Island's Racer, the decade saw a roller coaster arms race. New record-breaking heights were achieved, and in 1975, Knott's Berry Farm and Arrow Development Corporation built a steel Corkscrew looping roller coaster. Soon looping roller coasters were must-have attractions for successful theme parks. The intense competition sparked innovations in ride technology, which reached a level of complexity never before experienced. Most rides were now computer controlled and made by new high-tech manufacturing processes.

This was all very expensive, and rapidly increasing manufacturing costs, coupled with a downturn in the industrial economy, which provided the picnic business that so many traditional parks relied upon, brought about another wave of park closings in the late 1970s. By the end of the decade, nearly a hundred amusement parks had closed forever.

As the industry entered the 1980s, opportunities for new theme parks were limited, and the demand for large thrill rides was waning, with an aging population and increasing costs. The popularity of water attractions skyrocketed during this decade, however, as they could be enjoyed by the entire family and provided a fun way to cool off on a hot summer day. New concepts included the river rapids, (introduced in 1980), the splash-water (1984), and the "dry" water slide (1986). It was an era of tremendous growth for water parks, which eschewed traditional rides for water slides. The first water park, Wet 'n Wild, opened in Orlando in 1977, but the concept truly took off in the 1980s. In 1983, Geauga Lake became the first amusement park to add a full-scale water park to its lineup of traditional amusement park attractions.

The ride simulator was another attraction that many amusement parks thought would be the wave of the future during the 1980s. Small versions such as the Astroliner had been available since 1978, but the opening of Star Tours at Disneyland took the experience to an entirely new level. Industry observers predicted that simulators would supplant traditional thrill rides, because they could easily be reprogrammed into a new ride experience every few years. Most major theme parks added a simulator, but the lines at the roller coasters did not grow any shorter.

Many American theme park operators also turned their attention overseas. Disney became the first major American operator to expand overseas, opening Tokyo Disneyland in Japan in 1983. It soon became the world's most popular amusement park and set off a wave of theme park construction in Asia, turning it into the second-largest amusement park market in the world.

The Industry Today

By the late 1980s, amusement park operators realized something very surprising: As the "baby boom" generation got older, they were not retiring from enjoying thrill rides as previous generations had done. The roller coaster innovations in the late 1970s failed to satiate their appetite for thrills, and in 1988, the arms race began anew with the construction of the 170-foot-tall Shock Wave at Six Flags Great America in Gurnee, Illinois. It held the record for only a year, however. The following season, Cedar Point in Sandusky, Ohio, constructed Magnum XL 200, the first roller coaster to surpass 200 feet in height. The arms race continues unabated to this day, peaking in the year 2000 when about a hundred roller coasters opened around the world. In fact, that year the world's record for the largest and fastest roller coaster changed hands three times—from Goliath at Six Flags Magic Mountain (255 feet tall and 85 miles per hour) in February, to Cedar Point's Millennium Force (310 feet tall and 92 miles per hour) in May, to Steel Dragon 2000 at Nagashima Spaland in Japan (318 feet tall and 95 miles per hour) in August. That record stood until 2003, when Cedar Point opened Top Thrill Dragster, which stands 420 feet tall and has a top speed of 120 miles per hour. This was topped in 2005, with the opening of Kingda Ka at Six Flags Great Adventure in New Jersey, at 456 feet tall and 128 miles per hour. As for Shock Wave, the ride that reignited the arms race, it was dismantled in 2002 and sold for scrap as a result of declining popularity.

The year 1988 was also significant in that the development of new theme parks in the United States resumed, some being built in cities that had been considered too small for a theme park in the 1970s. These included Sea World Texas (1988) and Fiesta Texas (1992), both in San Antonio; Visionland, near Birmingham, Alabama (1998); Legoland, near San Diego (1999); and Jazzland, now Six Flags New Orleans (2000).

In the 1990s, the amusement park industry enjoyed a level of prosperity not seen since the 1920s. Theme parks were opening around the world and attracting record numbers of people. Although some parks did close, the traditional parks that survived the hard times learned to compete and have become beloved local institutions. The distinction between theme and traditional parks became blurred, with theme parks adding thrill rides that had little connection to their original themes and traditional parks adding themed areas. And the two continued to share a desire to entertain their customers and respond to an ever-changing society.

Consumers seemed to have less free time available for entertainment during this decade, so the industry responded with a new concept: the family entertainment center. Unlike larger parks, which required one or two days to fully experience, family entertainment centers emphasized activities that could be enjoyed in a short amount of time. Most cities now feature one or more of these facilities, which can range from a large game arcade to a miniature amusement park complete with go-carts and kiddie rides.

As with most mature industries, the amusement park industry in the 1990s became increasingly dominated by a few major players, led by Premier Parks, now Six Flags, which entered the industry in 1981 when it was a real estate development company known as Tierco. That year, it purchased Frontier City, a run-down theme park in Oklahoma City. The company intended to redevelop the land, but when the economy soured,

Enthusiasts' Groups

There are dozens of organizations for people interested in amusement parks or specific rides. The largest of these are listed here.

American Coaster Enthusiasts (ACE)

3650 Annapolis Ln.
Suite 107
Minneapolis, MN 55447

www.aceonline.org

Publications include *Roller Coaster!*, a quarterly magazine, and *ACE News*, a bimonthly newsletter. Normally hosts four national events and several regional events annually in North America.

Dark Ride and Fun House Enthusiasts

P.O. Box 484
Vienna, OH 44473-0484

www.dafe.org

Publishes *Barrel of Fun*, a quarterly newsletter, and hosts at least one event a year.

The Dark Ride and Fun House Historical Society

22 Cozzens Ave.
Highland Falls, NY 10928

www.laffinthedark.com

Features on-line newsletter.

European Coaster Club

Six Green Lane
Hillingdon, Middlesex UB8 3EB
England

www.coasterclub.org

Publishes *First Drop*, a bimonthly magazine, and hosts six to eight events a year, most often in Europe.

National Amusement Park Historical Association (NAPHA)

P.O. Box 83
Mt. Prospect, IL 60056

www.napha.org

The only club following all aspects of the amusement and theme park industry. Publishes *NAPHA News*, a bimonthly magazine, and *NAPHA NewsFLASH!!!*, a monthly newsletter. Hosts one to three events annually, primarily in North America.

(continued on page 20)

Enthusiasts' Groups
(continued from page 19)

National Carousel Association
P.O. Box 4333
Evansville, IN 47724-0333

www.nca-usa.org

Membership benefits include the quarterly magazine
Merry-Go-Roundup, a biennial census report of
existing carousels, and a biennial membership
listing. Hosts an annual convention and
a technical conference.

Roller Coaster Club of Great Britain (RCCGB)
P.O. Box 235
Uxbridge, Middlesex UB10 0TF
England

www.rccgb.co.uk

Publishes *Airtime*, a bimonthly newsletter,
and a yearbook. Hosts six to eight events a year,
primarily in Europe.

Wood Coaster Fan Club
338 East Portage Trail, Suite #4
Cuyahoga Falls, OH 44221-2876

www.woodcoaster.org

Publishes *Timber Tales*, a quarterly newsletter.

Additionally, a wealth of clubs around the world target specific regions or interests. These include CoasterBuzz Club, Coaster Enthusiasts of Canada, Coaster Zombies, Florida Coaster Club, Freundeskreis Kirmes und Freizeitparks e.V. (German Coaster Club), Great Ohio Coaster Club (GOCC), Mid Atlantic Coaster Club (MACC), Southern California Coaster Club, Western New York Coaster Club (WNYCC), and Wild Ones Coaster Club (Pacific Northwest).

it renovated Frontier City and successfully turned the park around. Seeing the opportunities that the theme park industry presented, the company then began purchasing other amusement parks around the country, culminating with the $1.8 billion acquisition of Six Flags Theme Parks in 1998. Today it operates thirty parks in three countries.

Although the industry is increasingly dominated by major corporations and large, high-tech thrill rides, there is a renewed sense of appreciation for the industry's heritage. Two amusement parks—Pittsburgh's Kennywood and Playland in New York—are now listed as national historic landmarks, as are numerous rides throughout the country, such as the Giant Dipper roller coaster at a revived Belmont Park in San Diego and Leap the Dips at Lakemont Park in Altoona, Pennsylvania, both saved as a result of grassroots preservation efforts. A few parks, most notably Arnold's Park in Iowa and Conneaut Lake Park in Pennsylvania, have found new life as nonprofit community assets. The few remaining family-owned parks have found ways to peacefully coexist with their large, corporate-owned competitors. Few regions of the country better reflect the industry today than New York. Of the sixteen major parks, only two are owned by major corporations, and both were started by the dream of an individual. Another is government-owned, and the remainder are family-owned.

In the twenty-first century, the amusement park industry is enjoying unprecedented popularity. People flock to their local parks throughout the world, and thanks to advances in technology, they are thrilled in ways never before imagined—400-foot-tall roller coasters with speeds exceeding 100 miles per hour; linear induction motors launching rides at unheard-of acceleration rates; 300-foot-high free falls; and dark rides in which riders become part of the action. More than 300 million people flock to American amusement parks annually, which is more than twice the number in 1970, despite the fact that the number of parks has remained consistent at around six hundred. The industry seems to have entered a new golden age.

A History of the Amusement Park in New York

THE EARLY DEVELOPMENT OF THE AMUSEMENT PARK INDUSTRY IN NEW York State can be traced to one source: water. From the Atlantic Ocean beaches along the metropolis of New York City, to the quiet lakes that dot the upstate region, to Lake Ontario, one of the Great Lakes, bodies of water, with their cooling properties, drew people from the earliest days. With people flocking to these lakes and beaches, it was only natural that enterprising businesspeople would seek to capitalize on the traffic by opening amusement resorts.

Though the appeal of the waterfront was the single most dominant reason for the development of the industry in the state, the concept of the amusement park was actually imported to New York from Europe, like the millions of immigrants that give that city so much of its energy. During the first half of the nineteenth century, small pleasure gardens similar to those in Europe were common throughout New York City. Most were short-lived enterprises, but one became an enduring destination. Vauxhall Gardens opened in Manhattan in 1805 on property owned by John Jacob Astor. Named after the famous London pleasure garden, the 3-acre site was a popular entertainment spot, with a restaurant, landscaped gardens decorated by statues, theatrical performances, fireworks, and two thousand colored lamps providing illumination. In 1845, the park was the location of the first carousel known to operate in the city. The park closed in 1856, hemmed in by an increasingly congested city.

Another popular early resort was Jones Woods, which opened along the East River in the early 1800s. Unlike the smaller pleasure gardens,

Jones Woods occupied 153 acres and is believed to have been the country's first large amusement resort. Its attractions included bowling, billiards, battle re-creations, a shooting gallery, donkey rides, music, dancing, and a beer garden. Like the pleasure gardens, however, Jones Woods succumbed to rising real estate values, and after briefly being considered as the location for what was to become Central Park, the location was redeveloped by the 1860s.

On the Waterfront

With land for recreation purposes in Manhattan increasingly scarce, amusement resort development soon spread to the outer boroughs, where the beachfronts were becoming ever more popular escapes from the hot, crowded conditions of the city. In most cases, the pattern of development of these waterfront areas started with the construction of a hotel or restaurant along a popular beach. This served as an anchor for smaller concessions that soon followed. Amusements typically started as separately owned businesses, followed by full-blown amusement parks as the area matured.

The most famous of these beaches was Coney Island, along the southern tip of Brooklyn. In 1829, the first hotel opened to accommodate visitors. It was soon followed by bathhouses, restaurants, dance halls, and amusement devices. Driven by the entrepreneurial zeal of immigrants who flocked to the burgeoning resort, by the end of the nineteenth century, Coney Island emerged as the world's top amusement resort, leading the amusement park industry into its golden age. Coney Island's first true amusement park, Sea Lion Park, was opened in 1895 by Paul Boyton. Its most enduring park, Steeplechase, followed in 1897. In 1903, Luna Park was opened on the former site of Sea Lion Park by Fred Thompson and Elmer Dundy. Luna Park revolutionized amusement park design with elaborate architecture outlined by 250,000 electric lights. The success of Luna Park inspired Dreamland, which opened in 1904, with a 375-foot-tall tower as its centerpiece and a million electric lights adorning its opulent buildings.

But Coney Island was not alone in providing entertainment to the citizens of New York City. Just east of Brooklyn, along the south shore of Queens, Rockaway became a popular resort in the mid-1800s. Initially accessible only by boat, Rockaway took off in the late 1800s when railroad service linked the area to the rest of the city. Its first amusement area, the Bowery, opened in 1886, followed in 1901 by L. A. Thompson's Amusement Park, which consisted of attractions that had operated at the Pan American Exposition in Buffalo.

South Beach was one of the original seaside resorts in the New York City area.

Establishment of railroad service to Staten Island's South Beach in 1882 set off a wave of development that included hotels, dance halls, concessions, carousels, and roller coasters. A boardwalk was built in 1892, followed in 1906 by Happyland, a large amusement park that was popular until it was destroyed by fire in 1917. Just north of South Beach, Midland Beach developed into a competing amusement area in the 1890s. It thrived until a fire destroyed much of the amusement area in 1924, and finally faded away in the mid-1950s.

In the northern part of Queens, where LaGuardia Airport now operates, residents were able to cool off at North Beach. Like other waterfront resorts, the beach attracted entrepreneurs seeking to cash in on the crowds flocking to the shore. The Bowery Bay amusement area opened in the late 1880s, and Gala Park followed in 1901. The onset of Prohibition did in North Beach in 1919.

One of the most elaborate of the early summer resorts was Glen Island, north of the city in Westchester County, where John H. Starin created a permanent world's fair consisting of five islands linked with piers and causeways. Each exhibited one of the major cultures of the world. Attractions included a zoo, natural history museum, bathing beach, and Chinese pagoda, along with the traditional amusements. The park was acquired by Westchester County in 1923 and now exists as a recreational park.

Spreading through the Empire State

Development of the amusement industry in the 1800s was not limited to New York City. In all of the major cities, amusement resorts were being developed, primarily along lakes and rivers, to provide places for the populace to cool off.

In the western part of the state, Olcott Beach, on the shore of Lake Ontario north of Buffalo, came into its own as a summer resort in the 1850s. Establishment of railroad service in 1875, followed by steamboat service four years later, cemented its place as one of western New York's leading amusement areas. Independent concessions were soon followed by Luna Amusement Park in 1898 and the Rialto in 1902.

The greatest concentration of resorts on Lake Ontario was just to the east, in Rochester. Starting in the 1870s, excursion trains brought people to Rochester from as far as Pennsylvania, Ohio, and New Jersey to enjoy the cooling lake breezes. Bartholomay Park was first, opened in 1874 by the owner of Rochester's largest brewery. In 1879, Glen Haven Park got its start with the construction of Griebels Hotel, while the Rochester and Lake Ontario Railroad opened Seabreeze, today the state's oldest operating amusement park. They were followed by Ontario Beach, one of the largest resorts of the late nineteenth century, in 1884; Manitou Beach in the early 1890s; and Summerville, with its large Shoot

Rochester's Ontario Beach was the largest of the amusement parks along Lake Ontario in the late nineteenth century.

the Chutes ride, in 1896. By the turn of the twentieth century, six amusement resorts were operating in Rochester on the shore of Lake Ontario.

Inland areas also saw a wave of amusement development along their waterfronts. Albany's Pleasure Island opened on an island in the Hudson River in the 1880s. Farther west, the lakes outside Syracuse became popular destinations. Sylvan Beach, along Oneida Lake, came into its own in the late 1870s, with amusements debuting over the next decade. Owasco Lake saw Lakeside Park open in 1891, while Onondaga Lake became a major hub for waterfront resorts. Starting with Lake View Point, which was linked to Syracuse by steamer in 1874, the lake became lined with amusement parks over the next three decades. These included Long Branch Park, which opened in 1882 and featured the area's first roller coaster; Iron Pier in 1888; and White City, which operated for nine years starting in 1906.

By the turn of the twentieth century, the amusement park industry in New York was well established. Led by the popularity of its waterfront resorts, the industry underwent a period of rapid growth. In just six years, from 1899 and 1905, the number of amusement parks in the state more than doubled, from around thirty to over sixty.

As the industry matured, amusement parks became as much destinations in their own right as the waterfronts that originally provided the traffic for them. As a result, more and more parks opened that did not depend on beaches for their traffic, many by trolley companies that

Among the many trolley parks to open across the state in the late 1800s was Jamestown's Celeron Park.

sought ways to stimulate ridership in evenings and weekends. Although Coney Island dominated New York City's industry, other parks opened there, including Fort George Park in Manhattan in 1895 and Golden City Park in Canarsie in 1908. The Albany area saw the opening of Forest Park on Ballston Lake in 1904, Luna Park in Clifton Park in 1906, and Altro Park in 1907. Suburban Park opened outside Syracuse in 1898. In the state's southern tier, Eldridge Park arrived in Elmira in 1902 and White City in Binghamton in 1906. In the western region, new parks included Celeron Park in Jamestown in 1891, Midway Park in Maple Springs in 1898, and Carnival Court in Brooklyn in 1904.

Supplying a New Industry

With parks opening at an unprecedented rate throughout the country, there was an increasing demand for rides. The same entrepreneurial zeal that made New York the center of the amusement park universe also made it a major hub of ride manufacturers during the early years of the industry.

Charles Dare was one of the first, making carousels in New York City from the mid-1870s until his death in 1901. Dare's rides were simple, but most of the city's carvers, primarily based at Coney Island, developed their own unique style of horses highlighted by flamboyant carvings, rich ornamentation, jewels, and flowing manes. One of the first was Charles I. D. Looff, a German immigrant who worked as a furniture carver. In 1875, he carved Coney Island's first carousel, launching a ride-manufacturing career that eventually led to the West Coast in 1910.

Another famed Coney Island carver was Marcus Charles Illions, who trained under English carousel manufacturer Frederick Savage. He carved for other manufacturers before setting up his own firm, M. C. Illions and Sons Carousell Works, in 1909. By the 1920s, he had sold carousels throughout the country and had ten in operation in the Coney Island amusement area. He produced his last ride in 1927.

The noted carousel manufacturer Stein and Goldstein started in 1912. Before going out of business after World War I, the company made seventeen carousels, including some of the largest ever.

William F. Mangels was the most enduring of the Coney Island manufacturers. His company got its start in 1888, when he built a steam engine for Pennsylvania carousel manufacturer Gustav Dentzel. In 1891, he was granted the first of his fifty amusement device patents for a circular attraction called the Razzle Dazzle. Over the next few decades, he developed updated carousels, roller coasters, and in 1914, his best-known ride, the whip, one of the first mass-produced spinning rides. Mangels sold more than five hundred of them by 1927. He was the first manufacturer to develop a line of kiddie rides and the industry's first true historian, operating the American Museum of Public Recreation at Coney Island from 1927 to 1940. In 1952, his *Outdoor Amusement Industry* became the first published history of the industry.

Coney Island was also home to the world's first roller coaster manufacturer, the L. A. Thompson Scenic Railway Company. The company was incorporated in 1888 by LaMarcus Thompson, who is credited with creating the first modern roller coaster ever at Coney Island in 1884. His fame created an international demand for his rides, and the company built dozens before liquidating in 1940.

But as active as Coney Island's manufacturing industry was, the state's largest manufacturer was located at the other end, near Buffalo. In fact, the Buffalo area is widely credited as having created more carousels than any other part of the world.

Most of the companies were short-lived, including Norman and Evans of Lockport, New York, which produced up to seventy-five carousels annually between 1898 and 1905; the American Merry Go Round and Novelty Company, which also operated in Lockport, between 1898 and 1901; and Gillie, Goddard and Company, in Tonowanda, between 1893 and 1900.

But it was Allan Herschell that put western New York on the carousel map. A Scottish immigrant who came to America in 1870, he formed the Armitage Herschell Company in 1873 to manufacture boilers. After being inspired by a carousel he saw on a business trip, he built his first ride in 1883. By 1894, the company was making three hundred carousels a year and selling them around the world. When the company went out of business in 1901 during tough economic times, Herschell was undaunted and teamed up with Albert Spillman to form Herschell Spillman. The company thrived, but in 1911, Herschell briefly retired for health reasons. He returned to form the Allan Herschell Company in 1916, and his former partner's company became Spillman Engineering in 1926.

Although Herschell died in 1927, his company continued to thrive, introducing other types of rides starting in 1929, including its first kiddie ride three years later. In 1945, the company purchased Spillman Engineering, which had also expanded its product lineup, forming the world's largest ride manufacturer.

The Golden Age

By the time World War I ended, the amusement park industry was well established in New York. The booming economy created an insatiable demand for entertainment, and the industry responded by adding new, more thrilling rides. Coney Island remained the center of the amusement park universe, despite the loss of Dreamland in a spectacular fire in 1911. But in the 1920s, it evolved from a high-end resort into the Nickel Empire, catering to the middle-class population. With the subway now linking Coney Island to the rest of the city, visitors flocked there in record numbers to enjoy the newest in thrill rides, including the now legendary Wonder Wheel (built in 1920) and Cyclone (1927).

The city's other major seaside amusement area, Rockaway, also underwent a major change when the L. A. Thompson Amusement Park was sold in 1928 to new owners, who completely modernized the facility. They renamed it Rockaway's Playland, upgraded the roller coaster, and built a 165-foot-long swimming pool. Others around the city also tried to cash in on the demand, with Starlight Park opening in the Bronx in 1918 and Paradise Park in Rye in 1921.

But the most influential amusement park to open in the New York City area during this period was Playland in Rye. Concerned about the honky-tonk nature of the Rye Beach waterfront, Westchester County condemned the old amusement area and constructed Playland. Every detail of the park was carefully planned, including the architecture, landscaping, ride selection, and a large parking lot to accommodate the increasingly popular automobiles.

After World War I, the state's amusement park industry underwent an evolution. Many older parks closed, often losing their customers to facilities more accessible by car. They were quickly replaced, however,

Sherman's Amusement Park was typical of New York's numerous lakefront amusement parks.

by others catering to the automotive public, particularly along the state's numerous lakes.

Along Caroga Lake, Sherman's Amusement Park opened in 1920. Farther west, Roseland Park opened in 1925 on the shores of Canandaigua Lake, on a 9-acre site that had been a former slaughterhouse.

Other parks opened away from water with ample facilities to accommodate cars. Among the most notable was Woodcliffe Pleasure Park in Poughkeepsie. Its main attraction was the Blue Streak, a massive roller coaster featuring a drop of 125 feet—the largest drop ever constructed until the coaster wars of the 1970s.

Hard Times

Unfortunately, the Blue Streak was a short-lived attraction. With the coming of the Great Depression, people in the 1930s just did not have the money to spend on entertainment. Woodcliffe Park struggled through the decade and quietly closed in 1941. Many other amusement parks in the state closed during this period as well, the number falling from about sixty at the end of the 1920s to thirty by the end of the 1930s. Other parks that fell victim to the economy included Forest Park at Ballston Lake and Sacandaga Park in Sacandaga in 1930; Starlight Park and Luna Park in Clifton Park in 1932; and Long Branch Park and Golden City in 1938.

In New York City, many of the parks had to deal with not only economic hard times, but also an aggressive public-works project undertaken by the city. Rockaway's Playland lost half its acreage to a boardwalk construction project in 1938; a new boardwalk opened on South Beach in 1939, closing many concessions and finally shuttering the amusement area in 1955. The city also began acquiring property around Coney Island for housing development, shrinking the size of the once huge amusement area.

Driving to New Heights

World War II prevented a full-blown recovery for New York's struggling amusement park industry, as materials to make repairs and expand were difficult to obtain. As the war ended, however, the industry entered a second era of growth, driven by the automobile. In 1950, the state had some forty parks, but by 1966, that number had increased to more than ninety. While some traditional amusement parks opened, such as the short-lived New Liberty Park in Buffalo and Long Point Park in Geneseo in 1948 and Boulder Amusement Park in Indian Falls in 1949, the postwar boom saw the emergence of two new types of amusement parks: kiddielands and theme parks.

Page's Kiddyland, near Buffalo, was part of the kiddieland boom of the 1950s and 1960s.

In the years following the war, returning veterans sought to realize the American dream by moving to the suburbs and starting a family. This created a demand for family-type entertainment in the suburbs, one answered by small amusement parks operating scaled-down rides for children. The kiddie park was not a new concept in New York. Dealing's Kiddie Park had been in operation near Buffalo since 1929, and the Nunley family, who had been operating carousels throughout the New York City area since the early twentieth century, opened Nunley's Amusements on Long Island in 1939. But development really took off in the 1950s, with dozens opening throughout the state through the mid-1960s.

New York City, with its large population, was one of the hubs of postwar kiddieland development. Among the parks that opened were Fairyland in Elmhurst (1949), Oceanside Kiddieland in Oceanside (1950), Smiley's Happyland in Bethpage (1951), Crossbay Playland in Howard Beach (1952), and Kiddy City in Douglastown (1954). Even shopping centers such as Long Island's Roosevelt Field and Yonkers' Cross Country got into the act, developing their own kiddielands.

Outside New York City, kiddieland development was much more moderate and largely concentrated in the Buffalo area, including Twin Fair Kiddieland in the late 1950s and Page's Kiddyland in 1964.

The Allan Herschell Company was a major beneficiary of the kiddieland boom, offering six different types of kiddie rides by 1950 and spending much of the decade introducing new models that it aggressively marketed to kiddieland operators. It even put together packages of rides to offer entrepreneurs a turnkey kiddieland operation and published a how-to guide titled *Kiddielands: A Business with a Future.* Unfortunately, the reality was not as bright as Herschell had hoped. Kiddielands, with their narrow target market and prime real estate, quickly fell out of favor and were largely gone by the early 1970s. A few do remain in the state, however, including Harris Hill Park in Elmira and Hoffman's Playland in Latham.

While kiddielands catered to families looking for entertainment close to home, New York's early theme parks were developed in reaction to the growing tourist market. In the postwar era, highways began crossing the countryside. Weekend drives and vacations became popular, and attractions sprang up to intercept the traffic. Unlike kiddielands, these facilities had to offer something to attract the attention of passersby, resulting in the development of unique themes. More than two dozen opened throughout the state over the next two decades, almost half being built along the U.S. Route 9 corridor, a heavily traveled highway running north of New York City through key vacation destinations such as the Catskills, Lake George, and the Adirondack Mountains.

The first such facility in the state was Santa's Workshop, near Lake Placid, developed in 1949 by Julian Reiss. Inspired by a story he told his daughter, Reiss sought to re-create Santa's North Pole village in the Adirondack Mountains. When it first opened, the groundbreaking theme park attracted nationwide attention. One of the key reasons for its early success was the influence of Arto Monaco, a local artist who had worked in Hollywood as a decorative set painter. Monaco enlisted in the army during World War II, where his experience was put to use building training aids. He staged mock battles at war bond rallies and even created a replica of a German village in the California mountains to train troops for the D-Day invasion, a project he considered his first theme park.

Monaco was the perfect person to bring a special brand of magic to Santa's Workshop, designing a North Pole village consisting of log buildings. The attention he attracted led him to design five more theme parks in the state, including his own, Land of Make Believe, which he opened in 1954. Land of Make Believe emphasized attractions in which kids actively participated. The park was filled with scaled-down buildings and rides made by Monaco, including a fire truck, antique cars, tugboat, and train. It remained a popular attraction until it closed in 1979 because of repeated flooding.

In 1954, Monaco also helped design Storytown USA, built outside Lake George by businessman Charley Wood. Considered one of the pioneering

Unique and Historic Attractions

Carousel, Seabreeze

Although this is a newer carousel, opened in 1996, it is one of the most beautiful around. In assembling it to replace a previous carousel lost to a fire, the park sought to recapture the nearly lost art of the hand-carved carousel. In addition, Seabreeze's carousel is unique for the large building that holds it, the band organ, and the famous red rocking chairs.

Carousels of Broome County

Broome County, located in the central part of the state along the Pennsylvania border, is home to the largest concentration of antique carousels in the country. George Johnson, founder of Endicott Johnson Shoes, never forgot the disappointment he felt as a child when he did not have the money to ride the local merry-go-round. When he made his fortune, he purchased six carousels for the municipal parks near his factories and decreed that the only price of admission be a piece of litter. Located in Binghamton (two), Endicott (two), Endwell, and Johnson City, the rides, manufactured between 1920 and 1934 by the Allan Herschell Company, remain free to all riders. It is a popular diversion to "ride the circuit," collecting cards at each ride and turning them in for a souvenir button at the end. For further information see www.binghamtoncvb.com/carousels.asp.

Crocodile Run, Adventureland

This ride is best described as controlled jet skiing. Riders board a two-person boat resembling a Jet Ski, which is attached to a turntable. As the turntable rotates, riders are able to steer their boat, throwing up waves at the other boats.

Cyclone, Astroland

This famous roller coaster, dating back to 1927, is one of the last reminders of Coney Island's golden age. The Cyclone packs twelve drops, including the first one of 85 feet at a 60-degree angle, and six turns into a 75-by-500-foot parcel, resulting in a nonstop thriller. The ride is among the few roller coasters that are operated like they were in the old days, allowing customers to reride as long as their money and stomachs hold out.

Derby Racer, Playland

This golden-age classic has been thrilling visitors at Playland since 1928. The ride simulates the thrills of a horse race, with fifty-six wooden horses sitting on a large turntable that rotates at a high rate of speed. The horses move up and down as well as back and forth.

Flying Skooter, Seabreeze

This classic spinning ride from the 1940s is a do-it-yourself ride in which you control your car via a large wing mounted in the front.

(continued on page 34)

Unique and Historic Attractions
(continued from page 33)

Laffland, Sylvan Beach Amusement Park
Built in 1954 by Pretzel Amusement Company, Laffland is probably the best-preserved vintage dark ride in the country. This lovingly cared-for ride beckons you with its one-of-a-kind facade. In addition, most of its original stunts still operate.

Old Mill, Playland
Commonly referred to as the Tunnel of Love, this ride was originally built in 1929 and features boats traveling through a tunnel. The ride underwent a multi-million-dollar renovation in 2001 and 2002 and is one of only two Old Mill rides still operating at an American amusement park.

Space Shot, the Fun House at New Roc City
This ride shoots riders up a 185-foot-tall tower using compressed air. The experience is intense, but what makes the Space Shot truly special is that it is located on the roof of the New Roc City shopping mall.

Spook A Rama, Deno's Wonder Wheel Park
When it opened in 1955, the Spook A Rama was billed as the "World's Longest Spook Ride." Although it has since been reduced in size, it remains a Coney Island classic and still retains many of its original scenes.

Whip, Playland
The whip was invented in 1914, and Playland's has been in operation since the park opened in 1928. It was one of the first high-speed circular rides, of which only about a dozen remain in operation.

Wonder Wheel, Deno's Wonder Wheel Park
This 150-foot Ferris wheel is one of the most unusual rides ever constructed. It has eight cars that travel in the traditional manner as the wheel rotates, plus sixteen more cars that slide on rails from the outer rim to an inner rim.

theme parks, Storytown has grown into one of the largest parks in the state, now known as the Great Escape. Wood and Monaco also collaborated in 1959, when Wood opened a second theme park, Gaslight Village, with a Gay Nineties theme. This park operated until Wood retired in 2000.

Frontier Town was another early theme park along the Route 9 corridor. Opened on July 4, 1952, it was one of the first theme parks with a Wild West theme. Frontier Town was built by Arthur Bensen, a Staten Island phone installer, who long dreamed of re-creating a Western town somewhere in the Northeast. He spent early 1951 looking for the right site. As he was about to give up, he found a 100-acre abandoned farm

Land of Make Believe in Upper Jay was owned and operated by New York theme park pioneer Arto Monaco. Many of the buildings were relocated to The Great Escape in 1981.

outside North Hudson and purchased it for $1,800. On July 6, 1951, he began construction on twelve log buildings, harvesting trees on the site. Although Frontier Town was initially a popular attraction, it failed to keep up with the times and finally closed in 1999.

While the Route 9 corridor was the focus of early theme park development in the state, new facilities did open elsewhere. Some attractions, such as Enchanted Forest in Old Forge (opened in 1956), Fantasy Island in Grand Island (1961), and Christmas City/Magic Forest in Lake George (1963), have managed to survive to the present day, but most had fallen by the wayside by the late 1970s.

Unlike the larger, multithemed corporate-owned parks that spread throughout the country in the 1960s and 1970s, these early facilities tended to be mom-and-pop operations focused on a single theme, such as storybook characters, the Wild West, or Christmas. There was one attempt to develop a major multifaceted theme park in the state during this era, however, but it was a miserable failure.

The Freedomland Fiasco

With the successful opening of Disneyland in 1955, entrepreneurs in New York City immediately began making plans to open a similar facility. By 1959, plans were announced by International Recreation Corporation to develop Freedomland on a 205-acre site in the Bronx. Unfortunately, the groundbreaking on August 26 seemed to be a sign of things to come. Despite an elaborate ceremony that included a specially chartered subway train from Manhattan, fifty bulldozers representing each state, and actors portraying historical characters, just nineteen spectators showed up. A fire during construction destroyed six buildings, costs zoomed from $16 million to $65 million, and on opening day, more than sixty thousand people visited the partially completed park, completely overwhelming area roads and park facilities.

By all projections, Freedomland should have been a success. C. V. Wood, a key figure in the development of Disneyland, was hired to guide construction. The park was themed after the history of the country, with seven areas—Little Old New York, Old Chicago, Satellite City, New Orleans, Great Plains, Old Southwest, and San Francisco—covering 85 acres arranged in the shape of the United States. The park was filled with numerous historical displays, such as a replica of the first Macy's store. Its two dozen attractions represented the latest in theme park technology and featured miniature antique cars; several boat rides, including one on a miniature version of the Great Lakes; a ride through a Civil War battlefield; a dark ride through the San Francisco earthquake; a sky ride crossing a 50-foot-tall re-creation of the Rocky Mountains; and a reenactment of the Chicago fire, where kids could help extinguish the flames.

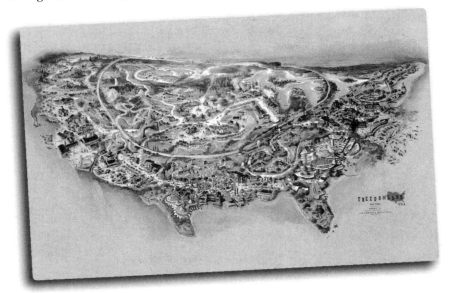

Freedomland, one of the first attempts to duplicate the success of Disneyland, was laid out in the shape of the United States.

But problems continued beyond the disastrous opening. Throughout the first year, the park experienced a stagecoach accident that injured ten people, a robbery of $29,000 from the cash control office, management turnover, and an increase in the admission price. The first season saw a total of 1.7 million visitors, one-third of initial projections. By the fall of 1960, Freedomland was looking for new investors. It also was faced with making expensive repairs to many of the buildings, as the park was constructed atop a former landfill that had been graded improperly during construction.

An attempt to turn around the operation in 1961 resulted in a pay-one-price admission, a dance floor for top-name acts, and kiddie rides, but attendance failed to increase. The next season, a $1 million improvement program included the addition of several traditional amusement park rides in an area themed as a State Fair Midway.

But by now the park was truly in decline. Many of the original sponsors were pulling out, as Freedomland had largely abandoned its original historical and educational focus to pursue the teen market. The 1963 season saw the addition of $3 million in new attractions, including the Meteor roller coaster and a waxworks replica of the Last Supper. The San Francisco section was blocked off, and many of the original themed attractions were closed. Attendance fell to 1.3 million.

In 1964, still more themed attractions were replaced by traditional rides, and many of the historical displays were converted into game concessions. In September, paychecks were bouncing and Freedomland filed for bankruptcy. Admission revenue that season totaled just $734,000, compared with $3 million in 1962. National Development Corporation acquired control of the facility during the season, and it announced plans to reduce the size of the park to 30 acres and convert the rest of the land into housing. But by February 1965, the brief history of Freedomland ended with the liquidation of the entire park in favor of a 15,500-unit housing development.

Trying to Keep Up

While the development of theme parks and kiddielands throughout New York was a bright spot in the postwar era, it was a very tough time for many of the state's older facilities. Coney Island was in the midst of a decades-long decline that started when Luna Park burned down in 1944. The city took over the land and developed a housing project on the property. Steeplechase closed in 1964, a victim of changing times and family disputes. The housing that had been built around the old resort was contributing to a crime problem that further strained the Coney Island. As a result, the 1960s and 1970s were marked by a general decline of the amusement area, with formerly great attractions closing on an almost annual basis. Were it not for the opening of Astroland in 1962 on the former site of the once legendary Feltman's restaurant, Coney Island likely would have faded away.

In fact, parks throughout the state were closing during these two decades. From a high of ninety amusement parks in the mid-1960s, just thirty-five were operating in New York by 1980. Most of the losses were short-lived kiddielands and theme parks that failed to adapt to changing tastes, but several of the parks that closed had earlier been the anchors of the industry.

In western New York, Celeron Park, one of the state's largest amusement parks, closed in 1960, never having recovered from a June 1959 tornado that knocked down its Greyhound roller coaster. Lakeside Park on Owasco Lake shuttered in 1967; Glen Park Actionland outside Buffalo failed to recover from a 1968 fire and closed in 1970; Boulder Amusement Park faded away in 1970; Olivecrest Park on Cuba Lake was shuttered in 1972, after nearly five decades of operation; Suburban Park outside Syracuse gave its final rides in 1973; and Sherman's Amusement Park on Caroga Lake closed in 1979.

Even the state's once great manufacturing industry faded away during this time. In 1970, the Allan Herschell Company was sold to Chance Manufacturing of Wichita. Though it had developed a full lineup of rides by the end of the 1960s, its products were increasingly falling out of favor in the theme park era. W. F. Mangels ceased operations in 1971 after scaling production back to solely kiddie rides.

While the 1980s did not see as dramatic a loss in parks as the 1970s, those that closed tended to be larger, older ones, and the loss hurt just as much. Rockaway's Playland was one such facility. Significantly reduced in size in the 1930s, the park nevertheless remained an important part of its neighborhood and kept up-to-date by importing several new European rides in the 1960s. But that decade, many of the summer cottages that provided much of its customer base were demolished in favor of year-round housing, although disputes caused much of the land to remain vacant for two decades.

By the early 1980s, the neighborhood was in decline, and in 1983, the owners considered closing the park. But a new ownership group purchased Playland for $2 million and launched a $1 million upgrade that included new rides and an eight-lane water slide. The park enjoyed success over the next two seasons. Then, in April 1986, the park's insurance premiums jumped from $50,000 to $400,000. This, combined with what the owners termed a "hostile political climate," led them to close

Gone but Not Forgotten

While New York is still blessed with a wealth of amusement parks, all too many are now memories. Throughout its history, more than three hundred different amusement parks have operated in the state. Here is a list of some of the better-known ones that no longer exist.

Adventure Town of the 1000 Islands, Alexandria Bay, mid-1950s to 1961.
Airport Kiddieland, Binghamton, 1959 to 1969.
Altro Park/Maple Beach Park, Albany, 1907 to early 1920s.
Amusement Park Department Store, Brooklyn, 1926 to 1977.
Bergen Beach, New York City, 1894 to 1925.
Boulder Amusement Park, Indian Falls, 1949 to 1970.
Bronx Funland, Bronx, 1951 to 1966.
Buy Rite Amusement Park, Peekskill, 1964 only.
Carnival Court/Luna Park/Athletic Park, Buffalo, 1904 to 1920.
Carson City, Catskill, 1958 to late 1990s.
Celeron Park, Jamestown, 1891 to 1960.
Cimarron City, Monticello, 1960 to mid-1960s.
Clason Point Park, Bronx, 1910 to 1935.
Cloud 9 Park, Olean, 1967 to early 1970s.
Coney Island Terminal Park, Brooklyn, 1896 to 1910s.
Cross Bay Playland, Howard Beach, 1952 to late 1990s.
Dealings Kiddie Park, Tonowanda, 1929 to 1980.
Dreamland, Brooklyn, 1904 to 1911.
Eldridge Park, Elmira, 1902 to 1989.
Fairyland, Elmhurst, 1949 to 1968.
Fairyland, Rego Park, early 1950s to late 1960s.
Fairyland Kiddie Park, Brooklyn, 1952 to 2002.
Fentier Village, Salamanca, 1966 to 1969.
Forest Park, Ballston Lake, 1904 to 1930.
Fort George Park, New York City, 1895 to 1913.
Freedomland, Bronx, 1960 to 1964.
Frontier Town, North Hudson, 1952 to 1999.
Fun & Games Park, Tonowanda, early 1970s to 1979.
Gaslight Village/Lake George Ride & Fun Park, Lake George, 1959 to 2000.
Glen Haven Park/Dreamland, Rochester, 1879 to 1923.
Glen Island Park, New Rochelle, 1879 to 1920.
Glen Park Actionland, Williamsville, 1920s to 1970.
Golden City Amusement Park, Brooklyn (Canarsie), 1907 to 1938.
Great Adventure/Adventurers Inn, Queens, 1957 to 1978.
Happyland, Staten Island, 1906 to 1927.
Holiday Mountain Amusement Park, Monticello, 1982 to 1986.
Island Park/Deauville Island Park, Auburn, 1889 to 1967.
Kaydeross Park, Saratoga Springs, 1912 to 1987.
Kiddie City, Douglastown, 1954 to 1964.
Krause's Half Moon Beach, Crescent, early 1930s to 1978.
Lake George Amusement Park, Lake George, 1956 to 1957.
Lakeside Park/Enna Jettick Park/Auburn Park, Auburn, 1891 to 1967.
Lake View Point, Syracuse, 1872 to 1915.

(continued on page 40)

Gone but Not Forgotten
(continued from page 39)

Lalle's Amusement Park, Angola, mid-1930s to mid-1960s.
Land of Make Believe, Upper Jay, 1954 to 1979.
Lollipop Farm, Syosset, early 1950s to late 1960s.
Long Point Park, Geneseo, 1948 to 1989.
Luna Amusement Park, Olcott Beach, 1898 to 1926.
Luna Park, Brooklyn, 1903 to 1944.
Massapequa Zoo and Kiddie Park, Massapequa, 1956 to late 1960s.
Mid City Park, Albany, late 1920s to late 1940s.
Midland Beach, Staten Island, 1897 to late 1920s.
Midway Beach Park, Niagara Falls, mid-1940s to late 1960s.
New Liberty Park, Buffalo, 1948 to 1955.
New Rialto Park, Olcott Beach, 1940 to 1992.
Nunley's Amusements, Baldwin, 1939 to 1995.
Oceanside Kiddieland, Oceanside, 1950 to early 1970s.
Olcott Amusement Park, Olcott Beach, 1942 to 1986.
Olivecrest Park, Cuba, late 1930s to 1972.
Olympic Park, Rochester, 1929 to 1980.
Ontario Beach Park, Rochester, 1884 to 1919.
Owasco Lake Park, Auburn, 1910s to 1968.
Paradise Park, Rye, 1921 to 1926.
Pine Lake Park/Lord's Amusement Park, Pine Lake, 1960 to 1982.
Rensselaer Park, Lansingburgh, early 1900s to 1917.
Rexford Park/Luna Park/Dolle's Park, Clifton Park, 1906 to 1933.
The Rialto, Olcott Beach, 1902 to 1928.
Rockaway's Playland/Thompson Park, Queens, 1901 to 1985.
Roseland Park, Canadaigua, 1925 to 1985.
Round Lake Beach, Round Lake, 1909 to 1955.
Rye Beach Amusement Park, Rye, 1917 to 1927.
Sacandaga Park, Sacandaga, early 1900s to 1930.
Sea Lion Park, Brooklyn, 1895 to 1902.
Sherman's Amusment Park, Caroga Lake, 1920 to 1979.
Skyline Amusement Park/Carousel Mountain/Adventure Mountain,
    Tioga Center, 1960 to 1987.
Smiley's Happyland/Nunley's Happyland, Bethpage, 1951 to 1978.
South Beach, Staten Island, 1886 to 1955.
South Beach Amusement Park, Staten Island, 1953 to 1999.
Starlite Amusement Park, Bronx, 1918 to 1932.
Steeplechase Park, Brooklyn, 1897 to 1964.
Steeplechase Park (new), Brooklyn, 1967 to 1981.
Sterling Forest Gardens, Tuxedo, 1960 to 1977.
Suburban Park, Manluis, 1898 to 1973.
Thunderbird Indian Village, Elmira, early to late 1960s.
Time Town, Bolton Landing, 1971 to 1982.
Twin Fair Kiddieland, Cheektowaga, late 1950s to mid-1960s.
Ulmer Park, Brooklyn, 1893 to 1899.
Ward's Kiddieland, Brooklyn, 1950 to 1980.
The White Beach, Ballston Lake, 1930 to 1960.
White City, Oswego, 1906 to late 1910s.
White City, Syracuse, 1906 to 1915.
Willow Point Park, Webster, mid-1940s to early 1970s.
Woodcliffe Pleasure Park, Poughkeepsie, 1928 to 1941.

Rockaway's Playland, a long-time institution in Queens, succumbed in the 1980s.

and sell the site to developers. For the first time in a century, there were no amusements in Rockaway.

Another major attraction lost during this period was Roseland Park on Canandaigua Lake. Since its opening in 1925, it had grown into one of the largest amusement parks in the central part of the state. But by 1985, the value of the property had exceeded the value of the business, and the 25-acre lakefront parcel was targeted for residential use. "Development in its place is a much greater asset to the community," owner Richard Boyce said at the time.

Like many cities in the Northeast in the 1980s, Elmira, in the southern part of the state, was affected by the decline in the country's industrial base. This took a toll on Eldridge Park, the city's main amusement park, started by a trolley company in 1902. The park went into a long decline as its picnic business dropped. The roller coaster was closed in 1983 because of increasing maintenance needs. By 1989, the rides were shuttered as a result of a lease dispute with the city, which owned the land, and were soon removed.

On the Rebound

By 1990, the number of amusement parks in the state had fallen to around thirty. But though the losses of the past few decades were sad, the industry in the state was far from dead. In 1977, entrepreneur Paul Snyder had started developing his Darien Lake campground into what would become the largest theme park in the state, Six Flags Darien Lake.

Throughout the 1990s, the remaining parks continued to grow, adding new rides and attractions. While some parks have closed, such as Nunley's Amusements in Baldwin in 1995, new facilities are being built. Many of these are family entertainment centers, the newest type of amusement park, which has spread throughout the state. The New York City area became the hub of an offshoot, the indoor family entertainment center. In a way, they replaced the old kiddielands, offering entertainment to suburban families, although they are much fewer in number.

Even Coney Island, after decades of decline, is on the rebound. The amusement area had reached rock bottom in the early 1980s. The boardwalk and beach were all but deserted, many of the old amusements and bathhouses were abandoned, and crime was a problem. But a few determined people took a stand and refused to give up. Astroland continued to add new rides and took over operation of the Cyclone, the area's last vintage roller coaster; Greek immigrant Denos Vourderis took over the Wonder Wheel and built a new amusement park around it; and the city finally realized the value of Coney Island and began making much-needed investments in infrastructure and crime reduction. Today Coney Island continues to serve the same role it always has, as a place to cool off on a hot summer day. Some things never change.

Coney Island

OPENED 1829

WHEN THE *NEW YORK TIMES* FIRST WROTE ABOUT CONEY ISLAND IN JULY 1866, it was hardly complimentary: "It lies low, is flat and unpicturesque, dreadfully sandy, and next to Jersey, and breeds the most ferocious mosquitoes." But even then its growing popularity was acknowledged as a result of the "splendid bathing."

Since being discovered by European settlers in the 1600s, this spit of land at the southern tip of Brooklyn held a unique appeal. The temperatures on the flat sand marshes typically were ten degrees below those in the crowded residential areas farther inland. It was this differential that launched the development of the most storied resort in amusement park history. Not a single amusement park, Coney Island is a Brooklyn neighborhood that long has had a collection of amusements and supporting businesses, including several independent amusement parks.

A Hotel on the Sands

By 1820, Coney Island's beaches were becoming increasingly popular. To accommodate the growing crowds, the first hotel, the Coney Island House, opened in 1829. It was joined by a dozen others within a few years.

By the 1840s, steamship service linked Coney Island to Manhattan, old farmhouses were converted into taverns, and bathhouses appeared. In 1845, a dance pavilion opened, the first building constructed for entertainment purposes.

The increasing crowds attracted the attention of entrepreneurs, who flocked to Coney Island to

Coney Island USA
Coney Island Museum and
Sideshows by the Seashore
1208 Surf Ave.
Brooklyn, NY 11224-2816
718-372-5159
info@coneyisland.com
www.coneyisland.com

cash in on the masses. During this time, many of the families who would build Coney Island to its greatest glory arrived. The Ravenhalls, who later operated one of the largest bathhouses, opened a restaurant in 1863. Peter Tilyou, whose son George would emerge as the resort's greatest showman, opened the Surf House hotel and restaurant two years later. In 1867, Charles Feltman arrived with his pie wagon and equipped it with a stove so he could sell boiled sausages in rolls, the first hot dogs. His creation enabled him to open a small saloon in 1871 and the 30,000-square-foot Ocean Pavilion three years later. It soon grew into the internationally renowned Feltman's, with a series of restaurants and beer gardens seating eight thousand diners at a time, along with live entertainment and rides such as the Ziz roller coaster and the Superba, one of the grandest carousels ever constructed.

Growing Up

By the 1870s, thirty thousand people were visiting Coney Island daily, and early amusements began arriving. Charles Looff built Coney Island's first carousel in 1875 at Balmer's Bathing Pavilion, a hotel and bathhouse complex. Next door, Andrew R. Culver built a terminal for his Prospect Park

and Coney Island Railroad, which included the 9-acre Culver Plaza, featuring a picnic area and hotel. Three years later, the 300-foot-high Iron Tower was purchased from the Philadelphia Centennial Exposition and erected at the plaza. It was Coney Island's first major amusement, with two steam elevators to transport visitors to the top.

Another railroad station opened down the street from Culver Plaza in 1879, when the Sea Beach Palace was relocated from the Philadelphia Exposition. With its terminal, restaurant, and hotel, it created a second center of activity at the burgeoning resort.

Relocated from the 1876 Philadelphia Centennial Exposition, the Iron Tower was Coney Island's first major amusement.

 **VISITING**

CONEY ISLAND

LOCATION

Coney Island is located on the southern tip of Brooklyn. The amusement area is bounded by the New York Aquarium, Surf Avenue, and KeySpan Park. Astroland is located at the corner of Surf Avenue and Tenth Street. Deno's Wonder Wheel Park is located on the Boardwalk at Denos Vourderis Place (formerly West Twelfth Street).

From the Belt Parkway, take Exit 7S, Ocean Parkway. Turn right and drive four blocks, to where Ocean Parkway ends at Surf Avenue. Parking is available at metered spaces along the streets and in pay lots at KeySpan Park and the New York Aquarium.

Coney Island is also easily accessible from the D, Q, F, and N subway lines. Get off at the Stillwell Station, located just across Surf Avenue from the amusement area.

OPERATING SCHEDULE

Palm Sunday is the traditional opening day for Coney Island, although some businesses might open later. Until mid-June, Astroland opens at noon on weekends only; closing depends on the size of the crowd and the weather. From mid-June through Labor Day, it is open every day from noon to midnight. From Labor Day, to mid-October, the park opens at noon on weekends, with closing time again depending on the crowds and the weather.

Deno's Wonder Wheel Park is open from noon to 9 P.M. on weekends and school holidays from Palm Sunday until Memorial Day weekend. From Memorial Day through Labor Day, the park is open daily from 11 A.M. to midnight. After Labor Day, the park is open from noon to 9 P.M. on weekends through October.

ADMISSION

There is no admission charge to Coney Island or the individual amusement parks. Astroland, Deno's Wonder Wheel Park, and the other rides and concessions maintain their own pricing policies, but rides typically cost $2 to $5 each.

In addition, Astroland offers pay-one-price wristbands for under $25 on weekdays, with an early session from 12 noon to 6 P.M. and a late session from 4 P.M. to 10 P.M. On Fridays, wristbands are available only for the early session.

FOOD

More than two dozen food stands are scattered throughout Coney Island, serving a wide variety of food. The most renowned is Nathan's Famous, a Coney Island institution since 1916. It is best known for its hot dogs but also serves other items, including burgers, seafood, chicken sandwiches, french fries, and onion rings.

Astroland has two Gregory and Paul's outlets, another Coney Island institution featuring a wide variety of food, including hot dogs, Italian sausage, pizza, seafood, knishes, corn on the cob, and french fries.

(continued on page 46)

VISITING (continued from page 45)

Deno's Wonder Wheel Park has four food stands. The largest is a McDonald's, offering its typical selection. The others serve a variety of snacks, including popcorn and cotton candy.

FOR CHILDREN

Coney Island has three kiddie areas. Astroland's Kiddie Park has fifteen kiddie and family rides. Many, including the merry-go-round, Scrambler, and Big Apple coaster, can be enjoyed by the entire family. Deno's kiddie park features seventeen kiddie and family rides, including the merry-go-round, Sea Serpent coaster, and Tilt-A-Whirl. McCullough's Kiddie Park, at the Bowery and Twelfth, is a smaller kiddieland, with a dozen family and kiddie rides.

SPECIAL FEATURES

Coney Island is the most storied amusement area in the history of the industry. Though significantly reduced in size from its peak, it nonetheless is an excellent example of the classic seaside experience. It also still has a number of vintage attractions.

The Wonder Wheel, at Deno's Wonder Wheel Park, is one of the most unusual Ferris wheels ever constructed. At 150 feet tall, it dates back to 1920 and has sixteen cars that travel on rails between an outer and an inner rim.

Astroland's Cyclone roller coaster is world renowned. Dating back to 1927, it is a true piece of history. Enthusiasts hold it in high esteem for its tight turns and steep drops.

The Coney Island Carousel is the last of more than two dozen classic carousels to have operated at Coney Island. Manufactured in 1919 by William Mangels and installed at Coney Island in 1932, it features fifty horses carved by Coney Island's greatest craftsmen. One of the fastest carousels in operation, it is among the few remaining where you can catch the brass ring. It was purchased by the city in 2005 and is undergoing restoration before re-opening along the boardwalk.

When Spook-A-Rama, now in Deno's Wonder Wheel Park, opened in 1955, it was billed as the longest dark ride in the world. Though it has been shortened since then, it remains one of the best-preserved examples of a classic dark ride.

Astroland's Log Flume was among the first flumes ever built and is an excellent early example of what is now an industry staple.

The Astrotower was the first observation tower of its kind in North America. It provides a fantastic view of Coney Island and the surrounding neighborhood.

TIME REQUIRED

Plan on spending most of the day to fully experience Coney Island. In addition to the amusement area, with its two major amusement parks, you'll also find the Coney Island Museum, Sideshows by the Seashore, the beach, and KeySpan Park, home of the Brooklyn Cyclones minor-league baseball team. If you are pressed for time, the major attractions can be enjoyed in about three hours.

TOURING TIPS

Coney Island consists of a series of independently owned businesses, so be careful when purchasing tickets that they are good on the rides you want to go on.

To avoid crowds, visit early in the afternoon, particularly on weekdays. The amusement area is a very popular destination in late afternoon and evening, particularly after the beaches close, so the rides can get quite crowded.

If you want to ride a lot, consider visiting on a weekday, when pay-one-price wristbands are available at Astroland.

Deno's Wonder Wheel Park sponsors free fireworks at 9:30 P.M. every Friday, starting in late June.

Coney Island is a big-city neighborhood. Though crime is not as bad of a problem as it used to be, use the same level of caution you would in any other urban area.

By 1882, the popularity of Coney Island was undisputed. Daily crowds of seventy-five thousand were common. Attendance for the season totaled 5 million, and spending was estimated at $9 million. Fireworks and pyrotechnic spectaculars such as the Destruction of Pompeii were popular draws. Also that year, the Tilyou family carved out an alley between the year-old Surf Avenue and the ocean to improve access to their new Surf Theater. The alley soon became known as the Bowery, and even today it is the heart of Coney Island.

New landmarks continued to appear. The most significant change in 1884 was the construction of a simple ride on the beach, the Switchback Railway, which changed the face of the industry. Considered the first modern roller coaster, the Switchback Railway was constructed by LaMarcus Thompson, a Sunday school teacher, who wanted to develop a cleaner source of amusement for kids than beer halls.

The ride consisted of a pair of wooden undulating tracks on a structure 600 feet long. A train started at its highest point and ran downgrade and then up until it lost momentum. Passengers got out while attendants pushed the train over a switch to a somewhat higher point on the second track. The passengers boarded the train again and rode back to the starting point. It cost just $1,600 to build, but it was hugely popular, and people lined up for three hours to ride. It was the first of a dozen roller coasters Thompson would construct at Coney Island.

In an age before movies, staged re-creations of famous disasters were a popular attraction at Coney Island. In 1893, a re-creation of the Battle of Vicksburg featured five hundred infantry, two batteries of artillery, two squadrons of cavalry, a lake full of boats, and a choir of one hundred. By the early 1900s, these shows were scattered throughout Coney Island, including the Galveston Flood, the Great Italian Earthquake, and the Sinking of the *Maine.*

Birth of the Amusement Park

In 1893, the hub of the amusement industry shifted temporarily from Coney Island to Chicago, where the World's Columbian Exposition was taking place. George Tilyou traveled to the fair to check out the new attractions and was enamored with the 250-foot-tall Ferris wheel. He attempted to purchase it but, failing that, leased a parcel at Culver Plaza and erected a sign stating, "On This Site Will Be Erected the World's Largest Ferris Wheel." Although not quite true, as the new ride would be only 125 feet tall, it created sufficient buzz that Tilyou sold enough concession space around the new ride to pay for it when it was delivered in the spring of 1894. It was the first of a number of rides he erected at Culver Plaza, signaling Tilyou's entry into the amusement park business.

The next year, Capt. Paul Boyton arrived from Chicago and changed the face of Coney Island. In Chicago in 1894, he had opened the highly successful Capt. Paul Boyton's Water Chutes, considered to be the first amusement park to emphasize rides as its major draw. He wanted to try his luck at Coney Island and opened Sea Lion Park, which featured a Shoot the Chutes water ride and a sea lion show. But the ride that attracted the most attention was the Flip Flap, one of the first looping roller coasters. It was quite uncomfortable for riders to negotiate the vertical 25-foot-diameter loop and typically had more watchers than riders.

Boyton's success caught the eye of Tilyou, who realized that his future rested in creating a facility similar to Boyton's. Tilyou secured a 15-acre parcel at the western end of the amusement area to one-up Boyton. At the time, Coney Island was the horse-racing capital of the world and Tilyou looked to the three racetracks operating in the area for inspiration. In an effort to compete with Boyton's chutes ride, Tilyou erected the one-of-a-kind Steeplechase ride. Costing $41,000, it was a gravity-driven ride with six wooden horses running along six parallel 1,100-foot-long tracks. The park also featured his Culver Plaza attractions, the airship tower, a canal boat ride, and a 1,500-foot-long boardwalk along the ocean.

Steeplechase, as he named the park, was different from anything seen before. It foreshadowed the theme parks by charging a pay-one-price admission to control crowds, paid attention to landscaping, and refused to sell alcohol. It even had early versions of the costumed characters seen at today's theme parks.

Tilyou was always on the lookout for unique new attractions to bring back to his park. In 1901, he traveled to the Pan-American Exposition in

Buffalo, where the sensation was a Trip to the Moon, an illusion ride operated by two partners, Frederic Thompson and Elmer Dundy. The ride was a spaceship, which sixty passengers boarded for a simulated trip to the moon, using what was the most advanced technology available at the time. Tilyou knew that the attraction would be a huge success at Steeplechase and struck a deal with the partners to bring it to his park.

It was fortunate for Tilyou that he was able to bring Trip to the Moon to Steeplechase for the 1902 season. It was a dismal summer, with rain and clouds plaguing the resort for seventy of the season's ninety-two days. With the popularity of Trip to the Moon, which attracted 875,000 patrons, Tilyou's business remained relatively stable, but Boyton, down the street, was not so lucky. Visitation dwindled to almost nothing, and he put his park on the market. Thompson and Dundy, seeing the success of Trip to the Moon, thought they could achieve even greater heights with their own amusement park and quickly struck a deal with Boyton.

With the exception of the Shoot the Chutes ride, Sea Lion Park was completely demolished. Trip to the Moon was jacked up on rollers and moved down Surf Avenue to the new park using elephants. In the place of Sea Lion Park, Thompson and Dundy built Luna Park, a 22-acre fantasyland of exotic architecture highlighted by more than a thousand spires, minarets, and towers and outlined by 250,000 electric lights. "Buildings can laugh quite as loudly as human beings," Thompson said of the architecture. The Court of Honor was an area at the heart of the

Luna Park and its elaborate architecture set new standards for Coney Island when it opened in 1902.

park with the chutes ride and a 200-foot-tall tower as its centerpiece. It was surrounded by elaborate attractions such as Trip to the Moon, the Dragon's Gorge roller coaster, Canals of Venice boat ride, Trip to the North Pole, Eskimo Village, and German Village.

One of the most unusual attractions was the Infant Incubators. Operated by Dr. Martin Couney, who devoted his life to developing methods for caring for prematurely born babies, the attraction featured a complete medical staff tending to real-live preemies. Though this may seem bizarre by today's standards, the technology he developed is now commonplace. Couney operated the attraction at various locations in Coney Island until 1943. During this forty-year period, he took in eighty-five hundred premature infants, seventy-five hundred of whom survived.

Coney Island at Its Zenith

Luna Park opened for the first time on May 16, 1903. Thompson and Dundy had put all they had into the park. With only $22 in working capital remaining, they had barely enough for change for the ticket booths. But the risk was worth it, as nearly sixty thousand people showed up that first night. By the end of the 1903 season, the $700,000 Luna Park had generated a $600,000 profit and attracted 4.8 million people. An additional 16 acres were soon acquired for expansion.

That type of success attracted the attention of others. In late 1903, a group of politicians and businesspeople pooled their resources to acquire Culver Plaza and several surrounding parcels to build Dreamland, the most spectacular amusement park to operate at Coney Island. Built at a cost of $3.5 million, Dreamland attempted to top Luna Park in every respect. Its centerpiece was a 375-foot-tall tower that dominated the neighborhood. The Shoot the Chutes ride was twice the size of Luna's. The buildings were adorned with a million electric lights, the ballroom measured 25,000 square feet, the wide midways could comfortably accommodate sixty thousand people, and a pier extended 2,000 feet into the ocean.

Attractions were equally spectacular, including Creation, an elaborate telling of the biblical creation of the world; Coasting through Switzerland, a themed roller coaster; the Haunted Swing illusion ride; Canals of Venice, a boat ride through Italy; Under and Over the Sea, a simulated submarine voyage; and Lilliputia, populated by three hundred little people, a complete city patterned after fifteenth-century Nuremburg, Germany, with a fire department, stores, and its own beach. The largest show was Fighting Flames. Inspired by a similar show at Luna Park, it featured a cast of four thousand battling a simulated fire in a six-story building.

As spectacular as Dreamland was, it never enjoyed the success of Luna Park or Steeplechase. Built as an investment, it lacked a showman

Dreamland, with its 375-foot-tall tower, was one of the most elaborate amusement parks ever constructed.

the caliber of Tilyou or Thompson and almost took itself too seriously with its high-minded shows, heavy classical influences, and a stark white paint job.

With three huge amusement parks and hundreds of other attractions, Coney Island reached its peak in the years before World War I. Elaborate roller coasters rose up across the resort: Deep Rift Coal Mine, Pike Peak Railway, and Rough Riders, all built in 1906; Drop the Dip, Over the Great Divide, Red Devil Rider, and Rocky Road to Dublin in 1907; and the Ben Hur Racer in 1908.

A Constant Menace

With Coney Island's abundance of tightly packed wooden structures, fire was a constant menace, with the very real risk of the flames growing into a full-blown conflagration. On an almost annual basis, a hotel, restaurant, or concession was lost. On July 28, 1907, in the still of the night, a fire broke out in the Cave of the Winds attraction at Steeplechase Park. Soon most of the park was ablaze, and the fire spread down the Bowery, engulfing dozens of wooden structures. It looked as if the entire resort would be lost, but just before 7 A.M., the flames reached the brick Stauch's hotel and bathhouse, which resisted the fire. Thirty-five acres of Coney Island lay in ruins, including ten hotels, a concert hall, a dance hall, and the Drop the Dip roller coaster. All that remained at

Steeplechase were the Ferris wheel and some smaller attractions. Damages totaled $1.5 million.

Ever the showman, Tilyou immediately reopened the undamaged corner of the park, built a fence around the wreckage, and erected a sign stating:

"I had troubles yesterday, that I have not today,
I have troubles today, that I had not yesterday.
On this site will be erected a bigger, better Steeplechase.
Admission to the burning ruins 10 cents."

By the end of the year, Tilyou announced plans to spend $1 million to rebuild the park. The centerpiece was the Pavilion of Fun, a 5-acre steel-and-glass building filled with rides and funhouse attractions such as the Human Roulette wheel, Barrel of Love, and Human Pool Table, intended to throw people together, allowing young couples to cuddle in public. Outside the Pavilion of Fun, new attractions included an expanded Steeplechase ride, the Figure 8 roller coaster, 15,000 square feet of formal gardens, and a 24,000-square-foot swimming pool. The fire actually had a positive effect on the rest of the burned area, as the ramshackle structures that had defined the old Coney Island were now being replaced by more substantial buildings.

With the damage from the 1907 fire repaired, Coney Island was more popular than ever. Crowds of three hundred thousand to five hundred thousand people were common, and annual revenues were estimated at

Steeplechase Park's Pavilion of Fun was one of Coney Island's most famous attractions.

$45 million. But Coney Island was badly underinsured. Total investment was valued at $100 million, but insurance was carried for only $10 million. This became a major issue in 1911, when Coney Island was hit with its next great fire.

On May 27, just after opening for the 1911 season, repairmen working late at night on Dreamland's Hell Gate ride accidentally spilled a bucket of hot tar. It set off a fire, which quickly spread throughout the structure and soon ignited neighboring buildings. Within an hour, the 375-foot-tall tower was ablaze, creating a giant torch that was visible from Manhattan. The Infant Incubators, which had moved over from Luna Park, were quickly evacuated, but the dozens of animals housed in the park were not as fortunate. Many were shot by their owners to keep them from burning to death, and one lion, Sultan, escaped from the park, ran down the street with his mane on fire, and climbed the Rocky Road to Dublin roller coaster, where he was killed by a fireman's ax. Another lion was discovered two weeks after the fire under Luna Park's Boardwalk, where it had been living off the park's chickens.

The fire then began consuming neighboring businesses. These included some of the area's oldest attractions, such as the Iron Tower and Balmer's Bathhouse, which housed Coney Island's first carousel. The newest ride, the Giant Safety Racer roller coaster, escaped only because of its steel support structure, although half a dozen other roller coasters were lost.

By the time the fire was brought under control at 5 A.M., 24 acres had been destroyed, and Dreamland and fifty other businesses were complete losses. Damage was estimated at $5 million, but the insurance on the damaged areas totaled less than $3 million.

Within hours, burned-out concessions were starting to rebuild to take advantage of the 350,000 people who came out to view the ruins. The Dreamland circus quickly reopened with fifteen surviving animals, and Sultan's body was put on display. Dreamland manager Samuel Gumpertz also opened the Dreamland Circus Sideshow along Surf Avenue.

Coney Island would never be the same. In 1912, Frederick Thompson declared bankruptcy and turned his beloved Luna Park over to creditors, although he remained as manager. The park had lost insurance coverage after the Dreamland fire. Across Surf Avenue, the city acquired the vacant Dreamland property for $3 million, with plans to turn it into a public park. The acquisition of the land signaled the beginning of increasing involvement by New York City in Coney Island, leading to a long, contentious relationship between the city and the area's private businessmen.

At the time Dreamland burned down, the city had constructed a bathhouse that started draining traffic from the private bathhouses. It also started making plans to reclaim the largely privately controlled beach for the public, announcing its intention to construct a 2-mile boardwalk along the waterfront. The property owners thought they had rights to the land extending into the ocean, however. Finally, in 1916, the New York Court of Appeals ruled that occupants have no land rights on the beach and ordered all structures and fences removed. When the businesses ignored the order, armed law enforcement officers visited the beach to enforce it. By 1919, the city was acquiring the needed property to return the beach to public use and build a boardwalk along the waterfront. The storied resort would be changed forever.

The decade also marked the loss of two of its most important showmen, George Tilyou in 1914 and Fred Thompson in 1919, probably the two people most responsible for elevating the standards at Coney Island into a first-class resort.

The Nickel Empire

Coney Island was completely transformed in the 1920s. The change was driven as much by the city's increasing involvement as by the evolution of the industry. In 1920, New York's subway was extended to Coney Island, making it accessible to millions of additional visitors for a 5-cent fare.

In 1923, the first sections of Coney Island's Boardwalk opened to the public. Eventually extending 3 miles, the Boardwalk was 80 feet wide

Surf Avenue has been Coney Island's front door for over a century. It is shown here following its widening in the 1920s.

The Tornado — Whirlwind Scenic Ride — Coney Island. N.Y.

16804   104

The Tornado anchored the Amusement Park Department Store when it opened in 1926.

and cost $2 million. As part of the project, the beach was increased by 2.5 million square feet by pumping sand in from other areas.

The infrastructure improvements moved to the heart of Coney Island after the 1923 season, when thirteen new streets were constructed between Surf Avenue and the Boardwalk to permit better access for firefighters. This meant the removal of 175 buildings and attractions, including the four roller coasters. By May 1924, Coney Island was completely rebuilt. The decade's final improvement was the widening of Surf Avenue in 1926, leading to the demolition of the Giant Safety Racer.

The loss of the old roller coaster hardly affected Coney Island, as it was replaced in 1927 by Coney Island's most famous ride, the Cyclone roller coaster. This was one of several rides opened during the 1920s that mirrored the evolution of the industry as a whole, changing its focus from live entertainment to thrill seeking.

The first of these new rides was the Wonder Wheel, a 150-foot-tall Ferris wheel that opened in 1920, featuring eight stationary cars and sixteen that rolled from the inner wheel to the outer wheel and back. In 1924, the Virginia Reel opened next to the Wonder Wheel. It consisted of a series of large tubs in which riders sat to cascade down a winding trough.

The 1920s was the decade of the roller coaster, however. With new technology allowing bigger drops and higher speeds, Coney Island's entrepreneurs raced to build the best ride. In 1924, the Mile Sky Chaser, the world's longest roller coaster, at nearly 4,000 feet, opened at Luna Park. The following year, John Miller, the most prolific roller coaster builder in history, constructed the Thunderbolt for George Moran. The Kensington Hotel, built in 1895, was already on the site, so the Thunderbolt was erected on top of the hotel, which was retained as a house for Moran.

In 1926, the L. A. Thompson Company developed the Amusement Park Department Store, a multifaceted amusement complex. It was anchored by the Tornado, a compact 71-foot-tall thriller designed by the firm of Prior and Church, featuring a wide array of twisting drops. Other attractions included a carousel, funhouse, bathhouse, shooting gallery, and glass house.

A Depressing Decade

With the onset of the Great Depression in 1929, Coney Island suffered along with the rest of the country. Although crowds continued to come, swelling to more than a million some days, they were not spending money. By the end of the 1932 season, tickets to some rides had been reduced to a penny, and the immense Feltman's restaurant saw employment fall from 1,200 to 350.

Luna Park struggled, with the lights dimmed and maintenance deferred. In 1933, the park declared bankruptcy. It was able to emerge by the following season, but only half the park was in operation. By 1935, new owners took over, promising to revitalize the operation.

While Steeplechase held on, it had its challenges. A 1939 fire caused $200,000 in damage, destroying the Flying Turns roller coaster after only five years of operation and damaging a section of the Steeplechase ride.

But as much of a strain as the Depression was on Coney Island, it was the naming of Robert Moses as parks commissioner in 1934 that sent the resort into a decades-long decline. Moses disdained Coney Island's atmosphere and declared that it "should be replaced by a Coney Island where mechanical amusement features would give way to scientific recreational facilities." His desires were actually the culmination of decades of tension between the amusement area and the city that dated back to 1899, when the first proposal was made to convert Coney Island into a public park, calling it "a blot on the face of civilization." Although that proposal went nowhere, the desire of some never died.

With control of the beach and the Boardwalk, Moses was able to impose new regulations on the resort regarding advertisements and noise. He announced plans to replace the amusement area with larger beaches, recreational spaces, and parking lots. "There is no use bemoaning the end of the old Coney Island fabled in song and story," said Moses. "The important thing is not to proceed in the mistaken belief that it can be revived. There must be a new and very different resort established in its place." With the owners of the amusements unsure of the long-term fate of the neighborhood, investments slowed considerably.

Still, Coney Island was big business, attracting 25 million people in 1939 who spent an estimated $35 million.

By 1941, the economy had improved to the point where Coney Island was looking to add new attractions. The World's Fair in nearby Queens had ended in 1940, providing a ready supply of equipment. Luna Park, which was taken over by new investors, brought in several new features. The Bobsled roller coaster was re-erected on the Bowery. Steeplechase acquired the Parachute Jump, a 262-foot-tall tower with twelve parachutes attached that offered customers a chance to experience a simulated parachute jump. It forever changed the Coney Island skyline.

World War II was a mixed blessing for Coney Island. New attractions and maintenance materials were hard to come by, and its eight hundred thousand lights had to be dimmed to avoid attracting enemy attention. The Pavilion of Fun was even closed in 1945 as a result of labor shortages. But Coney Island also served an important morale-boosting role, and people flocked there, leading to a record season in 1943. Despite the Depression and war, Coney Island was still an immense enterprise, with two large amusement parks, nine roller coasters, thirty-two other rides, eighteen bathhouses and swimming pools, six large restaurants, and more than two hundred other concessions.

The Decline

On August 12, 1944, at 3:30 P.M., a fire broke out in Luna Park's Dragon Gorge roller coaster. By the time it was extinguished, nearly half the park lay in ruins. The Mile Sky Chaser and Shoot the Chutes were severely damaged, and with material shortages because of the war, the park could not bounce back. While some portions of the park closest to Surf Avenue reopened, the remainder sat abandoned as insurance disputes were settled. Additional fires in 1946 and 1948 finished off much of the remainder of the park. At that point, the land had been sold for development into a housing complex, which finally opened in the late 1950s.

The loss of Luna Park was only the first of many setbacks that Coney Island would face over the next forty years. In 1946, Feltman's restaurant, which had been hurting since the Depression, was sold. It struggled on for another eight years before closing and being redeveloped. Thompson's Oriental Scenic Railway, the last of a dozen roller coasters he built at Coney Island, closed in 1954 after fifty-one years of operation. Meanwhile, many of the old-time business owners were dying off, and their properties were passed to absentee owners, contributing to an overall decline.

Robert Moses continued his plans to eliminate "shabby old Coney Island" in favor of "orderly public recreation." He succeeded in getting much of the neighborhood rezoned for residential purposes in 1953, and in 1957, the New York Aquarium opened on the former site of Dreamland.

By now the decline of Coney Island was evident. Steeplechase was the last major amusement park, and the number of roller coasters had fallen from nine in 1943 to four.

But in 1961, the Coney Island Chamber of Commerce proposed a $36 million rebuilding of the amusement area. The next year, Astroland opened on the former site of Feltman's, representing a bright spot in the troubled neighborhood. With its focus on modern rides, Astroland provided a reason to visit Coney Island during its bleakest years.

Still, many of the oldest anchors continued to disappear. The Ravenhall bathhouse burned down in 1963, and the Virginia Reel was demolished. In 1964, Coney Island was hit with its worst season in a quarter century, with concessionaires reporting drops of up to 90 percent. They were hurt not only by the New York World's Fair, but also by bad weather, increasing crime, and parking problems.

As the amusement area was preparing for the 1965 season, something was missing. Steeplechase was strangely quiet. Although the park had maintained the high standards that had made it a world-renowned attraction, by the end of 1964, family disputes, increasing costs, aging attractions, and the overall decline of Coney Island prompted the Tilyou family to close Steeplechase and put it up for sale.

The closing of Steeplechase Park following the 1964 season was a major blow to the struggling amusement area.

Throughout the 1965 season, Coney Island boosters desperately tried to find a buyer to reopen the park. Astroland and New Jersey's Palisades Park both expressed interest, but in the end, the Tilyous sold the 12-acre property to real estate developer Fred Trump for $2.5 million. Trump announced plans to redevelop the site into a housing complex, but his efforts to rezone the property were met with strong resistance.

The zoning fight continued through the 1966 season, while the abandoned Pavilion of Fun was leased to the operator of an animal display. But in the fall, Trump started to clear the site, and the rides and attractions were sold to parks around the world. In an attempt to win the rezoning, he proposed redeveloping the heart of the amusement area with a 7-acre, 160-foot-tall indoor amusement facility built atop two levels of parking.

As the battle continued, Trump leased the now vacant Steeplechase property to Norman Kaufmann, who opened his own version of Steeplechase Park in 1967. Although it featured a number of newer rides, such as a large Jumbo Jet roller coaster, added in 1972, it more resembled a carnival than an amusement park and came nowhere near recapturing the magic of its predecessor. By 1969, the city condemned the Steeplechase site and purchased the land from Trump for $4 million.

As Coney Island entered the 1970s, there were legitimate questions about whether the resort would survive the decade. The city was broke, crime was a problem, the boardwalk was deteriorating, landowners were abandoning their property, and arson was a constant threat. Subway traffic to Coney Island was 20 percent of what it had been in the 1920s.

Stauch's, the last of the big Coney Island bathhouses, closed early in the decade. The Bobsleds ride was demolished in 1974, and in December 1977, the Tornado was severely damaged by fire, leading to its demolition in 1979. Even the Cyclone was almost lost. The city had acquired the ride in 1965, and in 1972, it announced plans to demolish the ride to expand the Aquarium. But resistance to the plan prompted the city to lease it to Dewey Albert, owner of the adjacent Astroland, who proceeded to restore the ride. Perhaps there was life in the resort yet. Other people thought so as the Eldorado Bumping Disco opened along the Bowery in 1973, and today it remains among the best bumper car rides in the country.

The Slow Road Back

While the decline of Coney Island continued through the 1980s, signs slowly emerged that a revival was beginning. In 1981, the second Steeplechase Park finally closed after a decade-long battle with the city over its lease. This allowed the city to redevelop the site into a park for festivals and special events. The closure of the amusement park had a negative effect on neighboring businesses, however. In 1982, Fred Moran, owner

The Bowery has been the heart of Coney Island since 1882.

of the Thunderbolt and Tunnel of Laffs dark ride, died and the two rides were abandoned.

But there was still magic in the old resort. In 1984, Horace Bullard, a successful restaurant operator, reached an agreement with the city to take over the Steeplechase site and started acquiring additional property in neighborhood. He soon announced plans to build a new 17-acre Steeplechase Park for $65 million. Over the next few years, as the project worked its way through the approval process, it grew to 25 acres and $220 million. Unfortunately, the project lost its financing commitments in 1991, and the concept soon faded away.

While Bullard's dream died, a number of other revitalization initiatives were launched during the decade that started the slow comeback. Greek immigrant Denos Vourderis acquired Ward's Kiddie Park in 1981 and the Wonder Wheel and Spook-A-Rama rides in 1983 to form the basis of an all new amusement park, Deno's Wonder Wheel Park.

In 1981, an art group started by Dick Zigun, called Coney Island USA, started holding shows at Coney Island. That led to the launch of the Mermaid Parade in 1983, now one of the amusement area's largest events. The group followed up by opening Sideshows by the Seashore, an old-time sideshow, and the Coney Island Museum in 1985. By 1986, the city launched a major reconstruction and restoration of the Boardwalk and beach. The city even designated the Cyclone, Wonder Wheel, and abandoned Parachute Jump as historic landmarks.

By the 1990s, Coney Island was in the midst of a full-scale comeback. The city upgraded the Boardwalk, renovated the Stillwell Avenue subway terminal, and restored the Parachute Jump, now considered Brooklyn's Eiffel Tower. In 2001, a new baseball stadium opened on the Steeplechase site for the Brooklyn Cyclones, a minor-league team. Most recently, the city announced plans to enhance the remaining amusement area with a new restaurant complex adjacent to the Parachute Jump, the transformation of Stillwell Avenue into a public commons, and a restored B&B Carousel—Coney Islands last carousel—which the city acquired in 2005. The improvements are intended to inspire private developers to add new attractions to Coney Island. One such company, Thor Equities, has spent nearly $100 million to acquire 12 acres in the amusement area, where they intend to erect a resort hotel, entertainment facilities, and new amusements.

Coney Island Today

Coney Island is a true survivor. It has withstood decades of city negligence and urban decay and is once again on the rebound. Although it likely will never again achieve the stature that it had in the first half of the twentieth century, the appeal of its beach is not that much different than it was in 1829.

Coney Island has never been a single amusement park, but is a variety of independently owned amusements and concessions. Today its attractions include two full-scale amusement parks, Astroland and Deno's Won-

No trip to Coney Island is complete without a visit to Nathan's Famous hot dog stand.

der Wheel Park; a kiddieland, McCullough's Kiddie Park; a family entertainment center, Coney Island Batting Range and Go-Kart City; and a dozen other rides and attractions spread out over a five-block area along the Boardwalk.

The Cyclone roller coaster and Astroland amusement park anchor the eastern end of the amusement area. Next door to Astroland is Deno's Wonder Wheel Park, home of the world-famous Wonder Wheel and Spook A Rama dark ride. The Bowery is the heart of the amusement area and runs from Deno's to the western end. Among the attractions found along the Bowery are the Ghost Hole dark ride; one of the last Hurricane spinning rides in operation; McCullough's Kiddie Park, featuring a dozen kiddie and family rides; the Coney Island Museum and Sideshows by the Seashore; the Eldorado Bumping Disco; and Coney Island Batting Range and Go-Kart City, with two go-cart tracks, bumper boats, batting cages, and a miniature golf course. The original Nathan's Famous hot dog stand anchors the western end of the amusement area. Surf Avenue and the Boardwalk, which define the northern and southern boundaries, are also lined with a wide variety of concessions.

BROOKLYN

NEW YORK

Astroland
OPENED 1962

In the late 1950s, Coney Island was direly in need of a shot in the arm. The size of the amusement area was shrinking, in the face of city-sponsored urban renewal. Crime was increasing, traffic was starting to drop off, and the area's oldest institutions were beginning to fall by the wayside. One such place was Feltman's.

The Countdown

Starting as a small saloon in 1871, Feltman's had grown into the largest restaurant at Coney Island by the 1890s, covering 137,000 square feet, with several dining areas that could seat up to eight thousand patrons. It also had a wide variety of rides and attractions, including the Ziz roller coaster and a magnificent carousel dating to 1903 called the Superba. But by the 1950s, time and changing consumer tastes had caught up with Feltman's. The property was foreclosed on in 1952, and in June 1954, it was put up for auction.

Astroland
1000 Surf Ave.
Brooklyn, NY 11224
718-265-2100
www.astroland.com

With a bid of $490,000, control of the parcel—including a two-story restaurant, a recently erected steel-and-concrete cafeteria building, and twenty rides and concessions—passed to an investor group led by Dewey Albert and Herman Rapps. Albert, who was in the construction business, never intended to get into the amusement industry. But he joined the group at the encouragement of his friend Nathan Handwerker, owner of another Coney Island institution, Nathan's Hot Dogs, who wanted to keep the site for amusement purposes and away from the city's urban renewal program.

The new owners announced plans to eventually redevelop the site into an all-new amusement park, and they sought to make the most of their investment in the meantime. They leased the restaurant and amusements to new operators and added attractions such as a train, Tilt-A-Whirl and shooting gallery. By 1958, many of the older rides were being replaced.

Blastoff

During this time, Albert, who eventually bought out the other partners, started making plans to redevelop the site. When building-code violations closed the main building in 1961, he decided to make his move, having 30,000 square feet of old buildings demolished to make room for several new rides, including go-carts, a Flying Coaster, and the Space Ship. A predecessor to today's simulator attractions, the Space Ship consisted of a large aluminum rocket ship in which thirty-two riders could experience a trip into outer space through a movie projected onto a screen in the rocket's nose, with sound effects and seats that twisted and vibrated. Other attractions included a miniature golf course and a trout pond. Some older rides were retained, including Feltman's old carousel and the train. With the space race in full force, Albert decided to name the new amusement park Astroland.

Astroland opened for business in the spring of 1962 as Coney Island's first new major amusement park in more than fifty years. But that first season was primarily a transitional year between the old Feltman's operations and the true realization of Albert's vision. For several months, he and his son Jerome traveled to Europe to find the latest rides to bring back to Coney Island. On October 1, 1962, construction began to install nine major rides a cost of $3 million, including several that until that point had been seen only at major theme parks. The old carousel was removed to make room for an 80-foot-tall, 750-foot-long sky ride that linked the front of the park to the Boardwalk. The other anchor attraction was the Neptune Diving Bells. Costing $250,000, this unique ride featured two fifteen-passenger cabins that plunged into a 30-foot-deep tank where riders could view fish and dol-

This picture from Amusement Business *magazine shows construction at Astroland in 1963. Major attractions included the sky ride (1), the Space Ship (5), and the Diving Bells (7).* AMUSEMENT BUSINESS

phins. Rounding out the lineup were a number of spinning rides imported from Europe, including the Calypso, Cortina Bob, Satellite, and Himalaya, along with a seven-ride kiddieland.

After a successful season, Astroland completed the final phase of its redevelopment in 1964 with five more rides. The largest was the Astrotower, the first sky tower in the United States. Popular in Europe, the 275-foot-tall attraction featured a donut-shaped cabin that traveled up the tower. The massive $1.7 million ride required a foundation consisting of 1,100 tons of concrete and

The Astrotower was the first ride of its kind in the United States.

13 tons of steel reinforcing bars. Built by the Willy Buhler Company of Switzerland, the ride changed the skyline of Coney Island and still today provides a spectacular view of the city.

But the Astrotower was only the start. Replacing the go-carts was one of the first log flume rides ever constructed. Built by Arrow Development, the flume sent riders in fiberglass logs down a 1,052-foot-long trough into a splash-down finale. Other new rides included the Flight to Mars dark ride, Bumper Skooter, and kiddie roller coaster. But the 1964 season was a disaster because of competition from the New York World's Fair and bad publicity resulting from the decline of the neighborhood. That season, Steeplechase, Coney Island's other anchor attraction, closed, and Astroland was now the sole amusement park in the shrinking amusement area.

Albert's heavy investment in new rides, many of which did not exist outside of corporate theme parks, allowed Astroland to hold its own in a difficult period for Coney Island. New rides continued to be added, including a merry-go-round in 1965 and two rides purchased from the shuttered Steeplechase in 1966, the Caterpillar and Tilt-A-Whirl.

In 1971, the Flight to Mars was replaced by a new dark ride, Dante's Inferno, which remains a popular attraction, followed by three new attractions in 1972, the Round Up, Paratrooper, and Spanish Skooter, an electric go-cart ride.

Harnessing a Cyclone

By the mid-1970s, Astroland had become an established operation, and with its flashy modern rides, it remained a destination while businesses in much of the rest of the Coney Island amusement area were struggling. But the acquisition of a beloved antique that year changed the nature of Astroland.

Since Astroland opened, the Cyclone roller coaster was its neighbor across Tenth Street. When it debuted on June 26, 1927, at the height of the Roaring Twenties, it immediately achieved a reputation as one of the best roller coasters in the world. Charles Lindbergh even said that a ride on the Cyclone was "more of a thrill than flying." Standing 85 feet tall, the Cyclone was designed by Vernon Keenan and built by Harry Baker, one of history's most prolific roller coaster builders. Constructed on a 75-by-500-foot parcel, the Cyclone became known for its tight turns and steep drops along its 2,640 feet of track. It was owned by Jack and Irving Rosenthal, two brothers who got their start in the industry as youngsters selling pails and shovels at Coney Island. They later went on to turn New Jersey's Palisade's Park into one of the world's most famous amusement parks.

Coney Island's classic Cyclone now operates under the careful stewardship of Astroland.

After being sold by the Rosenthals in 1937, control of the ride eventually passed to the Pinto brothers in 1954, who operated and manufactured kiddie rides at Coney Island. In 1969, the city of New York condemned the ride and purchased it from the Pintos for $1.2 million, eventually planning to demolish it to expand the neighboring New York Aquarium. Until they were ready, however, they leased it back to the Pintos. But since the Pintos thought the ride would be torn down, they ceased making improvements, eventually wracking up 101 safety violations.

As a result, in April 1975, the city reopened the lease to new bidders. The Alberts immediately jumped at the chance to take over operation of the Cyclone, and on June 18, they received approval from the city to lease the ride. They immediately went to work around the clock renovating the Cyclone, spending $50,000 to upgrade it and make needed repairs. By July 3, the Cyclone was ready for eager throngs. Following the season, they invested another $60,000 on cosmetic improvements, including repainting the ride. Any talk of demolishing the Cyclone soon quieted. The Alberts have continued to care for the Cyclone, spending millions to keep it in top-notch condition. In 1988, just thirteen years after the city almost demolished it, the Cyclone was named a New York City landmark, and in 1991, it became a national historic landmark.

The Cyclone was not the only major change to hit Astroland that year. On July 11, 1975, just one week after reopening the classic, a midnight blaze broke out in the Astro Bar, a restaurant in the last remaining portion of the old Feltman's operation. Eighty firemen battled the blaze, which leaped 80 feet in the air and for a time endangered the Cyclone. By the time it was brought under control, the Astro Bar plus several games and concessions were destroyed. But fortunately, only one ride, the recently installed Music Express, was damaged. The construction crew that had just completed work on the Cyclone was pressed into service to clear the debris, and just three days later, the 10,000-square-foot area was blacktopped and ready for new attractions.

In a way, the fire was a blessing. The old building no longer blocked access to the park for passersby along Surf Avenue, and an area was opened up for new rides. Astroland began the 1976 season with $1 million in improvements, including two of the newest, flashiest rides in the industry: the Enterprise, a high-speed spinner, and the Wave Swinger, a colorful swing ride. These were followed in 1979 by the Astroliner, an updated version of the original Space Ship, which in 1972 was retired and placed atop a refreshment stand along the Boardwalk.

The Sky Ride was removed in 1975 and the Diving Bell was retired in 1982, but new rides continued to appear at Astroland. A swinging Pirate Ship opened in 1983, followed by the Rainbow in 1984 and the Himalaya in 1986. Another flashy, high-speed European-manufactured spinning ride, the BreakDance, replaced the Rainbow in 1988. It cost $1 million to install and was acquired after two years of research by Astroland on what type of ride to add.

Astroland's kiddie park also saw numerous changes during this period. The Cyclone received a smaller brother in the early 1980s with the addition of the Big Apple, a 13-foot-tall, 444-foot-long steel-track roller coaster with a unique turntable loading system. While one train is circling the track, a second is being loaded. A turntable then switches the trains, and the second train goes around the track while the first is loaded. Other new kiddie rides added during this period included kiddie boats in 1983, the Convoy truck ride in 1988, and swings in 1989.

Riding the Renaissance

By the 1990s, Coney Island was seeing the beginning of a renaissance. When the park saw the passing of its founder Dewey Albert in 1992, his son Jerome, who had worked with him almost since the beginning, stepped in along with daughter-in-law Carol. As the twenty-first century dawned, Astroland replaced the Spanish Skooter with the Hot Rods, billed as one of the largest bumper car rides in the world, and the Power

In operation for more than 40 years, Astroland's Log Flume is one of the world's original log flume rides.

Surge, which replaced the Music Express in 2001. The colorful 59-foot-tall ride spins twenty-four passengers in five different motions at the same time. Most recently, in 2004, Astroland brought in the Top Spin, another large European ride, in place of the Enterprise, along with the Tea Cups and Frog Hopper for kids.

Coney Island is now in the midst of a full-blown renaissance, sparked in no small part by the efforts of the Albert family and Astroland.

Astroland Today

As one of the anchors of the famed Coney Island resort, Astroland is the largest amusement park in New York City. Its two dozen rides include the Cyclone roller coaster, Dante's Inferno dark ride, and a dozen kiddie rides. The park occupies a rectangular block running between Surf Avenue and Coney Island's Boardwalk. The Cyclone is located across Tenth Street from the rest of Astroland. Entering Astroland from Surf Avenue, visitors are greeted by several of the flashy European rides for which the park is known, including the Power Surge, Top Spin, and Breakdance, along with Dante's Inferno. Next come the park's two oldest rides, the Astrotower and Log Flume. At the back of Astroland is the Kiddie Park, with fifteen family and kiddie rides, including the Tilt-A-Whirl, Scrambler, merry-go-round, Big Apple coaster, and Convoy.

Deno's Wonder Wheel Park

OPENED 1981

According to Denos Vourderis, his experience coming to the United States was different from those of others. Whereas most of the huddled masses looked to the Statue of Liberty for inspiration as their boats entered New York Harbor, Vourderis looked to the towering structures of Coney Island, in particular, the 150-foot-tall Wonder Wheel. Gazing upon the ride for the first time, he pledged to himself that he would realize his version of the American dream by one day owning it.

A Humble Beginning

Denos Vourderis was born in Aigion, Greece, in 1920, the eighth of twenty-two children. He emigrated to the United States in 1934 at the age of fourteen and joined the merchant marine. After serving in the army during World War II, Vourderis was honorably discharged in June 1946 and registered for a peddler's license. For the next several years, he sold food from pushcarts and even operated a restaurant. Whenever he could, he visited Coney Island, where he would claim a spot on the beach in front of the Wonder Wheel and marvel at the excitement of the Boardwalk. He even proposed to his wife, Lula, on board the Wonder Wheel, pledging that he would one day buy the wheel for her as a wedding present.

In 1962, Denos was able get closer to achieving his dream by purchasing the Anchor Bar and Grill, a restaurant on the Coney Island Boardwalk next door to the famous Cyclone. Denos worked hard to grow the business while raising his children in the restaurant. His business grew, and he opened a snack bar just a short way down the Boardwalk. In 1969, the city purchased the land under the Anchor to expand the New York Aquarium, and Denos lost the lease on the second location. But he was not deterred. He knew he could succeed at Coney Island and looked for his next opportunity.

He found it at Ward's Kiddie Park. Located on the Boardwalk in front of the Wonder Wheel, the park had opened in 1950 and featured nineteen

Deno's Wonder Wheel Park
3059 Denos Vourderis Place
(Formerly West Twelfth St.)
Brooklyn, NY 11224
718-372-2592
info@wonderwheel.com
www.wonderwheel.com

kiddie rides but no food service. Denos approached the owner, John Curran, and explained that Curran's customers were leaving when they got hungry, so he was losing them to other attractions. Denos opened for business in 1970 as the new food concessionaire, with an 8-by-16-foot concession trailer occupying a corner of the park. Though it was a small operation, it was extremely successful, prompting him to replace the trailer with a permanent building just three years later. But he did not get rid of the trailer, as he considered it the good-luck charm for what became a substantial empire. Even today, the trailer occupies a place of honor at Deno's Wonder Wheel Park, still fulfilling its original purpose. His children are under orders never to get rid of it.

By 1976, Denos had started to help Curran with the management of the kiddie park. He took to the amusement park business so well that in 1981, Curran, who was looking to retire, offered to sell him the park. Denos jumped at the opportunity. Although he did not have the money to cover the $600,000 asking price, Curran knew that his passion would allow him to run the business successfully and quickly pay off the debt. Denos's kids weren't as convinced, thinking he was crazy to take on such a large operation. But Denos, despite having only a third-grade education, was undaunted. "You got too much education and no guts," his son Dennis recalls him saying at the time. After all, it brought him even closer to his beloved Wonder Wheel.

It was not the best time to be investing in Coney Island. After several decades of decline, the resort was probably at its low point, with abandoned rides and buildings dotting the area. People still flocked to the beach across the Boardwalk, however, and were looking for clean, safe diversions. Denos knew that he had to invest to keep business viable, and his family went to work overhauling Ward's Kiddie Park.

The 1981 season was a learning experience for the family, but they knew they were on to something good. In 1982, they added their first new ride, the Mini Enterprise, a kiddie ride. Ward's Kiddie Park was soon on the rebound, which caught the attention of Denos's neighbor Fred Garms, owner of the adjacent Spook A Rama dark ride and, more important, the Wonder Wheel.

Claiming the Wheel

Since its opening on May 30, 1920, the Wonder Wheel had been one of Coney Island's most distinctive landmarks. Standing 150 feet tall, it was the tallest structure at the resort until the Parachute Jump opened in 1941. The wheel was invented by Charles Herman and is a true engineering marvel. Weighing 200 tons, it floats on a concrete slab, set in an underwater buoyancy tank 60 feet deep that also acts to diffuse any lightning that may strike the ride. But what makes the Wonder Wheel unique are its twenty-four cars, which hold a total of 144 people. While eight cars rotate anchored to the perimeter of the wheel, as on a traditional Ferris wheel, the remaining sixteen cars move on rails between the inner and outer rims, providing a one-of-a-kind, disconcerting ride experience, all the while offering panoramic views of Coney Island, the Atlantic Ocean, and the New York City skyline.

The Eccentric Ferris Wheel Amusement Company took two years to construct the ride, starting in 1918. A special forge was set up on-site to ensure that the best-quality steel was used, while Herman Garms led a group of eighteen co-owners who worked side by side with the construction crews to meet the highest standards. When Garms died in 1935, control of the ride passed to his son Fred.

The Wonder Wheel gained a neighbor in 1955 when Garms hired the Pretzel Amusement Company, the world's largest manufacturer of dark rides, to build the Spook A Rama on a strip of property adjacent to the wheel. When it opened, it was a quarter mile long and was advertised as the "World's Longest Spook Ride." It was truly a unique attraction. Riders boarded in a small building near the Bowery. After brief trip through that structure, the cars traveled outdoors past the Wonder Wheel, where they entered a larger building where most of the stunts were located. They then traveled outside, back to first building. In later years, the ride

The Spook A Rama dark ride originally opened in 1955, but was acquired by the Vourderis family in 1983.

was scaled back to the second building only, with the outdoor portion being removed in the late 1990s.

The two rides remained among the most popular in Coney Island, but by 1983, Garms was looking to move on. He was approached by several interested parties, some of whom wanted to move the Wonder Wheel elsewhere, but he knew that there was only one person to whom he would entrust what was essentially a huge family heirloom: Denos Vourderis, who by now had turned Ward's Kiddie Park into a successful operation.

When Garms decided he was ready to sell, Denos was in the hospital. As a result, his son Dennis relayed the message to him. Denos, realizing his lifelong dream was about to come true, responded, "If he sells that wheel to anyone else, I'll kill him." Needless to say, Garms had no intention of selling his operations to anyone else, and in June, the Wonder Wheel and Spook A Rama became the property of the Vourderis family for $250,000. It was the culmination of a dream for this immigrant from Greece, and he quickly went to work lovingly overhauling the ride for an additional $250,000. Largely as a result of his efforts, the Wonder Wheel was designated an official New York City landmark on May 23, 1989.

The Vourderis family holdings officially opened as Deno's Wonder Wheel Park in 1986. DENO'S WONDER WHEEL PARK

Although Denos's dream had come true, he was not done yet. In January 1985, an adjacent 12,000-square-foot building holding a Skooter and Scrambler ride burned down. For the entire summer, the burned-out shell sat there, deterring potential visitors. By the end of the season, visitation was down by half, and the Vourderis family knew that the future of their growing business depended on acquiring the property. They reached an agreement to gain control of the site and purchased three new rides to fill the area: the Balloon Race, Dragon Coaster, and Skooter.

A True Amusement Park

With the acquisition of the new property and addition of the new rides, the family felt that they now owned a true amusement park, rather than just a collection of attractions. At the suggestion of Peter Buxbaum, the owner of the nearby Eldorado Bumping Disco, the operation was named Deno's Wonder Wheel Park.

Like most seaside amusement parks, Deno's is a space-constrained operation, cramming nearly two dozen rides into a 100,000-square-foot parcel. As a result, once the park was established, the family rotated rides in and out to keep things up-to-date. In 1989, the Balloon Race was replaced by the Quasar, a flashy, high-speed circular ride, and four new rides debuted in the kiddie area: the Big Foot trucks, Rio Grande train, Elephants, and Spin the Apple. The Dragon Coaster was sold in 1991 to make room for the Thunderbolt, a spinning ride, and the looping High Flyer replaced the Quasar in 1994.

That year was a sad one for the Vourderis family, as Denos passed away. But he had seen his lifelong dream come true and played a major role in the burgeoning renaissance of Coney Island. The park was left in good hands, those of his sons Dennis and Steve, who continue to care for Denos's beloved wheel.

The first major attraction added by the brothers was a new roller coaster. Given that the park had the largest collection of kiddie rides in Coney Island, they knew that a kiddie coaster was just what they needed to round out their lineup of attractions.

Dennis Vourderis invited Fred Miler, owner of Miler Coasters, out to Deno's. Dennis pointed out a corner of the park and asked Miler to design a ride that would provide the maximum amount of thrills for the space. The result was the Sea Serpent, a custom-designed, 13-foot-tall, 312-foot-long, steel-track ride complete with a spiral.

Most recently, the park added two tower rides. In 2001, a kiddie free-fall debuted, and in 2005, the High Flyer gave way to the 100-foot-tall Super Shot tower.

Deno's Wonder Wheel Park features a large kiddieland.

All along, the Vourderis family has stuck to its roots, offering clean, safe family entertainment. As Dennis Vourderis once told the *New York Times*: "It's more than just business, or the money. It's the promises Steve and I made to my father. And the history is here too."

Deno's Wonder Wheel Park Today

Deno's Wonder Wheel Park stands as testament to one man's realization of the American dream. Through sheer hard work and guts, Denos Vourderis built an amusement park from a disjointed collection of attractions and played a key role in revitalizing the storied Coney Island amusement area. Today the park has two main sections featuring nearly two dozen rides, including the fabled Wonder Wheel. Along the Coney Island Boardwalk is the kiddie park, home to seventeen kiddie and family rides, including the Sea Serpent roller coaster. A ramp leads from this area down to the Wonder Wheel. Next door is the Spook A Rama dark ride and a walkway, along which the major rides such as the Super Shot are arranged, that leads to the Bowery, the heart of Coney Island.

Seabreeze Amusement Park

OPENED 1879

ALONG THE SHORES OF LAKE ONTARIO ON THE EASTERN SIDE OF ROCHESTER sits the inlet to Irondequoit Bay. The beach at the convergence of these two bodies of water is a popular destination for people to enjoy the water and cooling breezes on hot summer days. Its timeless appeal has attracted people for more than 150 years and led to the founding of Seabreeze, the country's fourth-oldest operating amusement park.

Enjoying the Sea Breeze

Since the mid-1800s, Sea Breeze, this spit of land dividing Lake Ontario from Irondequoit Bay, has served as a recreation spot for residents of Rochester. The breezes generated by the two bodies of water provide relief from the heat of the city. Boating, fishing, and picnicking initially were popular pastimes. Hotels began appearing in the 1860s, but the area remained largely inaccessible to big crowds because of a lack of transportation infrastructure.

But in 1876, when Rochester resident Michael Filon attended the Centennial Exposition in Philadelphia, he spotted a train transporting passengers around the grounds and thought that a similar line would be a great way to connect the Sea Breeze area with downtown Rochester. After returning home, Filon lined up forty-one other investors to acquire two locomotives and eight passenger coaches from the exposition. The new railroad was officially called the Rochester and Lake Ontario Railroad but was more widely known as the Dummy Line,

Seabreeze Amusement Park
4600 Culver Rd.
Rochester, NY 14622
585-323-1900
info@seabreeze.com
www.seabreeze.com

referring to a structure over the locomotive's boiler built to prevent the engine from scaring off horses.

The new company also purchased 50 acres of land on the Sea Breeze bluff overlooking the lake and bay, and set about turning the property into a first-class resort. A railroad terminal was erected, along with a large pavilion for dining and dancing, a hotel overlooking the lake, and a boathouse. A large picnic area, linked to the main part of the park by a bridge over a ravine, was the main attraction. On August 5, 1879, the first train arrived at the new resort from downtown Rochester.

With Sea Breeze now more widely accessible, people flocked to the area, and more attractions soon were added. A boat dock was constructed so that steamboat excursions could reach the resort. In 1883, the park's first ride, a steam-driven carousel, appeared.

The young park suffered a major fire in 1885, the first of several that it would experience during its history, which destroyed the hotel and train station. In many instances, this would have quickly put an end to a fledgling operation, but the patrons were undeterred. They continued to flock to the park and growth continued. A new train station was constructed almost immediately, a structure that still stands as the park's main concession area.

In 1887, Stahley's Switchback was built along the Lake Ontario beach. A primitive roller coaster, the ride consisted of two parallel undulating tracks down which a car coasted. But the ride was destroyed by a storm the following winter, and it would be sixteen years before a roller coaster again operated at Sea Breeze. By 1889, the park had fully recovered from the fire, and a new hotel and dance hall overlooking Irondequoit Bay and Lake Ontario opened.

The resort was thriving, but its owner, the Rochester and Lake Ontario Railroad, was struggling. Though the trains the railroad purchased had run successfully on the level grounds of the Philadelphia Exposition, the more rolling terrain of Rochester took its toll on the equipment. In 1899, one of the trains was rounding a curve on the way to Sea Breeze when it toppled over, killing one person and injuring fifty. The accident brought the railroad into bankruptcy, and the resort was put up for auction.

Sea Breeze soon found a new owner, the Rochester and Suburban Railway Company, which had established service to the park just a few years earlier. Many trolley companies of the era, including the Rochester and Suburban, saw the development of amusement parks at the ends of their lines as a way to generate ridership on evenings and weekends. The company already operated Ontario Beach, a rival amusement park just west of Sea Breeze that had opened in 1884.

LOCATION

Sea Breeze is located on the east side of Rochester on Culver Road. To reach the park, take I-590 North to its end at Lake Ontario, and turn left onto Culver Road. The park is 500 yards ahead on the left.

OPERATING SCHEDULE

Seabreeze opens at noon on weekends from mid-May to mid-June. From mid-June through Labor Day, the park is open daily. The water park is open from 11 A.M. to 8 P.M., and the amusement park is open from noon to 10 P.M. weekdays and 11 P.M. on weekends.

ADMISSION

Pay-one-price admission of less than $25 entitles visitors to all rides and attractions, with the exception of games. Discounts are available for children under 48 inches tall and for visitors after 5 P.M. In addition, a spectator pass for less than $10 is available for visitors who do not wish to ride. Ride tickets also are available.

FOOD

Seabreeze Amusement Park features about ten different food outlets. The Seabreeze Grill, located next to the park office, is the main stand, offering hot dogs, Italian sausage, burgers, french fries, and onion rings. The California Café, in the water park, has a similar menu, as well as grilled chicken, pretzels, and nachos. Other stands serve made-to-order submarine sandwiches, pizza, fresh-cut french fries, and ice cream. Don't miss the Waffle Stand, home of Seabreeze's famous sugar waffles.

Outside food and beverages are permitted in the public-use picnic groves, located between the log flume and wave pool. Tables and grills are available on a first-come, first-served basis.

FOR CHILDREN

Kiddie City is the main kiddie area. Located in the center of the park, it features five of the park's kiddie rides. Don't miss Bear Trax, a custom-designed roller coaster just for kids and their parents. Many of the other rides in the park can be enjoyed by the entire family, including the carousel, Scenic Train, Flying Scooters, Spring, and Bobsleds. In the water park, kids can splash around in Looney Lagoon.

SPECIAL FEATURES

Although things have been kept up-to-date, Seabreeze Amusement Park has managed to maintain its classic traditional amusement park atmosphere. Many of the structures, including the game colonnade, park office, and bumper car building, date back to the late nineteenth and early twentieth centuries. The

(continued on page 78)

VISITING (continued from page 77)

SEABREEZE AMUSEMENT PARK

park still has several classic rides, including the Jack Rabbit, Flying Scooters, and Scenic Train.

Few carousels are more beautiful than the one at Seabreeze. Although it dates only to 1996, it harks back to the hand-carved masterpieces of yesteryear and is a work of art in its own right. Topped off with the band organ and the famous red rocking chairs, this magnificent ride provides one of the greatest carousel experiences anywhere.

For a park of its size, Seabreeze boasts one of the most complete roller coaster lineups. Dating back to 1920, the Jack Rabbit is a classic wooden roller coaster; the Bobsled is a one-of-a-kind steel-track ride; the Whirlwind represents the latest in roller coaster technology; and Bear Trax is an excellent starter coaster.

TIME REQUIRED

Seabreeze Amusement Park, with its rides and water park, can easily fill an entire day. If you are pressed for time and visit on a day when crowds are light, the major attractions can be enjoyed in about four hours.

TOURING TIPS

Visit on a weekday, as crowds tend to be lighter. Seabreeze hosts a lot of large group picnics on weekends.

Start the day at the north end of the park, where you'll find the Whirlwind and Bobsled roller coasters and the Gyrosphere. They are among the most popular attractions in the park, and their lines can get quite lengthy on crowded days.

The water park opens one hour before the rest of the amusement park during much of the summer. Consider starting your visit there and moving to the amusement park as the water park becomes more crowded in the afternoon.

Sea Breeze's new owner set about to transform the park from a quiet resort focused on picnicking and other passive activities into a full-blown amusement park to meet changing consumer tastes. The first major attraction to open was the Figure Eight in 1903, a common type of roller coaster in that era, with cars that traveled down a gently sloping track in the shape of a figure eight.

A Long Relationship

It was the simple addition of a carousel the next year that changed the fate of Sea Breeze. It was common during the era that amusement parks did not purchase and operate the rides and attractions, but leased space to concessionaires who built and operated their own attractions.

When the trolley company put out a request for a carousel operator, it attracted the attention of George Long, whose family had been building and operating carousels for nearly three decades. When Long came

The Figure Eight roller coaster was the first major attraction added to Seabreeze as it transformed into a full blown amusement park. SEABREEZE AMUSEMENT PARK

across the solicitation, he had just concluded an unsuccessful season in Norfolk, Virginia, where he had taken a carousel his family built in 1899. The park he had contracted with, Pine Island, was hit with construction delays, and Long and his son, George Jr., spent the summer living in a shack on the beach while their ride sat idle.

Long jumped at the chance to spend the summer in Rochester, where his brother operated a carousel at nearby Ontario Beach, and he moved his ride to Sea Breeze. This began an association between the park and the family that lasts to this day. The park had no electricity, so the carousel ran on steam power. The family lived in a room in the back of the carousel building, and during the winter, they stayed in Philadelphia.

Sea Breeze was evolving under its new ownership. A circle swing ride was added in 1908. The original pavilion, the last of the park's buildings from 1879, was lost to a fire in 1909. The Mirror Gallery, a fun house attraction, arrived in 1914.

In 1915, the twenty-three-year-old George Long Jr. returned to Sea Breeze. After graduating from high school, he had studied electrical engineering at the Drexel Institute and went to work for Bell Telephone. But once summer arrived, the amusement industry that he had known all his life called him back. His father told him that the carousel could not support two families, so he took on other jobs in the park. The young George had always been a builder, so his first project was constructing a new carousel building for the family's ride, since they had leased the existing building to another concessionaire for conversion into a dance hall.

That same year, the Long family responded to a solicitation to operate a carousel at Rochester's Seneca Park Zoo. Since the family was no longer building carousels, they purchased a new ride from the Philadelphia Toboggan Company (PTC #38) for $7,800. Representing the latest in carousel technology, it featured forty-eight horses that moved up and down. Again, George Jr. was pressed into service to construct a building for that ride.

The more modern carousels, like the one the Longs operated at Seneca Park, were starting to have a negative impact on their original ride at Sea Breeze, whose horses did not move. In 1917, George Jr. used the skills he learned in a woodcarving class in high school to make new legs for the horses so that they could be converted into jumpers.

Roaring through the Twenties

With the closing of Ontario Beach in 1919, Sea Breeze was coming into its own as the dominant amusement park in Rochester. During the prosperous twenties, Sea Breeze entered its greatest era of growth.

Starting off the decade was the addition of a new roller coaster, the Jack Rabbit. Representing the latest in roller coaster technology, it used a new technique to lock the train to the tracks, allowing for higher speeds and bigger hills. The Jack Rabbit was built by the team of John Miller and Harry Baker, two of history's most prolific roller coaster builders. At 2,130 feet long and 60 feet tall, and featuring a 75-foot drop

The Jack Rabbit has anchored the south end of the park since 1920.

The PTC carousel was Seabreeze's most beloved attraction until it was destroyed in a 1994 fire.

into a ravine, a helix, and a 265-foot tunnel, the Jack Rabbit was an immediate hit and remains as the second-oldest operating roller coaster in the United States.

George Long Jr. was very much involved in the park's growth during the decade. In 1921, he teamed with two concessionaires to replace the Figure Eight with the Virginia Reel, a unique attraction on which riders in large tubs travel down a switchback track. The following season, he constructed a building for a new Dodgem ride next to the Jack Rabbit.

With the Roaring Twenties at its peak, the 1925 season saw the arrival of Sea Breeze's largest attraction, the Natatorium. Measuring 300 by 125 feet, it was billed as the largest saltwater swimming pool in the world. The $300,000 project also included a stage for entertainment, bleachers for observers, a toboggan slide, a water merry-go-round, 6,500 lockers, an ultraviolet water purification system, and a massive heater that kept the water at a constant 72 degrees.

More new features were added that year as well. As the industry matured, kiddie rides were starting to appear in amusement parks. Sea Breeze jumped on the bandwagon, building the Jack 'n' Jill Scenic, a small, powered roller-coaster-type ride, along with several other kiddie rides.

Expansion continued in 1926 with the Wildcat, a huge roller coaster built by the Philadelphia Toboggan Company that stood 93 feet tall with 2,800 feet of track. The roller coaster was an important addition, but it was a seemingly innocuous move by the Longs that would have the longest-lasting impact.

For a number of years, Seneca Park, where the Longs operated their newer carousel, had been in decline. At the same time, it was harder for their older Sea Breeze carousel to accommodate the park's growing crowds. As a result, in 1926, they swapped the two rides. At Sea Breeze, the former Seneca Park ride was joined by a new Wurlitzer 165 band organ, and it became the park's most beloved attraction. Unfortunately, the older carousel was destroyed by fire in 1942.

By that time, Sea Breeze was at its peak. Billed as Rochester's Million Dollar Playground, it featured three major roller coasters, the Virginia Reel, a huge swimming pool, a dance hall, and numerous other attractions. To cater to the increasingly important automobile trade, the park advertised three thousand parking spaces. But this glory was not to last.

Troubled Times

In 1929, America entered the Great Depression. With money in tight supply, the amusement industry was especially hard hit, and Sea Breeze was no exception. Steamboat service to the park was halted. To add to the problems, a series of fires cost the park many of its major attractions.

The first fire was in 1930 and destroyed the Virginia Reel and the Greyhound, a roller coaster that had opened in 1918. The Greyhound, which operated as a concession, had been losing customers to more modern rides for years. It even turned one of its cars around to allow visitors to ride backward as a last-ditch attempt to attract business. Its station was

The Virginia Reel and Greyhound were popular attractions that were both destroyed by fire in 1930. SEABREEZE AMUSEMENT PARK

spared from the flames and later converted into the park's bumper car ride. The next year, fire claimed the Jack 'n' Jill Scenic, while the Natatorium was abandoned because of high operating costs.

The run of bad luck continued in 1933, when flames consumed the Danceland dance hall after ten years of operation and nearly claimed the adjacent Jack Rabbit. The Jack Rabbit survived, but the Wildcat did not, falling victim to fire in 1935.

By 1936, Sea Breeze was truly a troubled operation. Some attractions, such as Danceland, were replaced, but the park was full of holes where other features used to be. The trolley company wanted to get out of the amusement park business and turned to George Long Jr.

Despite the park's troubles, Long remained committed to the operation, having taken over ownership of the carousel in 1932 when his father died. His work ethic, which is still legendary at the park, made him an ideal candidate to take over the operation. A story handed down through the family recalls a time when George Sr. was sitting in front of the carousel, and Jack Kirby, who owned the Jack Rabbit, strolled by. The elder Long said, "Jack come over and sit down, take it easy. Don't be like my son, jumping around, running here and there, doing this and that. He doesn't enjoy life. You should sit down and enjoy yourself."

On the Rebound

In 1937, George Long agreed to lease the park from the trolley company, and he jumped headlong into revitalizing the operation. He staged twice-daily live shows to attract crowds and began filling the empty spaces with the park's first new attractions in nearly a decade. These included the Loop-O-Plane; the Sky Ride, an updated version of the circle swing; and the Lightning Bug, a large ride on which circular cars traveled on an undulating track, on the former location of the Virginia Reel. The abandoned Natatorium was converted into a bingo hall in 1938. To give the park a fresh image, he changed its name to Dreamland in 1939.

Another unique attraction added during this period was the Subway. For a number of years, the Old Mill, a boat ride through a tunnel, operated in and around the Jack Rabbit's structure. For much of its existence, it had been plagued by leaks. As a result, the park drained the water, took the cars from the demolished Greyhound, and pulled them through the tunnel using a converted Model A Ford. Eventually, in 1970, it was converted into the Kaleidoscope, with a new set of cars that each had an eight-track tape player for sound effects. The ride lasted until the early 1980s.

Rationing brought about by World War II severely limited park improvements. By the time the war ended, the trolley company was looking to fully divest the operation and approached Long about buying the park. The initial asking price was $100,000, to which Long responded, "If I had that hundred thousand, I wouldn't even bother with you." The trolley company persisted and sent an appraiser to the park, resulting in a reduced asking price of $85,000. Long had spent off-seasons since 1925 building houses throughout Rochester and had $50,000 saved up, and he was able to get a loan for the balance just on a signature and his good name because of his past dealings with the bank. It turned out to be a wise investment, as Long paid off the loan in just two seasons.

With Long now in full control of the park and America experiencing a period of postwar prosperity, he set about rebuilding Dreamland. Although he lost 16 acres of the park in 1952 to the state for highway construction, he was undeterred and spent much of the decade erecting new attractions that he designed.

He built a Junior Coaster for the park's younger visitors in 1954, the same year he installed Fairyland, a petting zoo and storybook attraction. Two years later, the Scenic Train was built using track and cars acquired from a local shipyard. The Delta Queen, a riverboat ride, also debuted during this period, but it was never popular because the pond that held it was too small, and it was removed in 1964.

One of the park's most notable attractions, Over the Falls, a shoot-the-chutes ride, was built in 1958. The park purchased the plans for the ride from Euclid Beach Park in Cleveland, which had previously built an identical attraction. There was an error in the plans, however, and the boats were a little too wide to fit through the turns. Some of the concrete had to be chipped away to allow the boats to pass before more permanent modifications could be made the following winter. The 1950s closed with the installation of the Crazy Cups and several kiddie rides to serve the children born in the postwar baby boom.

Expansion continued into the 1960s with the addition of the Hot Rods, a go-cart ride, in 1961. But times were changing, and the park began struggling in the face of urban unrest and changing consumer tastes. Long did what he could to hold on and continued to make improvements. One of his major projects was to convert the Junior Coaster into the Bobsleds in 1968. Inspired by a visit to Disneyland, where he was enamored with the Matterhorn roller coaster, Long enlarged the structure and replaced the wooden tracks with tubular steel. The result is a zippy 31-foot-tall, 1,240-foot-long ride that remains one of the park's most popular attractions.

During this period, Long used his woodcarving skills to take up a new hobby. In 1965, his son-in-law, Merrick Price, purchased an old carousel carving machine from the Philadelphia Toboggan Company. It was the same machine Long had used half a century earlier, when he briefly

Over the Falls was built by George Long in 1958. It was converted into the Log Flume in 1984. SEABREEZE AMUSEMENT PARK

worked at the company, and he started carving full-size replicas of carousel horses. One of the few people at the time still proficient in this lost art, George Long was profiled in 1969 by Charles Kuralt on *On the Road.*

Passing the Torch

By the 1970s, Long was tiring of the daily grind of running an amusement park. In 1973, he briefly considered selling the park for a waterfront condominium development. But his family, especially his five grandchildren, could not bear to see his life's work plowed under. As a result, the grandchildren started learning the business, and by 1975, control of the park was transferred to a new company run by Anne, George, John, and Rob Norris and Suzy Hoffsass.

The youthful owners brought renewed vigor to the amusement park. They revived the Seabreeze name, using a one-word contraction of the original, as Dreamland never really took hold. They spent the first several years upgrading the park's infrastructure. In the late 1970s, the park started adding new attractions. In keeping with family tradition, many were created by the grandkids.

One of the first was the Gyrosphere, constructed in 1977 on the former site of the Lightning Bug, which has been removed several years earlier. The $75,000 Gyrosphere was a unique attraction in which a Scrambler spinning ride was placed inside a large, air-supported dome. An elaborate light and sound show using two 200-watt speakers and nine projectors accompanied the ride. The inaugural song was "Fire on High," by Electric Light Orchestra (ELO). The ride has become such a local institution that even today local radio stations call "Fire on High" the "Seabreeze Gyrosphere Song."

Other new additions included the Animal Crackers kiddie ride and Manhandlers, a tub ride themed as Campbell soup cans, in 1978. The next year saw the Round Up and the conversion of the 1940s-era Ghost Train dark ride into the Merlin-themed Enchanter. In 1981, the park's youngest visitors were able to enjoy Kids Kingdom, a large interactive play area featuring a pool of balls, cube maze, log mountain, bounce, slides, and cargo nets to climb on that replaced the Hot Rods.

The upgrades continued in 1984, with the replacement of Over the Falls by a new log flume ride. The ride was lengthened to 1,200 feet, and the original 40-foot-tall hill was maintained and renovated to accommodate the flume. Its 55-degree drop is the steepest found on any log flume. The 1985 season saw the addition of the Bunny Rabbit, a steel-track kiddie roller coaster.

As 1985 wound down, the reinvigorated amusement park ended its first decade under the direction of George Long's grandchildren. What had been a struggling operation was now thriving and becoming a regional destination, while many of its former competitors went out of business.

Sliding in a New Direction

It seemed to be the perfect time to take Seabreeze to a new level by launching the largest expansion the park had seen in sixty years. During the 1980s, water parks had become increasingly popular attractions, and Seabreeze viewed the addition of one as the perfect way to grow their market. The result was a new, 4-acre, $1.2 million water park for the 1986 season, featuring five water slides all extending from a 50-foot-tall tower. The new water park also led to another major change to the park: For the first time ever, admission was charged. Seabreeze knew that there might be some initial resistance, because it had been a free-admission facility for 107 years. As a result, they distributed vouchers that could be turned in for cash or used as a discount on pay-one-price admission. The water park was a huge success. Seabreeze followed it up in 1988 with a kid's water area that featured two slides and an activity pool, followed in 1990 by a 600-foot-long lazy river.

Growth also continued in the amusement park. A Yo Yo swing ride was added in 1989, and the Sea Dragon, a swinging ship ride, replaced Kids Kingdom in 1991.

Seabreeze was now firmly in control of George Long's grandchildren, but he remained close to the operation. Long was a regular presence at the park and had a particular fondness for the carousel. He had a workshop in the basement of the carousel building, where he kept busy maintaining the ride and carving miniature carousel horses. By the time he died on September 27, 1988, at age ninety-six, Long had carved five hundred miniature horses, including two complete miniature carousels each measuring eight feet in diameter.

Continuing a Family Tradition

Seabreeze's carousel was held in special esteem at the park because of the family's history. The carousel pavilion was not just a building to hold a ride, but the veritable heart of Seabreeze. With historical displays, George Long's carvings, and three dozen rocking chairs, it was one of the most popular gathering places in Rochester. The ride was considered such a gem that it was voted one of the top five carousels in America by the National Carousel Association.

On March 31, 1994, the heart of Seabreeze was torn out. As the park was making preparations for its 115th season, workers repairing the roof of the neighboring arcade building ignited a fire that quickly engulfed the arcade, an old building that for many years had been a roller rink. By 3:06 P.M., the first of 175 firefighters arrived at the park. Thanks to past drills at Seabreeze, the firefighters knew how to position equipment to keep the fire from spreading, but it was too late to save the beloved carousel.

By the time the fire had been brought under control at 4:47 P.M., 10 percent of the park had been lost. All that was left of the carousel was the twisted remains of the center pole. George Long's miniature rides were reduced to ashes. The Goofy House fun house, arcade, and shooting gallery were gone. The Gyrosphere's dome had been torn open by the heat, and the Tea Cup, Yo Yo, and Bobsled had all sustained damage. To complicate things, many ride vehicles had been stored for the winter in the maintenance shop, located in the basement of the arcade.

The industry rallied to support Seabreeze. Many amusement parks and manufacturers provided surplus ride vehicles to help get the park open. In the end, opening for the 1994 season was delayed by just two weeks. But there was still a hole that needed to be filled.

Seabreeze's owners also knew that they had to do something to prove to their customers that the fire would not put them out of business. Before the fire, they had been shopping for a new roller coaster for the 1995 season and had just located one for sale in France that suited their needs. The 840,000-pound ride arrived in Rochester from France just after July 4 and opened only two weeks later. Named Quantum Loop, the new ride stood 75 feet tall and had 2,822 feet of track, two 58-foot-tall loops, and a 720-degree horizontal spin.

With the 1994 season behind them, the family turned their attention to rebuilding the attractions destroyed by the fire. Seabreeze was able to quickly have a new 5,000-square-foot arcade building ready for the 1995 season, but George Long's grandchildren deliberately took their time finding a replacement carousel.

It would have been easier to purchase an off-the-shelf merry-go-round with fiberglass animals, but they knew it would not be a fitting legacy for the beloved lost carousel. Acquiring another antique ride would prove problematic, because few were available and their cost was prohibitive. As a result, the family decided to continue tradition and create their own carousel. The intent was not to replicate the lost carousel, but to recapture the spirit of the original ride by creating horses in similar styles.

Rob Norris headed a team that evaluated eight different manufacturers and a dozen carvers before coming up with a concept for the new ride. As the heart of the new carousel, Seabreeze was able to locate a frame from an antique Philadelphia Toboggan Carousel machine dating to 1914 that had been stripped of its horses many years ago. It was completely overhauled by a team headed by George Norris.

To repopulate the ride, Ed Roth of Lakewood, California, was hired by Seabreeze to hand-carve thirty-eight new horses and two chariots. For eighteen months, Roth worked almost around the clock to create horses reflective of vintage carving styles. Six horses that were not on the original machine at the time of the fire, four from the original PTC #38, and

Seabreeze opened its new wooden carousel in 1996.

The park celebrated its 125th anniversary in 2004 by opening the Whirlwind roller coaster.

two that were carved by George Long were also included on the new $500,000 ride.

A new $300,000 building, measuring 86 feet wide and 42 feet tall, was constructed to house the new carousel. Since a Wurlitzer 165 band organ was not available, Seabreeze contracted with J. Verbeek Organ Manufacturing of Belgium to create a new version. The park was fortunate to discover parts of an original Wurlitzer 165 to incorporate into the new organ.

With the carousel and band organ in place, replacements for the famous red rocking chairs were still needed to make the new ride complete. No plans existed for the chairs, and it took three different prototypes to get them just right. But on June 1, barely two years after the fire, the ninth carousel created by the Long family opened to a grateful public.

A carousel was back in its rightful place and Seabreeze was whole again. The family could now focus on adding new attractions. In 1997, Bear Trax, a 12-foot-tall, 380-foot-long custom-built kiddie roller coaster, replaced the Bunny Rabbit. The Screamin' Eagle, a 70-foot-tall looping thrill ride, debuted in 1998. The next few years focused on the water park. The Soak Zone, a water play area anchored by a 1,000-gallon tipping bucket, debuted in 1999. That was followed by a 15,000-square-foot wave pool in 2001. In 2003, the Spring, a bouncing tower ride, joined the lineup.

As Seabreeze approached its 125th anniversary in 2004, Quantum Loop's popularity was declining. A new roller coaster would be the perfect way to celebrate the anniversary. The family wanted something that would be thrilling but still appeal to a wide variety of visitors. The result was the Whirlwind, a 51-foot-tall, 1,400-foot-long steel-track roller coaster with a series of tight turns, manufactured by the German firm of Maurer Sohne. What made the $2 million ride unique was its cars, which spun freely up to twenty times per minute based on the weight distribution of the four riders. Quantum Loop was sold to an amusement park in Bogotá, Columbia.

Seabreeze Amusement Park Today

In an era dominated by large corporate-owned theme parks, Seabreeze Amusement Park is alive and well as a family-owned traditional amusement park. On its 35 acres are fourteen major rides and eight kiddie rides, including four roller coasters, along with a full-scale water park.

The park has three entrances: the main entrance off parking lot 1, another next to the park office, and a third at the water park. Coming in through the main entrance, visitors find the Jack Rabbit and Bear Trax roller coasters to the right. To the left is the main game area, along a covered promenade that dates back to the late 1800s. Continuing down the midway, visitors enter the north end of the park, home to the carousel, Gyrosphere, Sea Dragon, and Bobsled and Whirlwind roller coasters.

Heading toward the back of the park from the game area, visitors pass Kiddie City, home to most of the kiddie rides, bumper cars, and log flume. At the back of the park is the water park, featuring nine water slides, a lazy river, wave pool, Soak Zone wave pool, and Looney Lagoon, a special area just for kids.

Sylvan Beach Amusement Park

OPENED 1895

NEW YORK STATE IS FILLED WITH LAKES, AND IN THE PAST, MANY OF THEM had amusement parks hugging their shores. But as the years went by, they slowly faded away, falling victim to changing times and rising property values. Now few remain; Sylvan Beach Amusement Park, on the shore of the 57,000-acre Oneida Lake is one.

Down the Canal

At 20 miles long, Oneida Lake is an immense body of water. In 1816, the developers of the Erie Barge Canal incorporated the lake into the canal system. Hundreds of tugs and barges used the lake yearly throughout the mid-1800s, and the town of Sylvan Beach on the lake's eastern shore became an active canal port.

By the 1870s, the canal era had passed, and Sylvan Beach became increasingly popular with vacationers, who flocked to the 5 miles of beaches around the town. The first hotel, the Forest House, opened in 1879. In 1886, access to the fledgling resort was improved when the Ontario and Western Railroad completed a rail line into the village. Until that time, people had to ferry or swim across the canal to get to the resort.

With Sylvan Beach now accessible from all of central New York, things really took off, with the resort attracting up to four thousand picnickers and ten steamships on busy days. Sylvan Beach now called itself the "Coney Island of Central New York," and independently owned amusements started appearing on the beach, including a prim-

Sylvan Beach Amusement Park
P.O. Box 149
Sylvan Beach, NY 13157
315-762-5212
www.sylvanbeach.org/
amusementpark/index.html

The Toboggan Slide was a popular early attraction at Sylvan Beach. The single story bathhouse to the left was later converted into the Laffland dark ride.

itive roller coaster. In 1893, the resort's most famous early attraction appeared in Oneida Lake: the Toboggan Slide, an early water slide on which small sleds carried riders into the lake.

As the area matured, the collection of independently owned amusements were supplanted in 1895 by Carnival Park, the area's first full-scale amusement park, which formed the basis of today's Sylvan Beach Amusement Park. It was followed a few years later by a second, Luna Park.

Carnival Park's most enduring attraction arrived in 1896, when Joseph Cottman opened a new carousel, carved by Charles Looff, in a large building erected especially for the ride. It was the third carousel manufactured by the man who would become one of the most famous carvers in history.

After the Algonquin Hotel, the resort's first large lodging facility, burned down in 1899, Carnival Park took over the land for expansion. At this time, there were few permanent buildings in the amusement area; instead, concessionaires would erect tents for the summer.

Ups and Downs

Sylvan Beach's amusement area entered its greatest era in 1902, when Dr. Martin Cavana acquired Carnival Park. Cavana arrived at Sylvan Beach in 1891, planning to open a recuperative hospital offering a "gold cure" for virtually any kind of affliction. As he built his sanatorium and a nursing school, he saw the potential of the resort and decided to diversify.

 **VISITING**

LOCATION

Sylvan Beach Amusement Park is located in the village of Sylvan Beach. From I-90 (the New York Thruway), take NY Route 13 (Exit 34) North about 8 miles to Sylvan Beach. The park will be on the left. Village parking is free but limited. Pay parking is available at a municipal lot near the beach.

OPERATING SCHEDULE

From early May through early June and in September, the park is open Fridays at 6 P.M. and weekends at noon. From early June through Labor Day, the park is open at noon daily. Closing time varies depending on weather and crowds.

ADMISSION

Admission to Sylvan Beach Amusement Park is free, with rides available on a pay-as-you-go basis. Ride tickets cost about 80 cents each, with rides taking two to four tickets.

FOOD

The park has six food outlets. The main stands in the park include Galaxy Pizza; Fries and More, which serves french fries and onion petals; and the Beach Hut, with sandwiches, hot dogs, burgers, and fried clams. Yesterday's Royal, located across Canal Street from the rest of the amusement area, is a full-service, sit-down restaurant featuring an extensive menu of American classics and appetizers. An ice cream bar offers sixteen flavors of homemade ice cream.

FOR CHILDREN

This park focuses on families, and its rides can be enjoyed by most members. The park's kiddieland features eight kiddie rides, including several vintage models that are rare in today's amusement parks.

SPECIAL FEATURES

Sylvan Beach Amusement Park is one of the last of the dozens of amusement parks that used to line the lakes of New York State. It still has a nostalgic atmosphere that is difficult to find today.

Laffland is one of the best-preserved vintage dark rides in the country. Lovingly maintained, the ride dates back to 1954 and still features most of its original scenes.

TIME REQUIRED

A visit to the amusement park can be part of a full day's visit to the village. Enjoy the rides, lounge on the beach, and dine at Yesterday's Royal. If you are pressed for time, the major attractions can be enjoyed in about two hours.

TOURING TIPS

Visit on a weekday, when crowds tend to be lighter.

Cavana launched a major expansion of Carnival Park, increasing live entertainment offerings and adding attractions such as the Ocean Wave, a circular ride, the Cave of the Winds walk-through, the Trip Thru Hell dark ride, and in 1908, the Figure Eight roller coaster. Eventually he absorbed Luna Park into Carnival Park. By now the town of Sylvan Beach was one of the leading resorts in the state, attracting crowds of up to thirty thousand and featuring eleven hotels, twelve rooming houses, 360 cottages, and three boat docks.

Unfortunately, this fame was fleeting. Prohibition drained customers from the hotels, and as the automobile became more popular in the 1920s, Sylvan Beach's working-class customer base started traveling to more distant resorts. Cavana sold Carnival Park to Emory Sauve Jr. in 1924 and died soon after. By the end of the decade, the Figure Eight had been demolished.

Through the 1930s and early 1940s, Carnival Park and Sylvan Beach struggled in the face of the Depression and World War II. But by the late 1940s, the park experienced a rebound as peacetime America had a pent-up demand for recreation and entertainment. Sylvan Beach adjusted to life as a destination for day-trippers rather than as a vacation resort. Russell's Danceland, a local nightclub, became a popular place for its big-band music.

New attractions were added, including the Playland arcade in 1947, now a local landmark with its neon and stainless steel facade. In the early 1950s, the Carnival Park name was retired in favor of Sylvan Beach

Figure 8, Sylvan Beach, N. Y.

The Figure Eight opened during the park's great expansion in the early 1900s.

Sylvan Beach's kiddieland replaced the miniature golf course in 1954.

Midway. It now featured about twenty rides, including the Octopus, Silver Streak, Caterpillar, and Whip. In 1954, in response to the postwar baby boom, a five-ride kiddieland replaced the miniature golf course.

Also that year, the Laffland dark ride was built by James Donlon, a concessionaire who came to own much of the amusement area by the 1960s. Donlon was able to acquire the long, narrow bathhouse that had served the toboggan slide, which had been removed several years earlier. He pulled the bathhouse up from the water, cut it in half, moved it from the lakeshore on rollers, and placed the halves side by side along the midway to form the basis for the dark ride. He then hired the Pretzel Ride Company, history's leading manufacturer of dark rides, to outfit the building with cars, a track, and twenty stunts. It has survived to this day and is one of the best-preserved vintage dark rides.

In 1959, three new rides were added: the Scrambler, Bomber, and Tilt-A-Whirl. But the town of Sylvan Beach was entering another period of decline, which had negative effects on the amusement park. In the early 1960s, after Joseph's son William Cottman died, their carousel, which dated back to 1896, was shuttered and the animals sold off to collectors. Several other rides, including the Whip and bumper cars, were sold off in 1964, and lease disputes led to the abandonment of a portion of the park. Meanwhile, many of the old dance halls in the village became destinations for rock-and-roll acts, chasing away the family trade.

As the park entered the 1970s, it was a fraction of the size it used to be. But there were still some bright spots. In the fall of 1972, Larry

Laffland continues to operate as one of the country's best preserved vintage dark rides.

Carello, who owned a nearby french fry stand, purchased the abandoned carousel. He spent the winter overhauling the mechanism and acquired new aluminum animals from Theel Manufacturing of Leavenworth, Kansas. The ride was reopened in 1973 to an appreciative public. In 1975, an attempt was made to revitalize the portions of the park abandoned in the 1960s with the addition of rides, but it was unsuccessful, and in 1977, the property was sold to the town for a parking lot.

Bouncing Back

By the early 1980s, what remained of Sylvan Beach Amusement Park was a shell of its former self. More than a dozen concessionaries controlled portions of the 8-acre property, and the ride lineup was reduced to Carello's carousel, the Bomber, Scrambler, Laffland, a fun house, and five kiddie rides.

But Pat Goodenow, a schoolteacher who had worked at the park as a game attendant in the 1960s and 1970s, saw potential in the old amusement park. In 1981, he teamed up with John Clements and reached an agreement with the Donlon family to purchase their holdings for a $15,000 down payment, with the balance to be paid over seventeen years.

He immediately went to work to expand the depleted ride lineup, and as amusement parks closed in the area, he was able to acquire rides from them. In 1981, he purchased a new Tilt-A-Whirl from Olympic Park in Rochester, and the next year, he rescued a kiddie boat ride from a junk pile at Pine Lake Park in Caroga Lake and restored it.

The new owners suffered a setback in 1983, when a fire destroyed the 1920s fun house. But Goodenow was undaunted, immediately clearing the site and erecting a bumper car ride. Other new rides soon followed, including bumper boats, the Rock-O-Plane, and the Tip Top. In 1987, the Crazy Dazy teacup ride was salvaged from Eldridge Park in Elmira after it was damaged in a flood. A kiddie Ferris wheel and turtle rides were acquired in 1988 from the defunct Mountain Park in Massachusetts. By now the ride lineup had doubled.

As important as expanding the ride lineup was, the new owners also knew that they had to gain greater control of the property and made efforts to buy out the other concessionaires. In 1984, they acquired several of the game concessions, including Playland. By the end of the 1980s, they had acquired everything but Carello's carousel.

As the 1990s dawned, Sylvan Beach Amusement Park had grown to the point where Goodenow thought it needed a roller coaster. For three years, he searched for a ride that would appeal to the park's family-oriented crowd. In the summer of 1992, he heard that Fun Forest Amusement Park in Seattle was replacing its Galaxi roller coaster with a larger

The Galaxi was Sylvan Beach's first roller coaster in over six decades when it opened in 1993.

ride. Goodenow visited the park and knew that the 45-foot-high, 1,650-foot-long steel-track ride would be the perfect fit and immediately reached an agreement to purchase it.

When the season closed in Seattle, the ride was dismantled and placed on six trailers for the 2,800-mile journey to its new home. But only five trailers arrived at Sylvan Beach. For a week, there was no word on the missing trailer. When it finally arrived, the driver explained that he had become sick during transport and had to park the truck in Colorado while he sought medical attention. Now that all the pieces were there, the roller coaster underwent an extensive restoration despite severe winter weather, and it was ready to go in the spring of 1993.

With Sylvan Beach Amusement Park completely revitalized, Goodenow purchased the former Hotel Royal, next door to the park, in 1998. Built in 1912, it is the last of the many hotels that once lined the lakeshore. It now operates as the Yesterday's Royal restaurant.

Sylvan Beach Amusement Park Today

After a roller coaster life, Sylvan Beach Amusement Park has survived to be a nostalgic reminder of a time when any self-respecting lake in New York State had its own amusement park. The park is closely integrated into the surrounding village and features twenty-one rides, including eight just for kids, along two main midways. When visitors face the park from its main entrance on Canal Street, the midway to their right leads past most of the larger spinning rides, including the bumper cars and Scrambler, along with several game arcades, to Carello's carousel and the kiddieland. The left-hand midway goes past a number of midway games, the walkways to the Galaxi and bumper boat rides, past Carello's carousel and the Playland arcade to Laffland, which fronts on the village's municipal park.

Midway Park

OPENED 1898

THIS IS A GREAT PLACE TO SPEND A SUMMER AFTERNOON, WITH THE COOL-ing breezes of Chautauqua Lake, lakeside picnic grove, merry-go-round pavilion, and the large two-story waterfront building with its conces-sions and open-air roller rink. Midway Park is a survivor, a nostalgic throwback to a simpler time.

A Stop on the Line

Midway Park is one of the few remaining trolley parks in the country. In the early days of the industry, hundreds of parks like this were opened along trolley lines on the outskirts of cities to stimulate ridership on the weekends.

In 1898, the Jamestown and Lake Erie Railway started a search for a place to build a resort for their business. They located a 17-acre parcel on the shores of Chautauqua Lake known as "midway," a name given by a local steamboat company when it erected a dock there in 1894, between Point Whiteside and Maple Springs. The new park officially opened on July 12, 1898.

Midway Park was similar to many of the other trolley parks of this era. Five acres were cleared to allow activities such as baseball, tennis, croquet, swimming, and boat-ing. The park also had 500 feet of lake frontage, a dance pavilion, beach, dining room, and row-boats. Patrons could visit the park either by trol-ley from nearby Jamestown or Mayville, for a round-trip fare of 25 cents, or via steamship.

Midway Park
4859 Route 430
P.O. Box E
Maple Springs, NY 14756
716-386-3165
midwayinfo@yahoo.com
www.midway-park.com

Although the park changed little during its early years, it was nonetheless a popular escape for area residents. The park's owners incorporated in 1899 as the Jamestown and Chautauqua Railway Company. In 1907, they acquired the Chautauqua Steamship Company, which had built the original steamboat dock and had been providing boat service to the area since 1894. In an effort to allow more people to visit the park, an expanded 450-foot-long steamship dock was constructed.

In 1913, the railway and Midway Park were purchased by the Broadhead family, and the railway became the Jamestown, Westfield and Northwestern Railroad Company. They electrified the rail line, providing a twenty-eight-minute trip from Jamestown, compared with two hours by boat. At this time, many people visiting the park took the steamships out in the morning and rode the trolleys home in the evening.

Ownership of the park changed again in 1915, when the Chautauqua Lake Navigation Company bought the park. The new owners built a 40,000-square-foot pavilion on the shores of the lake, with a roller-skating rink and dance hall on the second floor and a bathhouse, dining room, kitchen, shooting gallery, and other games on the first floor. The pavilion remains the heart of the park to this day and has its original maple floor on the second level. Midway Park also added a major attraction on the lakeshore, a water toboggan slide from Sellner Manufacturing. A forerunner of today's water slides, it had a large ramp down which people rode small sleds into Lake Chautauqua. It lasted until the 1940s.

In 1924, during the peak of the golden age of the wooden roller coaster, Midway Park constructed its largest ride, the Jack Rabbit. Most

This view of Midway Park from Chautauqua Lake has changed little since the 1920s.
MIDWAY PARK

 **VISITING**

LOCATION

Midway Park is located on NY Route 430, 3 miles north of Exit 10 off I-86. The park is also accessible from Exit 60 off I-90 (New York State Thruway). From Exit 60, take NY Route 394 East to NY Route 430 East in Mayville, and follow for 6 miles to the park.

OPERATING SCHEDULE

Midway Park opens Memorial Day weekend and is open weekends through June. In July and August, the park is open Wednesday through Sunday. It closes on Labor Day. The park opens at 11 A.M., with rides operating from 1 to 7 P.M.

ADMISSION

Admission to Midway Park is free. Rides and attractions are available on a pay-as-you-go basis, with tickets costing $1 each and rides requiring one to four tickets. Discount ticket packs are available. Pay-one-price wristbands, which include all rides and attractions except Water Wars, go-carts, and bumper boats, are available for about $15.

FOOD

The main food stand is located in the pavilion along the lakefront. It serves a wide variety of items, including burgers, hot dogs, Italian sausage, chicken sandwiches, and pizza.

Outside food and beverages are permitted in the park, and picnic pavilions are available on a first-come, first-served basis.

FOR CHILDREN

Midway Park is geared to kids and their families. As a result, almost all of the rides and attractions can be enjoyed by young and old.

SPECIAL FEATURES

This is one of the last trolley parks in the country and still features its nostalgic lakefront atmosphere.

The park has one of the best collections of vintage Allan Herschell kiddie rides around. The company was the leading kiddie ride manufacturer in the 1950s, and Midway Park was a major customer.

TIME REQUIRED

The park can be enjoyed in about three hours, although families with small children will likely want to spend longer.

TOURING TIPS

If you have small kids with you, consider purchasing the pay-one-price wristbands. You will easily get your money's worth.

The Jack Rabbit was a mild roller coaster that bordered the park's ball field.
MIDWAY PARK

likely erected by the legendary roller coaster team of Miller and Baker, the Jack Rabbit was a relatively large, though mild ride constructed in an out-and-back layout. The loading station was located near the pavilion, the lift hill traveled up a bluff near the lakeshore, and most of the ride was in the upper half of park by the ball field.

Expansion continued in 1928, when Midway added a large carousel manufactured by William Dentzel. It too was located near the pavilion, in an all-new carousel building. Like most of the country's amusement parks, Midway Park experienced hard times when the Depression hit in the 1930s. The owners, primarily concerned with their trolley and steamship interests, decided to get out of the amusement park business.

Changing Hands

In 1934, the trolley company, struggling during the tough economic times, leased the park to Thomas Carr, who immediately commenced renovations. Unfortunately, there were setbacks. Ice flows on the lake demolished the steamboat pier in 1935, and Carr was forced to tear down the deteriorating Jack Rabbit in 1939. He pressed on, however, and purchased the park that same year, restoring the pavilion.

Carr died in the late 1940s, and in 1951, brothers Martin and Frank Walsh bought the park from his estate. Martin "Red" Walsh started working at Midway in 1927, overseeing food concessions. He soon expanded his involvement to the arcade operations and built a flight trainer ride that gave people the opportunity to pilot a miniature airplane.

The Walshes immediately went to work to expand Midway Park. By now the trolley tracks were gone, and the park was dependent on the nearby highway to deliver its patrons. At the time, the only ride was the carousel, so expanding the ride lineup was a top priority. Since America was in the midst of the postwar baby boom, the new owners decided to develop a new area near the highway focusing on kiddie rides. In the mid-1950s, they purchased several rides from the Allan Herschell Company of nearby North Tonawanda, including a kiddie roller coaster, Sky Fighter, wet boats, and handcars. Also added were a Chair Plane swing ride and Ferris wheel, both manufactured by Smith and Smith of nearby Smithville, New York.

Expansion continued throughout the decade, with larger picnic areas and a miniature golf course. In 1955, a used miniature train ride, manufactured in 1946 by the Miniature Train Company of Rensselaer, Indiana, was added on half a mile of track that completely encircled the burgeoning ride area. A Roto Whip followed in 1957, and a Dodgem ride in 1958. The Ferris wheel was replaced in 1960 by a larger version from the Eli Bridge Company.

Throughout the 1960s, new rides continued to be added at Midway Park. A Tilt-A-Whirl and Fly-O-Plane appeared in the ride area, while the old ball field was replaced by a go-cart track. In 1967, a Scrambler ride was leased for two seasons. The next year, the park's aging Dentzel carousel was sold and replaced in the lakeside carousel pavilion with a 1946 Allan Herschell merry-go-round with thirty aluminum horses, pur-

Amusement Area, Chautauqua Lake, New York

Midway Park started developing a new ride area in the 1950s.

chased from the shuttered Owasco Lake Park in Auburn, New York. As the decade ended, the Scrambler gave way to a Giant Slide.

With traditional parks around the country succumbing to competitive pressures in the early 1970s, Midway was still able to thrive in its lakeside location. Expansion continued in 1972, when a Paratrooper and two kiddie rides—the Roadway and helicopters—were purchased from Sunset Bay Park, a defunct amusement park in Irving, New York. During this period, the Ferris wheel gave its last rides.

Passing the Torch

Expansion slowed considerably during the next decade, although Midway remained a charming escape. The park came under new management in 1984, when Martin's son and daughter-in-law, Michael and Janis, took over the operation. They made a major commitment to the future of the park in 1985 by adding one of America's first Dragon coasters, a compact roller-coaster-type ride with self-propelled trains. Bumper boats followed in 1990. As the park neared its hundredth anniversary, the Walshes started to upgrade the facility, replacing the aging bumper cars in 1995, updating the arcade in 1997, and completing extensive restorations of the merry-go-round and miniature train in 1998.

To celebrate the new century, in 2000, Midway Park replaced its Chair Swing and Paratrooper rides with the Tidal Wave, a rotating boat ride, custom built for Midway Park by the Italian firm of Sartori.

Midway Park's ride area in the late 1990s.

By 2004, the Walshes were looking to retire, but wanted to find a way to ensure that the park would be preserved for future generations. The following year, they reached an agreement to sell Midway Park to the state of New York, which would maintain it as part of the state park system, assuring that this charming reminder of yesteryear will create memories well into the future.

Midway Park Today

Even today Midway Park maintains much of the nostalgic lakefront atmosphere that has attracted customers for more than a century. It features eighteen rides, including nine just for kids, a miniature golf course, and a large picnic area. The park is divided into two sections. The front of the park, near the road, is home to the miniature golf course and most of the rides, including the kiddie rides, bumper cars, bumper boats, and slide. The go-carts are located on a hill behind the bumper car building. Along the lakefront is the oldest part of the park, including the pavilion that has served as its heart for more than ninety years, arcade, merry-go-round, and picnic area.

Playland

OPENED 1928

A VISIT TO PLAYLAND IS LIKE STEPPING BACK IN TIME. PULLING INTO THE parking lot, you are greeted by graceful Art Deco style buildings leading to a boardwalk that hugs the shore of Long Island Sound, and a spacious tree-lined mall that serves as the heart of the amusement park. Surrounding the lushly landscaped mall are several antique rides interspersed among their newer cousins, important links to the industry's golden age. Playland is indeed reminiscent of an earlier time, but it is also one of the most important amusement parks in the history of the industry.

Along the Shores of Long Island Sound

For centuries, this piece of land has been a popular recreation spot. Before Europeans came to the area, Indians gathered here for festivals. Later, as America was being established, the shore became a popular picnicking retreat. Toward the end of the nineteenth century, hotels started to appear along what was then known as Rye Beach. In the early 1900s, a trolley line was extended to the shore, leading to the opening of several amusements, including Rye Beach Pleasure Park.

But as the popularity of the resort increased, its previously high standards started to slip, with fly-by-night operators setting up ramshackle bathhouses, dance halls, and concessions along the sound to cash in on the crowds. As the quality of the amusements decreased, so did the crowds. The 1921 opening of Paradise Park, with its new amusements such as the Blue Streak roller coaster

Rye Playland
Playland Parkway
Rye, NY 10580
914-813-7000
www.ryeplayland.org

and Old Mill, failed to stem the tide. Rye Beach had become a blight in the community.

Around this time, the Westchester County Park Commission was formed to develop a $47 million countywide recreation system. One of its first purchases was Manursing Island, 160 acres of salt marsh adjacent to Rye Beach, in 1923. As much as the commission would have liked to, it resisted purchasing the Rye Beach because of high cost of removing the amusements, but local residents had had enough. In 1925, citing the "disreputable and honky tonk" nature of the area, they petitioned the park commission, urging that it replace Rye Beach.

In 1925, the commission authorized $2.5 million to acquire 54 acres of Rye Beach, including three hotels and Paradise Park. The 13-acre Rye Beach Pleasure Park was acquired soon after. Later purchases increased the total land area to 270 acres. The commission announced plans to create an "unequalled seaside public park to provide clean, wholesome recreation for the people of Westchester County." But it had to honor the existing leases and wound up operating Paradise Park and Rye Beach. Paradise Park was largely wiped out by fire in the fall of 1926, but Rye Beach continued operating through the summer of 1927. But now the park commission controlled the land, and it was time to make a change.

Breaking New Ground

The park commission wanted to create something new: "an amusement park possessing artistic merit to attract a class of people who before, resented going to summer amusement resorts of the 'Coney Island' type and to educate the habitual amusement park goers to an appreciation and a desire for things beautiful." The commission hired the noted Manhattan architectural firm of Walker and Gillette to design the facility and enlisted Frank Darling, president of the L. A. Thompson Scenic Railway Company at Coney Island and an experienced designer and builder of amusement parks and rides, to guide construction. Gilmore Clark, the commission's head landscape architect, went on a nationwide tour of amusement parks to get ideas. Operations were to be overseen by an independent commission that owned a core group of rides and attractions and leased additional space out to concessionaires.

Every detail of Playland was carefully planned. A 40-foot-wide, 1,200-foot-long boardwalk ran along the water's edge. A 1,600-foot-long beach was created by pumping 350,000 cubic yards of fine-grained sand from the bottom of Long Island Sound. A ten-thousand-space bathhouse served not only the beach, but also a nearby Olympic-size swimming pool. An 80-acre boating lake was carved out of the salt marsh, and a 110-acre

Playland's 110-foot-tall Music Tower is the focal point of the 1,200-foot-long central mall.

nature area was created. At the heart of the operation was a broad, 1,200-foot-long, intricately landscaped mall running from the beach to the lake, around which a carefully selected assortment of amusement rides was clustered. Rides were linked by covered walkways called colonnades. A separate amusement park, just for small children, was created with half a dozen scaled-down rides, a wading pool, a playground, Mary's Garden, and attendants to care for children while their parents enjoyed the larger rides. A 110-foot-tall music tower piped "restrained harmonious music" throughout the park. Seaplanes could land at a special bay, and a pier became a popular stop for steamships that made regular trips from Manhattan and New Jersey. Even the type of hot dogs to serve and the uniforms for employees were carefully evaluated. This attention to detail had never been seen before in the industry and foreshadowed the carefully planned theme parks that would spring up thirty years later.

Playland foreshadowed the theme park era in another important area. While facilities were included for buses, Playland was clearly designed to serve an automobile-loving public. Playland Parkway, a broad 1.5-mile-long boulevard, extended from a nearby highway directly to a large parking lot, replacing the maze of one-way streets and "insuring a middle-class clientele arriving by car," according to one newspaper.

Work progressed rapidly on the new amusement park. On the day after Labor Day 1927, a thousand workers began demolition of the old

LOCATION

Playland is easily accessible from I-95. Just look for the Playland Parkway exit (Exit 19) in Rye, which leads directly to the park entrance. Playland is also accessible via the Bee-Line bus system and Metro North rail line.

OPERATING SCHEDULE

Playland opens at noon on weekends in May and September. During June, the park opens at 10 A.M. Wednesday through Friday and noon on weekends. In July and August, it opens at 11 A.M. on Tuesdays and noon Wednesday through Sunday. Closing time is typically 11 P.M. on weekdays and midnight on weekends, but it can vary based on the time of year. With the exception of holidays, Playland is closed on Mondays.

ADMISSION

Admission to Playland is free. Visitors have the choice of purchasing a Fun Band for less than $40, which is good for six hours of unlimited rides, or a Fun Card. Points can be purchased for the Fun Cards for about $1 each, with rides requiring two to four points. Discounts are available for multiple point purchases.

FOOD

The park features about twenty food outlets, including Burger King, Nathan's Famous, and Carvel, with a wide variety of offerings such as hot dogs, hamburgers, chicken, pizza, Mexican food, and ice cream. Most are walk-up stands, but Captain Hook's outdoor restaurant on the Boardwalk offers seafood, live entertainment, and a view of Long Island Sound.

Outside food and beverages are permitted in the park, and a public picnic area is available on a first-come, first-served basis along Playland Lake. Barbecue grills are also available.

FOR CHILDREN

Playland prides itself on being a family amusement park, and many of its rides, including the Log Flume, whip, Carousel, and Family Flyer roller coaster, can be enjoyed by most members of the family.

The park's Kiddyland, with two dozen family and kiddie rides, is one of the largest in the country and has something to appeal to almost anyone. Favorites include the Kiddy Coaster and Kiddy Carousel, which date back to the park's opening; the Arctic Flume; Convoy; Up, Up and Away Balloons; Crazy Submarine; Fun Slide; and Playland Express train.

SPECIAL FEATURES

Playland is one of the most historically significant amusement parks in the world. When it opened in 1928, it represented a dramatic departure from the haphazard nature in which amusement parks had been constructed up to that point. Every element of Playland was carefully planned, from its placement close to major

(continued on page 110)

PLAYLAND

VISITING (continued from page 109)

roads to its carefully selected lineup of attractions, covered colonnades that link the rides, broad landscaped mall, and separate Kiddyland offering children their own scaled-down amusement park. It foreshadowed the carefully planned theme parks, such as Disneyland and Six Flags, that came three decades later.

Playland is one of only two operating amusement parks in the United States to be listed as a national historic landmark (the other is Kennywood in West Mifflin, Pennsylvania). Much of its nostalgic atmosphere and several rides from its earliest days remain lovingly maintained links to another era. They should not be missed and include the following:

- The Carousel, carved in 1915 by Charles Carmel, is a work of art featuring four rows of 66 hard-carved, bejeweled horses, three chariots; and a Gavioli band organ. It originally operated at Savin Rock in Connecticut before being relocated to Playland in 1928.

- The Derby Racer, one of the last three rides of its kind in the world, is a high-speed carousel with four rows of fifty-six horses mounted on a large platform that rotates at speeds up to 25 miles per hour. Watching the operators leap on and off the spinning ride is almost as entertaining as the ride itself.

- The Dragon Coaster, a 75-foot-tall wooden roller coaster, is one of the last operating rides built by Fred Church, one of the greatest roller coaster designers of the 1920s. Its long, dragon-shaped tunnel is an attraction in itself.

- The Old Mill, a dark boat ride, travels through a 1,200-foot-long tunnel to visit the land of gnomes and trolls.

- The whip, a classic spinning ride, is increasingly hard to find in today's amusement parks.

- The Kiddy Coaster, built by Playland designer Frank Darling, is the oldest operating kiddie roller coaster in the world.

- The Kiddy Carousel, House of Mirrors, and Zombie Castle dark ride are other antique classics.

TIME REQUIRED

With all of its rides and attractions, a visit to Playland can easily occupy an entire day, particularly if you have small children. If you are pressed for time, the major attractions can be enjoyed in about three hours.

TOURING TIPS

Try visiting during the week or late afternoon in June to avoid the biggest crowds.

Make a day of your visit, and take along a swimming suit to enjoy the beach on Long Island Sound and a picnic lunch to soak in the atmosphere along Playland Lake.

If you are traveling to Playland from New York City, consider taking the Metro North rail line. Special packages are available that offer round-trip transportation and tickets. For more information, call 800-METRO-INFO or 212-532-4900.

facilities, taking down the ramshackle collection of flimsy wooden buildings, and piling up the debris on the beach and burning it. More than a million square feet of pavement were poured in three weeks, and on May 26, 1928, four days ahead of schedule, the $6 million Playland was ready to open to an enthusiastic crowd of more than a hundred thousand. Advertisements stated: "Playland is not an amusement park, it is a greater, finer, better thing. Playland is the start of a modern recreation center such as the world has never known."

The park featured two dozen of the latest in amusement rides. The undisputed king of the park was the Aeroplane, a towering wooden roller coaster. Built on a tight, triangular piece of land, it was nearly 100 feet high with 2,970 feet of track. The ride was distinguished by tight turns, sudden drops, and two high-speed spirals, including a particularly intense one known as the Whirlpool, which soon made it legendary.

Some of the rides, such as the Noah's Ark fun house and Jack and Jill slide, were short-lived. Others, including as the Airplane Swing, Caterpillar, Dodgem, Tumble Bug, and Magic Carpet fun house, lasted several decades. Several remain in operation: the Derby Racer, a high-speed merry-go-round that simulates a horse race; whip; House of Mirrors; and kiddie carousel and roller coaster.

Patrons could dine at Café des Colonnades, modeled after a Parisian sidewalk café; a thousand-seat clambake pavilion; and a Japanese Tea House. Live entertainment included a dance hall and circus.

The Aeroplane was Playland's most exciting attraction until it was demolished in 1957.

The Dragon Coaster opened in 1929 and remains the park's most popular ride.

Playland's first season was a success by every measure. Gross revenues exceeded estimates by 80 percent, and attendance topped 3 million, including a reported 320,000 on July 4. Media and recreation consultants from around the world traveled to Rye to see the groundbreaking amusement park.

To accommodate the crowds, the county launched another phase of development for the 1929 season. The largest project was the development of the Casino, a large mixed-use building located at the park entrance on the waterfront that featured a dance hall, roller rink, bowling alley, game room, and in the winter, an ice rink. Along the Boardwalk, an Olympic-size swimming pool was constructed, and two major rides, still in operation today, were added to the amusement park: the Old Mill, a 1,200-foot-long boat ride through darkened tunnels, and the Dragon coaster, which has become one of Playland's most popular rides.

During the first season, park management noticed that the intense nature of the Aeroplane, with its high-speed turns, kept many people from riding it. As a result, they went back to Fred Church, the ride's designer, and asked him to build a milder roller coaster across the midway. The result was the Dragon, which stands 85 feet tall and has 3,400 feet of track, a top speed of 45 miles per hour, and a long tunnel shaped like a dragon. With its milder dips, the Dragon was the perfect complement to the Aeroplane.

As Playland was closing a second successful season, America was plunged into the Depression. Despite the hard times, an occasional new attraction did appear. In 1931, the *Benjamin F. Packard*, a retired clipper ship, was anchored along the shoreline and turned into an entertainment complex with a pirate show, aquarium, naval museum, and dining and dancing on the deck. The *Packard* remained a major Playland attraction until 1938, when it was pushed ashore by a hurricane. The following spring, it was towed away and sunk.

While amusement parks around the country were confronted with plunging attendance during the difficult economic times, Playland, with its unparalled atmosphere, still enjoyed strong visitation. In 1932, attendance increased by 400,000 to a record 3.87 million, but those people were watching their pennies and revenues dropped. Though it was able to eke out small profits throughout much of the decade, Playland also was forced to economize. For example, because the cost of paint was prohibitive, buildings were washed to keep them looking fresh, using towels since sponges were too expensive.

When the economy started improving in the mid-1930s, new attractions began appearing once again, including Laff in the Dark, a dark ride manufactured by R. E. Chambers of Beaver Falls, Pennsylvania. The ride has remained in operation and is now called Zombie Castle.

As the Depression wound down, it looked as though Playland could begin to make permanent improvements. But soon World War II diverted everyone's attention. In 1942, the first season under wartime restrictions, gas rationing severely affected business, with attendance dropping 18 percent. In addition, because of the park's waterfront location, the lights had to be dimmed to thwart any potential enemy attack. The park owners briefly considered closing it for the duration of the war, but realizing it had a positive impact on morale, they kept it open.

Holding On

The 1950s were a quiet decade for Playland. Changes were minimal, and most new rides arrived in the form of concessions. Unfortunately, the decade saw the loss of Playland's most famous attraction in 1957, when Westchester County changed its insurance company. The new insurer inspected Playland and determined that the Aeroplane needed $100,000 in repairs to make it "safe," even though it had no problems during three decades of operation. The park decided that it could not afford the improvements, and in November 1957, unceremoniously demolished the roller coaster. In

1958, visitors were instead greeted by a Wild Mouse roller coaster. Though it represented the newest type of roller coaster, with its sharp turns, the small ride paled in comparison to its legendary predecessor.

Playland kicked off the 1960s with a number of improvements, including a Caterpillar, Flying Scooter, Rock O Plane, and Octopus spinning rides in 1961. That year also saw a major overhaul of the Kiddyland, with the playground removed in favor of several new kiddie rides.

By now some factions within Westchester County wondered whether an amusement park was the optimal use for this seaside parcel. Many nearby residents were being inconvenienced by the traffic generated by Playland, amusement parks were in decline nationwide, and because of the Depression and World War II, the facility had seen little major maintenance since it opened.

In 1962, a committee was formed to study alternative uses for the park, including selling or leasing the facility to a private operator. But by 1964, it was decided not to make any major changes. Another study in

Although many of the rides have changed, Playland's basic layout has changed little since the park opened. It is shown here in the years after World War II.

1965 recommended an $8.4 million improvement plan, including a $1.3 million renovation of the Casino, a $2.3 million marina, a $1.5 million poolside restaurant, beach improvements, and two golf courses. But as the proposal was being evaluated, plans were announced to build a bridge across 7 miles of Long Island Sound, connecting Oyster Bay, Long Island, to Playland Parkway. The bridge would cut through Playland, meaning the loss of the pool and part of the Boardwalk and beach. All long-term planning or major capital improvements were put hold until the early 1970s, when the project was canceled.

Further complicating the situation was a July 1966 fire, which destroyed almost 20 percent of Playland, including part of the colonnades, 300 feet of the Boardwalk, several concession stands, the Magic Carpet fun house, and four rides.

The fire stirred hope among some that it would be the start of the eventual removal of the amusements, but the county decided that the amusement park should continue because "it does the greatest good for the greatest number of people." County Commissioner Charles Pound stated, however, that the Magic Carpet should not be rebuilt "because its dark rooms and tumbling rides were hazardous to the morals of teenagers." Because of an insurance dispute, it was several years before any new rides occupied the burned area.

Playland saw a new roller coaster arrive in 1967, when the Monster Mouse replaced the Wild Mouse. Built by the Allan Herschell Company, the Monster Mouse, was an expanded Wild Mouse, with the customary tight turns of the older ride plus two large drops along its 1,200 feet of track.

The park launched the 1970s with a major improvement program that finally filled the burned area with new rides, including the Flying Witch, a large three-story dark ride; the Zyclon, a small steel-track roller coaster; and the Tumbler, a one-of-a-kind Ferris wheel acquired from Six Flags Over Georgia in Atlanta, with two large wheels on either end of a boom that rotated as the wheels spun. In addition, the famous colonnades received a $200,000 "modernization" in 1971 that replaced much of their Art Deco ornamentation.

Modernization continued in 1974 with the $6 million conversion of the Casino into a three-rink ice-skating facility that served as the practice home of the New York Rangers until 2001. In 1978, the amusement park saw $1 million in improvements, including a $200,000 renovation of the Derby Racer; a new Auto Skooter ride; two new spinning rides, the Yo Yo and the Rotor; two kiddie rides; and Sensavision, a wrap-around movie attraction. Unfortunately, to make room for the new attractions, two of Playland's original rides, the Tumble Bug and the Airplane Swing, were scrapped.

Moving in the Wrong Direction

By the late 1970s, time was catching up with Playland. While it remained a popular destination, much of its infrastructure dated back to 1928. It was starting to lose money, and questions continued about whether an amusement park was the best use for the parcel continued. The oversight of the park by the Playland Commission was set to expire at the end of 1980, and the county saw an opportunity to move in a new direction.

That year, Playland was placed on the National Register of Historic Places, and the commission started soliciting proposals for outside companies to operate the facility. By the end of the summer, sixteen companies had submitted proposals, including other amusement park operators, Radio City Music Hall Productions, and a group of Playland's concessionaires. In September, the commission decided to offer a management contract to the Marriott Corporation, a successful operator of hotels, food service, and two Marriott's Great America theme parks, opened in 1976. Marriott promised to retain the historical character of the park, use its experience to improve the operation, and eventually invest $20 to $30 million in upgrades. Under the agreement, Marriott would operate Playland for two years to evaluate the operation, with the option to renew for ten more years.

Marriott initially wanted to close the park for a year to have time to make all the changes it wanted, but the county did not want to see Playland out of service for that long. So Marriott went to work cleaning up the facility, painting rides and buildings, and making desperately needed improvements to food service. In addition, many features that made theme parks successful were implemented, including uniformed employees, an extensive lineup of live entertainment, and costumed characters such as Bugs Bunny and Daffy Duck. But it was the implementation of two changes characteristic of theme parks that offset all of this good work.

In order to better control the flow of visitors, Marriott fenced in Playland and for the first time ever charged admission. They also banned visitors from bringing picnic lunches into the park. For customers who for generations were used to free access to Playland and its picnic groves, the changes were heresy. The public stayed away, attendance fell by one-third, and a $1.3 million profit in 1980 turned into a $2.6 million deficit in 1981.

With more time to prepare for the 1982 season, Marriott was optimistic that it could turn around the bad impressions created in 1981. The company added two new rides, the Enterprise and Bayern Kurve; launched a more aggressive group sales program; and increased marketing. Also, for the first time ever, a pay-one-price ticket was introduced, and county residents with a parks pass were admitted free. But the public still resisted and attendance dropped even further, to 621,000, less than half the number admitted just three years earlier. It was obvious that the Marriott management was not working out.

At season's end, Marriott bowed out and the county started looking at alternative plans for the park. A consulting firm was hired to develop a master plan for Playland. It proposed four different alternatives: convert Playland into a $78 million theme park; upgrade the existing facilities for $40 million; redevelop Playland into a hotel and conference facility; or remove the amusement rides and convert the land into recreational facilities. The general consensus was that, although Playland had seen its share of troubles and was in need of repairs, it still played an important role in Westchester County life. As a result, the county advisory board decided to upgrade the existing facilities.

On the Rebound

Playland opened for the 1983 season under control of the county with $200,000 in improvements. The reviled fence was removed, and the free admission and picnic policies were restored. The Old Mill was renovated, a new miniature golf course was constructed, and seven rides were added: Bumper Boats, a Himalaya, and five kiddie rides. The public was happy to have the old Playland back, and attendance jumped 12 percent, to 930,000.

Following a successful 1983 season, Playland started making more elaborate plans for the future. Upgrades costing $2 million were made to the electrical and plumbing systems, much of which dated back to 1928. New rides were added: a Music Express; the Sky Flyer, a looping ride; and the Thriller, an enclosed spinning ride featuring a light and sound show. The Monster Mouse, removed in 1981, and the aging Zyclon were replaced with the Whirlwind, a 1,200-foot-long, 64-foot-tall double inversion roller coaster, and the Wildcat, a 45-foot-tall, 1,500-foot-long steel-track ride. The improvements were well received. Revenues jumped 26 percent and attendance grew another 12 percent, surpassing a million for the first time since 1979.

Playland was on its way back. In 1985, a five-year, $11 million improvement program was launched, resulting in several much-needed upgrades. Management replaced the aging water and electricity systems, rehabilitated the 1,300-foot-long Boardwalk, repaved walkways, upgraded landscaping, and made improvements to the Casino. Many of the historic rides and buildings were restored, including the Dragon coaster, Derby Racer, Old Mill, and Boat House. In addition, the 600-foot pier, which once hosted steamships from as far away as New Jersey, was rebuilt in 1992. Playland now had recovered to the point where the park was named a national historic landmark in 1987.

Management also knew that Playland had to remain exciting. New rides were added to complement the old, including a Tilt-A-Whirl and go-cart track in 1985; the Mind Scrambler, an indoor spinning ride in 1987; and the Thunderbolt, another spinning ride, in 1988. In 1990, the park's Auto Scooter ride was upgraded with a new building reflective of the park's Art Deco architecture, and the Big Wheel was added. Kiddyland received a major upgrade in 1991, with the addition of six new kiddie rides, including a scaled-down water flume ride. Two additional major rides, the Sea Dragon swinging ship and Wipeout spinning ride, debuted in 1992, a year that saw the carousel and band organ restored.

But the rebounding Playland suffered a blow on December 11, 1992, when a major storm struck the park. Winds of up to 60 miles per hour inundated Playland with as much as 4 feet of seawater. Initial television reports said the park had "all but been wiped out." Though this proved to be false, damage was extensive and estimated to total nearly $5 million. While damage was evident throughout Playland, it was most severe along the waterfront, where the pier was destroyed and the boardwalk severely damaged.

Playland quickly bounced back, however. In 1993, construction began at the former site of the Whirlwind and Flying Skooter on a major new

Playland's kiddieland is a mix of old and new rides.

The Log Flume opened in 1994 as part of a major improvement program.

attraction, the Log Flume. Manufactured by O. D. Hopkins, the world's leading manufacturer of water rides at that time, the ride is 1,150 feet long and features two drops of 25 and 40 feet. The Log Flume opened in 1994 and proved to skeptics that Playland was here to stay.

With the removal of not only the Whirlwind, but also the Wildcat in 1991 when its lease expired, Playland needed another roller coaster. That hole was filled in 1995 with the addition of the Hurricane. Built by the Italian firm of S&MC, the compact 50-foot-tall, 1,430-foot-long ride was characterized by a series of twisting drops. The Hurricane was one of four new rides to debut that year, along with the Starship 2000, a new Sky Flyer, and a spinning balloon ride in Kiddyland called Up, Up and Away.

Playland spent much of the late 1990s reinforcing its history. The bathhouse was restored in 1995, and a $2.7 million rebuilding of the pier and a $45,000 renovation on the Hall of Mirrors were completed in 1997. The following season, a new museum tracing the history of Playland opened along the Boardwalk, while the Derby Racer was restored in 1999. This was just the start of a $7 million improvement program that lasted through 2002.

As the twentieth century was nearing its end, Playland was preparing for a big 2000 season. The Double Shot, which shoots riders up and down an 85-foot-tall tower, was constructed. Also added were the Inverter and Fun Slide. The Wild Wind roller coaster was also slated to open, but as it was undergoing testing, the park's engineers determined that the ride's forces were too intense for Playland's family-oriented crowd, and it was removed without giving a single ride. Taking its place in 2001 was the Family Flyer, a much smaller roller coaster that could be enjoyed by small children and their parents. The Family Flyer was just one of seven new rides to debut at Playland that year. Others included the Playland Plunge, a 50-foot-tall water ride; the Dream Machine, a swing ride; and the Power Surge, a six-story-tall ride that spins riders on three different axes concurrently.

The 2002 season was also a year of growth. Two new family rides, the Kite Flyer and Sky Skater, were added. The highlight of the year was the refurbishment of the Zombie Castle and reopening of the Old Mill after a two-year, $2.7 million renovation. While maintaining the historical integrity of the ride, Sally Industries, a leading dark ride manufacturer, put in all new scenes. Riders now visit the Playland Waterworks and Crystal Mine, operated by a band of friendly animatronic gnomes; travel past an explosion and a downpour through the Point of No Return; and enter Troll City, where trolls try to capture intruders with water cannons, swinging logs, and other tricks.

As Playland celebrated its seventy-fifth anniversary in 2003, it was clearly on the rebound. The season kicked off with a $1.5 million reconstruction of the Music Tower Theater, permitting the park to book more popular musical acts; $1 million in plumbing and electrical upgrades; and the addition of the Crazy Mouse, a 38-foot-tall, 900-foot-long roller coaster reminiscent of the Wild Mouse and Monster Mouse.

Upgrades to Playland's roller coaster lineup continued in 2004, when the Hurricane was replaced with the 50-foot-tall, 1,282-foot-long Super Flight. Super Flight represented a new generation of roller coasters, where riders boarded the four passenger cars standing up. As the ride started, the cars swung down, putting the riders into a "flying" position under the tracks. In addition to Super Flight, the Inverter was replaced by the Twister, which flips riders in numerous directions. The historic attractions were not forgotten. The Dragon Coaster's famous tunnel was restored to its original appearance, receiving a new fearsome face that resembled a dragon, complete with menacing red eyes, gigantic teeth, and smoke spewing from the mouth.

Playland Today

Playland has changed to remain relevant to today's thrill seekers, yet the same carefully planned layout and cream-colored Art Deco buildings with sea green trim remain as reminders of the amusement park's golden age. The Playland of today features more than fifty rides, including five roller coasters, two water rides, and nearly two dozen kiddie rides, a number

The carousel, carved in 1915, is one of eight rides dating back to Playland's earliest years.

matched by few amusement parks in the country. Playland also has a museum, pool, beach, boardwalk, and a 178-acre wildlife sanctuary.

Playland's main entrance leads into the fountain plaza, which is surrounded by the miniature golf course, boardwalk leading to the beach and pool, Ice Casino, and 1,200-foot landscaped mall that is the heart of the amusement area. It's easy for visitors to find their way around the mall, with most of the rides and attractions clustered around it.

On the left, the first area visitors come across along the mall is the Kiddyland. Featuring two dozen kiddie and family rides, the area is anchored by the Kiddy Coaster, one of Playland's original rides, and the Playland Express train. Adjacent to Kiddyland are the Big Wheel, Derby Racer, and Super Flight roller coaster. Across the mall from these attractions are the go-carts, Family Flyer roller coaster, Carousel, and Auto Scooter.

At this point, the mall intersects with another midway featuring the Old Mill and Dragon Coaster to the left. To the right is the waterfront area that features most of Playland's contemporary rides, including the Log Flume, Thunderbolt, Twister, Sea Dragon, and Playland Plunge.

Continuing down the main mall, to the left are the whip, House of Mirrors, Zombie Castle dark ride, and Crazy Mouse. To the right are the Double Shot, Flying Witch dark ride, and Mind Scrambler. The Music Tower and Boat House anchor the mall's far end. Beyond the Boat House are Playland Lake for boating and the Edith G. Read Wildlife Sanctuary.

Santa's Workshop

OPENED 1949

MANY PEOPLE CONSIDER DISNEYLAND TO BE THE FIRST THEME PARK, BUT in actuality, its opening represented the culmination of an evolutionary process. Before Disneyland opened in 1955, several parks claimed title to the first theme park by creating environments not found in the everyday world. Included in this group is Santa's Workshop in the aptly named town of North Pole. It's hard to imagine the real North Pole being much different from this.

A Spark of Inspiration

One December evening in 1946, Long Island automobile dealer Julian Reiss was driving to the family's vacation home in Lake Placid. Reiss had been coming to the area since 1925, when he contracted tuberculosis and went to the mountains to recuperate. As he wound his way through the small towns of upstate New York, which were decorated for the upcoming Christmas season, he began telling his five-year-old daughter Patricia, one of his six children, a story about a baby bear that wandered from his den and discovered Santa's home. Patricia was enthralled and begged her father to take her to visit Santa's house. He had to explain that the story was only pretend, but he thought to himself, "Why couldn't such a place exist?"

Santa's Workshop
P.O. Box 1768
North Pole, NY 12997
800-806-0215
www.northpoleny.com

It would not be easy for Reiss to bring his dream to reality. The idea of creating an amusement park around a single theme had not yet taken hold in the country. He formed a partnership with two other individuals, Harold Fortune,

122

a contractor who specialized in constructing log cabins, and Arto Monaco, a former animator and Hollywood set designer. With nothing to compare their project to, it was difficult to develop a business plan. They arrived at their business projections by counting the cars that drove past the 25-acre site they had acquired at the base of Whiteface Mountain.

The lack of information did not deter the trio, and soon the park took shape. At the foot of a hill, eight log cabins created the heart of the new park. The cabins held attractions such as Santa's house, shops selling gifts for boys and girls, a post office, and refreshment stand. Herds of deer, sheep, and goats roamed the grounds. Reiss knew that Santa's house had to have an icy North Pole nearby, but how could that be achieved? His son Bob came up with a solution. A student at the U.S. Naval Academy, he had just completed a class in refrigeration and developed a system using a steel pipe with a coil in the middle. Sending coolant through the coil would cause a thick layer of ice to build up on the pipe. Even today, it remains one of Santa's Workshop's most popular features.

In June 1949, Santa's Workshop opened for business, attracting 250 visitors the first day. In the era before theme parks spread throughout the country, the new park created a sensation. Curiosity seekers flocked to this remote corner of upstate New York to visit Santa, feed the animals, and marvel at the ice-covered pole. Reiss tried to keep commercialism out of the park and created a unique system in which visitors paid for their admission and purchases on the way out of the park. But

North Pole Village is the heart of Santa's Workshop and has changed little since 1949.

this system became an administrative headache and was discontinued after a few seasons.

Marketing that first season was limited to posters tacked on utility poles and placed in area hotels. As fate would have it, a photojournalist from New York City passed by Santa's Workshop a couple weeks after it opened for business. Intrigued by the collection of log buildings nestled in the pine grove, she went in. Her story was picked up by the wire services, and people as far away as California soon knew about the new facility. By the end of the first season, Santa's Workshop was attracting two thousand to three thousand people a day, nearly ten times their initial projections. "We didn't have to start advertising until the mid-1960s," recalls Bob Reiss. In fact, the park was considered so groundbreaking that Walt Disney sent a team out to New York to evaluate it when he was planning Disneyland.

There were a few problems that first season, however. It had not occurred to the developers to build a souvenir shop, so a barn was soon converted into one. Also, the goats would try to chew on the customers' skirts, and as a result, their insurance company had to pay damage claims. But these were only minor distractions for an increasingly successful business. The national media attention continued. The *Saturday Evening Post* called Santa's Workshop one of the most novel attractions on the eastern seaboard and mentioned that it redirected Adirondack travel patterns. On the Sunday of Labor Day weekend in 1951, more than fourteen thousand people flocked to the park. By the end of the fifth season, the park had attracted more than 2.5 million patrons.

The partners wanted to build on their initial success. For their second season, they added a pony ride and a stage for puppet and magic shows, along with a real souvenir shop. The following season, the true meaning of Christmas was remembered with a nativity pageant.

The national prominence of Santa's Workshop in those first few years attracted the attention of the Macy's department store chain, which was looking for a herd of live reindeer for its famous Thanksgiving Day parade. The park did not yet have any, so Macy's helped finance the acquisition. During the park's 1953 season, a herd of reindeer was flown in from Golovan, Alaska, to Newark, New Jersey, and then trucked up to park. The herd appeared in the Macy's parade, but the animals had trouble adapting to the climate and began dying. Santa's Workshop worked hard with the University of Vermont to develop ways to properly care for the reindeer and brought in additional head, whose ancestors still live at the park. The reindeer continued to appear in the Macy's parade for several years and even attended the White House Pageant of Peace in 1955 and 1956.

LOCATION

Santa's Workshop is located just outside the town of Wilmington at the foot of Whiteface Mountain on NY Route 431, 1.5 miles northwest of the intersection with NY Route 86.

From the south, take I-87 to Exit 30, then follow NY Route 73 to Keene. At the Elm Tree Inn in Keene, take the right fork (NY Route 9 N) and follow signs to the Wilmington/Whiteface Area.

From the north, take Exit 34 off I-87 and follow NY Routes 9 N and 86 to the Wilmington/Whiteface Area.

OPERATING SCHEDULE

Santa's Workshop opens for the season the last weekend in June and operates daily from 9:30 A.M. to 4:30 P.M. through Labor Day. After Labor Day, the park is open only on weekends from 9:30 A.M. to 4 P.M. It is also open from 10 A.M. to 3:30 P.M. on weekends between Thanksgiving and Christmas.

The entrance remains open until thirty minutes prior to closing time. Reentry passes are available for those who are unable to complete their visit in one day.

ADMISSION

Pay-one-price admission of less than $20 entitles visitors to all rides and attractions.

FOOD

Santa's Workshop features two food outlets. Mother Hubbard's Cupboard, the main restaurant, features submarine sandwiches, chicken tenders, hot dogs, and grilled cheese sandwiches. Jack Sprats Snacks, located in North Pole Village, offers cookies, ice cream, and pretzels.

Visitors can have breakfast with Santa at Mother Hubbard's Cupboard on Tuesdays, Wednesdays, and Saturdays in July and August from 8:30 A.M. to 10 A.M. Santa is present for breakfast from 8:30 A.M. until 9:15 A.M.

FOR CHILDREN

The summer home of Santa Claus, Santa's Workshop is built with small children in mind. All of the rides and shows were installed to appeal to children and their families.

SPECIAL FEATURES

Santa's Workshop was one of America's first amusement parks to embrace a themed environment, and it predates the opening of Disneyland by six years. As a result, it played a crucial role in the development of the theme park industry. The park was originally designed and built by Arto Monaco, who designed several of the region's theme parks.

(continued on page 126)

VISITING (continued from page 125)

(continued from page 125)

SANTA'S WORKSHOP

TIME REQUIRED

For families with small children, Santa's Workshop can easily occupy much of the day, with its wide array of entertainment.

TOURING TIPS

Since the park is located on a hillside, plan your visit carefully. To avoid tiring climbs up and down the hill, try to fully enjoy the attractions at either the bottom or the top before moving on to the rest of the park.

Santa plays a key role in many of the live shows, so he is unavailable for personal visits several times during the day. Check at the front gate for his availability.

Don't miss the Reindeer Barn, where you can feed the park's herd of reindeer.

Rain passes are available in case inclement weather hits the park.

For the Christmas season, the park offers Yuletide Family Weekends. Designed for families with children aged two to ten, the weekend packages include lodging, breakfast and dinner, two evenings of entertainment at local motels, visits to the park, and gifts.

Along with the debut of the reindeer herd came the introduction of a reindeer sleigh ride. In reality, a golf cart had been renovated to resemble a sleigh. A few of the reindeer were trained to trot as fast as the self-propelled cart to make it appear as if they were actually pulling the cart. The sleigh held only a few riders at a time, leading to its removal after just a few seasons.

The park always had a place on the grounds where people could drop off letters and postcards to Santa. On December 16, 1953, Santa's Workshop officially established its home in the North Pole, with its own post office and zip code of 12924, gaining a rural substation designation. Today thousands of people forward their Christmas cards to Santa's Workshop to be stamped with the North Pole postmark.

Passing the Torch

As Santa's Workshop celebrated its tenth anniversary in 1959, Julian Reiss died at age sixty. With his passing, the family pulled together to keep Julian's dream alive and even added new attractions. In 1961, Julian's son Bob put his career as an industrial engineer on hold to help out the family. He took to the family business with the same passion as his father and added several more attractions. A half-mile-long train ride manufactured by the Allan Herschell Company opened in 1961, followed in 1962 by a merry-go-round built by the Theel Manufacturing of Leavenworth, Kansas. Unlike most merry-go-rounds, the Santa's Workshop version featured reindeer rather than horses. In 1964, two more

Santa's Workshop's merry-go-round features reindeer instead of horses.

rides debuted, including the Christmas Tree, on which riders pilot orna-
ments, and the Bobsleds, a kiddie ride.

In 1967, Reiss reconfigured the shops at the village and added a number of craftsmen, including a glassblower, a blacksmith selling reindeer
shoes, and a dollmaker. In addition, shows were upgraded to appeal to

The Christmas Tree is one of the park's unique Christmas-themed rides.

an increasingly sophisticated customer. By the time Santa's Workshop celebrated its twentieth anniversary in 1969, 12 million visitors had walked though its gates.

With the dawn of the 1970s, Santa's Workshop was facing a changing world. The theme park genre that it helped create had become more competitive. Numerous theme parks dotted the Northeast, and inter-state highways made it easier for vacationers to travel to more distant destinations. The gas shortages of the early 1970s hit the park hard. It responded by expanding its season in 1973 with the addition of Yuletide Family Weekends. Taking place over the Christmas season, the weekend package includes two nights' lodging, meals, gifts, park admission, and two evenings of entertainment. It remains the park's most popular event.

In 1976, Santa's Workshop added the Slide-A-Boggan. Meant to simu-late the thrill of tobogganing in the summer, the ride consisted of two plastic troughs down which people could ride toboggans. Unfortunately, after the ride was set up, it was discovered that changes in temperature and humidity resulted in a very temperamental attraction. On some days, the toboggans would stop before the end; on others, they overshot it. Despite several attempts to correct the problems, the park never could get it to work right, and the ride was soon removed.

Vacationers continued to be drawn to places farther away. By the early 1980s, attendance had dropped to seventy thousand annually, just one-third the visitors of the park's peak years. By the late 1990s, attendance had fallen even further, to fifty thousand. Reiss stopped taking a salary and even considered shuttering the venerable facility. But in 1997, he was joined by his niece Martha Reiss Colon and her husband, Clarke, who brought renewed energy to the park. By updating technologies and increas-ing marketing, they succeeded in stemming the attendance decline.

On the Rebound

The operation had stabilized by the end of the 1990s, and Reiss thought it was time for new blood to take over. He wanted to take his time to find the right buyer, someone who could bring new ideas but still respect the park's history and be a proper guardian of the memory of Santa. In order to maximize exposure for the facility, Reiss showcased the park on the QVC shopping network on Thanksgiving Day 1999, with an asking price of $650,000. Santa's Workshop received dozens of phone calls, and Reiss narrowed it down to eight serious bidders.

One of those bidders was Gregory Cunningham, a hotel owner from the central part of the state. By the end of 2000, he had reached an agree-ment with Reiss and announced a major improvement program. Cun-ningham felt that the park's target market had become too narrow, and he planned to broaden its appeal by adding attractions such as a hot-air balloon ride, an interactive 3-D theater, virtual reality games, miniature golf, new shops, and a series of festivals.

Cunningham started to upgrade the park, but he had legal problems with some of his other business investments, and the deal fell through. It took several months to sort out the mess, and Santa's Workshop failed to open for the 2001 summer season. The park's future again was up in the air, and the small community that surrounded the park suffered from the decreased attendance. By fall, however, Reiss was able to get things straightened out, and the park opened for its Christmas Preview to anxious throngs.

Fortunately, another buyer soon emerged. Douglas Waterbury, a businessman from Oswego, purchased a controlling interest in the park from Reiss in 2002. For 2003, Waterbury launched a $500,000 improvement program that included infrastructure upgrades, new shows, an arcade, and three new kiddie rides—a roller coaster, Ferris wheel, and Flying Sleighs—in a new area dubbed Frosty's Fun Park.

Santa's Workshop Today

Santa's Workshop is a true pioneer in the amusement park industry. One of the first parks ever built around a theme, it maintains many of the original attractions that created a national sensation when it opened in 1949. Today the park features eight rides, its famous collection of log buildings, and Santa Claus, all nestled in a pine forest at the base of Whiteface Mountain. Ten live shows are performed thirteen times a day at four locations.

At the top of a hillside, visitors enter Santa's Workshop, home to Mother Hubbard's Cupboard restaurant, the train, and the Christmas Tree ride. Beyond the restaurant are most of the park's rides in the Frosty's Fun Park area, including the Bobsled, Sleigh Ride Coaster, Reindeer Carousel, and playground.

Winding down the hill, visitors pass the reindeer barn and petting zoo. At the bottom of the hill is the heart of the park, North Pole Village, consisting of a series of log buildings, many of which date back to the park's opening in 1949. In addition to Santa's House, visitors can enjoy a variety of shops and craftsmen, as well as the famous North Pole, which is covered in a thick layer of ice no matter what the temperature.

Hoffman's Playland

OPENED 1952

ENTREPRENEURSHIP RUNS DEEP IN THE HOFFMAN FAMILY. SINCE GERMAN immigrant Charles Hoffman set up an ice business nearly a century ago, the family has sought to capture their portion of the American dream. As the ice business started to decline, one of Hoffman's five sons, Adam, acquired a 61-acre parcel of land in Latham, where he constructed a diner and bowling alley. During World War II, the bowling alley was appropriated by the government for a defense plant, and Adam started a turkey farm. A few years later, as America was enjoying postwar economic prosperity, he decided it was time to pass the torch.

A Piece of the Farm

Adam Hoffman wanted to instill the entrepreneurial sprit in his three sons, so in the late 1940s, he split a portion of the farm into three 8-acre pieces and told each to start his own business. Paul started first, opening a restaurant in 1948. He was followed by Robert, who built a miniature golf course in 1950. In 1952, it was William's turn. In postwar suburbia, he looked to the baby boom families in need of low-cost entertainment for his inspiration. Kiddielands were rapidly spreading throughout the country, and William thought these small amusement parks with scaled-down rides would be the perfect fit for his 8-acre parcel.

Hoffman's Playland
Route 9
608 Loudon Rd.
Latham, NY 12110
518-785-3842
www.hoffmansplayland.com

Hoffman's Playland started small, opening with just a miniature train from the Miniature Train Company and a merry-go-round manufactured by the Allan Herschell Company, two major suppliers of rides during the kiddieland boom. In order to give customers the most value for their money, the train made two laps around the track, a tradition that continues today. The only building at the time was a small ticket booth, which, though retired, still has a place of honor at the park.

The small amusement park was an immediate hit, and in 1953, the park expanded to include a kiddie boat ride and ponies. Hoffman was on a roll. Adding new attractions drew more people, which necessitated the addition of still more rides. A kiddie Caterpillar opened in 1955, followed by a Sky Fighter in 1956, a Helicopter in 1958, and a kiddie roller coaster and turnpike auto ride in 1960. All were provided by the Allan Herschell Company, and with the exception of the turnpike, they are still in operation today, looking as good as they day they first opened.

As the baby boom began to wane in the 1960s, Hoffman wanted to expand his appeal by adding some larger rides. The first "big kids" ride he added was bumper cars in 1962. Manufactured by Lusse Brothers of Philadelphia, this ride is still a favorite and represents one of the last

In its earliest years, Hoffman's Playland had just four rides, two of which remain in operation. HOFFMAN'S PLAYLAND

Hoffman's Playland started adding larger rides in the 1960s and 1970s.

old-style bumper car rides of its kind in the country. Other big rides followed, including a Scrambler in 1965, a Ferris wheel in 1971, and a Paratrooper in 1974.

Passing the Torch

By now William Hoffman was tiring of the business and looking to move on. His son David, who was just finishing college, initially was not interested in taking over the operation, but when his father considered liquidating the business, he decided it would be a great place to begin his career. He started out keeping a low profile, but he did make one critical change that first season, putting a phone in the office, something his father did not believe in.

As the 1980s began, Hoffman gave the park a new face with the addition of a large building in the front that housed a gift shop, ticket booth, and train station. The park had grown substantially since its earlier days, and the original train could not accommodate the increased crowds. Hoffman decided to add a larger train, but increased costs for rides made it difficult to afford a new model. So he went shopping for a used train looking for a good home and found one at Smiley's Happyland, an amusement park in Bethpage, New York, that was going out of business. It was selling an Iron Horse train, manufactured by the Allan Herschell Corpora-

 **VISITING**

HOFFMAN'S PLAYLAND

LOCATION

Hoffman's Playland is located on U.S. Route 9 in Latham, just outside Albany. From I-87, take Exit 5 (Watervleit Shaker Road) east to Route 9. The park is approximately 1 mile south on the right.

OPERATING SCHEDULE

The park opens at noon on weekends in April and September. During May, it is open daily, at 3 P.M. weekdays and noon on weekends. From mid-May through Labor Day, opening time is noon daily. Closing time depends on the crowds and the weather.

ADMISSION

Admission is free, with all attractions priced on a pay-as-you-go basis. Tickets cost about $1 each. Major rides require two tickets, kiddie rides one ticket.

FOOD

The park features five food stands. The main one in the heart of the park offers burgers and chicken, peanut butter and jelly, and grilled cheese sandwiches. Others include a Subway sandwich shop, pizza stand, and ice cream stand.

FOR CHILDREN

All of Hoffman's Playland is designed for kids and their parents. Almost all of the rides can be enjoyed by the entire family.

SPECIAL FEATURES

Hoffman's Playland is one of the last classic 1950s-style kiddielands still in operation. Throughout the 1950s, parks like this were a staple in suburban America. Today only a handful remain.

Don't miss the bumper cars. Manufactured in 1962 by Lusse Brothers, it is one of the last old-style bumper car rides still in operation.

TOURING TIPS

As an amusement park serving the local market, Hoffman's Playland is very dependent on the weather, so call ahead to confirm operating hours if the weather is questionable.

tion. Hoffman completely overhauled the ride and put it in operation for the 1980 season. Eight years later, he found another train sitting on the boardwalk at Funtown USA in Seaside Park, New Jersey, that he was also able to rebuild and place in operation.

The new owner had hit his stride, and through the 1980s, he continued to add new attractions. A kiddie space ship ride opened in 1983, followed in 1985 by a Tilt-A-Whirl from Hanson's Amusement Park, a

The park today features a wide array of rides.

defunct operation in Harvey's Lake, Pennsylvania. In 1989, the aging kiddie turnpike was replaced by the 4x4 truck ride.

The park continued to grow, and in 1994, food service was added for the first time. Initially, Hoffman brought in a small concession trailer to test the waters. It was so popular that he quickly replaced it with larger facility, along with three other food stands.

Hoffman traveled to Shreveport, Louisiana, in 1996 for the auction of Hamel's Amusement Park. He was the winning bidder for a colorful Balloon ride, one of only eight made by Bradley and Kaye. Since the compact ride would take up only half of a tractor trailer, Hoffman decided to make the most of his shipping costs and purchased a second ride to fill the rest of the trailer: a Rock Spin-N-Roll spinning tub.

Hoffman's Playland Today

In operation for more than half a century, Hoffman's Playland has become an institution in the Albany area. Its eighteen rides, including ten just for kids, are maintained in top-notch condition, as are its neatly landscaped grounds. From the entrance, visitors find the original merry-go-round, kiddie boats, and Balloon ride to the right. Most of the larger rides, including the train, bumper cars, Scrambler, Paratrooper, and Ferris wheel, are to the left, as are the kiddie roller coaster and 4x4 trucks. Several more kiddie rides are found toward the back of the park.

The Great Escape & Splashwater Kingdom

OPENED 1954

IN 2001, THE GREAT ESCAPE & SPLASHWATER KINGDOM UNVEILED A NEW marketing slogan: "My, how we've grown!" Truer words have never been spoken in the amusement industry. In just five decades, the park has evolved from a 5-acre collection of storybook displays connected by dirt paths to a full-scale theme park that takes at least a full day to enjoy completely. And to think, it started with a road trip to California.

One Man's Dream

The Great Escape & Splashwater Kingdom was the culmination of a dream by Charles Wood. His spark of inspiration came in 1937, when he noticed an article in *Reader's Digest* about California's Knott's Berry Farm and how it was able to generate $500,000 in annual profits despite the Depression. Wood immediately set out from New York to California to check out the operation and returned with a burning desire to create his own version. It was not the right time, however. The Depression was soon followed by World War II, which deferred, but did not kill, his dream.

In 1947, Wood traveled from his native Lockport, New York, across the state to Albany to look at a skating rink he was interested in buying. But the deal fell through during a meeting at a downtown hotel. As he was leaving the hotel, Wood noticed a newspaper advertisement offering the Holiday House, a hotel in Lake George, about 60 miles north of Albany, for sale. He asked a policeman for directions and embarked on a journey that would change his life.

> **The Great Escape & Splashwater Kingdom**
> P.O. Box 511
> Lake George, NY 12845
> 518-792-3500
> www.sixflags.com/parks/greatescape

Wood discovered that the hotel was out of his price range, but he was referred to another that was for sale in the area, the Arrowhead Lodge. He was able to buy this one and quickly turned it into a successful operation—so much so that four years later, he sold it and bought the Holiday House.

While he was becoming a successful hotelier, Wood continued to pursue his dream of opening a theme park. But rather than have an Old West theme like Knott's Berry Farm, Wood wanted to base his park on the storybook characters he loved, allowing visitors to relive cherished children's tales. Wood's daughter Barbara recalled that he had a closet full of storybooks he used for reference.

By 1953, Wood's hotel business had grown to the point where he could now bring his park to life. He purchased 230 acres of marshland 4 miles south of Lake George and set about carving a park out of 5 acres along U.S. Route 9, the area's major north-south route. Wood toiled throughout the winter, doing most of the work himself, and on June 27, 1954, Storytown USA opened. He struggled with doubts the night before it opened: "I sat on the Mother Goose hill and I cried, 'What have I done? I'm not gonna have anybody pay and see what I've done.'"

The Never-Never Land of the Adirondacks

Built at a cost of $75,000, Storytown that first season was a simple operation. Dirt paths connected two dozen storybook displays, including the Old Woman's Shoe, a little red schoolhouse, Peter's pumpkin, a ginger-

The Swanboats were one of The Great Escape's first rides. DEAN COLOR SERVICE

 VISITING

THE GREAT ESCAPE & SPLASHWATER KINGDOM

LOCATION

The Great Escape & Splashwater Kingdom is located between the towns of Glens Falls and Lake George on U.S. Route 9. From I-87, which runs parallel to Route 9, take Exit 20 to Route 9 South.

OPERATING SCHEDULE

The Great Escape & Splashwater Kingdom is open weekends from 10 A.M. to 6 P.M. from mid-May until Memorial Day weekend. From Memorial Day weekend through June, the park opens at 10 A.M., closing at 6 P.M. on weekdays and 8 P.M. on weekends. From July through Labor Day, the park opens at 10 A.M., closing at 8 P.M. on weekdays and 10 P.M. on weekends. The park opens at noon on weekends in September and October.

ADMISSION

Pay-one-price admission of less than $40 entitles visitors to all rides and attractions, with the exception of games and some attractions, including the Sky Coaster, Turbobungy, go-carts, and Climbing Wall. Children under 48 inches tall and senior citizens receive a discount. Half-price admission is available after 4 P.M. Discounted tickets can also be purchased through the park's website.

FOOD

The Great Escape & Splashwater Kingdom has two dozen food outlets, ranging from sit-down restaurants, many of which are air-conditioned, to portable carts. The Character Café in Looney Tunes National Park serves a variety of sandwiches; the German Beer Garden in the Fest Area features German specialties, burgers, and hot dogs; the Chicken Chalet has chicken specialties; and Saddle Rock Café in Ghost Town offers burritos and burgers. Other outlets have pizza, submarine sandwiches, funnel cakes, turkey legs, ice cream, and cotton candy.

Outside food and beverages are not permitted in the park. A public picnic area is located near the front gate.

FOR CHILDREN

Looney Tunes National Park offers eight rides for kids, many of which can be enjoyed by the entire family, and the Fest Area also has a number of kiddie rides. Families with children should be sure to visit Arto's Small World, a collection of quarter-scale buildings, and the Alice in Wonderland and Jungleland walk-throughs.

Noah's Sprayground in the water park is a great place for kids to splash around, featuring two wading pools and dozens of fountains, geysers, slides, and places to climb.

The park also has a number of other rides and attractions for the entire family, including the Cinderella Coach, Storytown Train, Grand Carousel, swan boats, Giant Wheel, and Thunder Alley.

(continued on page 138)

VISITING (continued from page 137)

THE GREAT ESCAPE & SPLASHWATER KINGDOM

SPECIAL FEATURES

The Great Escape & Splashwater Kingdom was one of the country's first theme parks, and many of the storybook displays that gave the park its original name are still scattered throughout the Storytown area. The Cinderella Coach and swan boats are two of the park's original rides.

Arto's Miniature World is a collection of miniature buildings created by Arto Monaco, one of the theme park industry's pioneers. Many of the early theme parks in New York State owe their existence to him.

The Comet is the Great Escape's flagship attraction. It is one of the few wooden roller coasters to have been moved from another location and is highly regarded for its high speed and "airtime."

TIME REQUIRED

With all of its rides and attractions, plus the water park, the Great Escape & Splashwater Kingdom will easily fill an entire day. If you are pressed for time and visit on a day when crowds are light, the major attractions can be enjoyed in about four hours.

TOURING TIPS

Try to visit The Great Escape & Splashwater Kingdom on a weekday, particularly before mid-June, when the park tends to be less crowded.

Arrive just before the park opens and start your day either in the Ghost Town or by the Comet. These areas are the farthest from the front entrance and the last ones to get crowded.

If you want to ride the Nightmare at Crack Axle Canyon indoor roller coaster, try to hit it first thing in the morning. It tends to have long lines most of the day.

bread house, Humpty Dumpty, Little Boy Blue, and Noah's Ark. People dressed up as storybook characters and animals were scattered throughout the park. A creek called the River Dee ran through the property.

Wood's fears were soon alleviated, as Storytown became a popular stop for the region's tourists. In fact, he was soon forced to expand the park office, because every time the employees tried to count the money, someone would open the door and it would blow all over the place.

Storytown continued to grow over the next two seasons, with new scenes, including a chapel, Moby Dick, the Three Bears, and the Cow Jumping over the Moon, and rides such as a train, swan boats on the River Dee, and the Cinderella Coach. The last two remain popular attractions today.

As popular as Storytown was, some people could not be coaxed into visiting. "I noticed that all the men stayed in the parking lot when families arrived," Wood remembers. "They wouldn't go through the gates,

Ghost Town was the park's first major expansion.

and that bothered me." As a result, he added a new area for the 1957 season: Ghost Town. Modeled after an early American mining community, Ghost Town featured several Old West buildings, such as a blacksmith shop, livery stable, and saloon. The area was filled with live entertainment—dancing girls in the saloon, the Medicine Wagon Show, and gunfights on the street—as well as a stagecoach, surrey, burro train, and a mine tunnel linking Ghost Town to the storybook area. The main ride was the half-mile-long Ghost Town Train, built by Arrow Development, which had just established itself as a major force in the industry by providing many of Disneyland's rides. Overseeing the town was Marshal Wild Windy Bill McKay. Today McKay, well into his eighties, still walks the streets of Ghost Town.

Ghost Town was an immediate hit, and soon Storytown USA was the leading attraction in the Adirondacks. In 1962, another new attraction opened in a swampy area in the back of the park: Jungleland, a 60,000-square-foot walk-through featuring a variety of elevated walkways, suspended bridge, and mechanical animals. By now, Storytown had grown to 56 acres and welcomed its 2 millionth visitor.

Growing Up

Charley Wood was a compulsive collector and filled his park with items acquired from around the world. In 1964, Freedomland, one of the first attempts to duplicate the success of Disneyland, closed in New York City

after a disastrous four-year run. Wood was a major purchaser at the liquidation and brought several rides back to the park, including a mule-pow-
ered merry-go-round for Ghost Town; Danny the Dragon, a dragon-shaped
trackless train; a mirror maze walk-through; and a magnificent, huge
antique carousel, featuring seventy-two animals hand-carved by William
Dentzel. The addition of the rides from Freedomland marked a new phase
in the growth of Storytown, in which traditional amusement park rides
joined the more sedate attractions. Others included the Flying Carpet sky
ride, Turnpike car ride, Astrowheel, and Trabant spinning ride.

The major new attraction in 1965 was not the rides, however, but a
new walk-through themed to the story of Alice in Wonderland, created
to provide kids with things to climb in and around and a place to blow
off steam. Alice in Wonderland, situated in a grove of tall trees, was the
first major attraction on the hill above River Dee, which became a main
area of growth for the park over the next few years. Wood closed out a
very successful 1965 season by purchasing an additional 115 acres
across Route 9 from the rest of the park, which he turned into a much-
needed parking lot.

Storytown added another major attraction in 1967, when the Tornado
dark ride, themed as a journey through a midwestern tornado, opened
in Ghost Town. Wood acquired the ride from Kennywood, near Pittsburgh, although it had originally operated at Freedomland.

*The Italian Roller Coaster was The Great Escape's first roller coaster when it opened
in 1971.* DEAN COLOR SERVICE

By the 1970s, Storytown had grown from a small kiddie park into a full-fledged theme park. In 1971, the park installed its first roller coaster, the Italian Roller Coaster, which operated until 1988. Other attractions soon followed, including a dolphin show in 1973; a thousand-seat theater and the Calypso spinning ride in 1974; a trackless train constructed by theme park designer Arto Monaco in 1975; and the Magical Mystery Ride, an enclosed scrambler ride, in 1977.

Inspiration for improvements often came from unexpected sources. In the mid-1970s, while on vacation on Gatlinburg, Tennessee, Wood became enamored with one of the town's shopping villages and its European-style architecture. Considering the growth of Storytown over the past decade, he knew that the park needed a new front entrance and felt that a similar type of shopping village would be the perfect entrance for the ever-expanding park. International Village opened in 1977, a $1.25 million project with fifteen shops that sold everything from park souvenirs to $30,000 Tiffany lamps. Resembling a small European village, the area featured more than $100,000 in decorative items, such as streetlamps, stained-glass windows, gargoyles, and cast-iron benches. Anchoring the area is an Italian bronze boar sculpture that Wood purchased on one of his travels.

Wood's collecting abilities proved beneficial again the following year when Busch Gardens in Van Nuys, California, closed. He purchased the park's 1,500-foot-long log flume ride and relocated it to Storytown, where it was erected in Ghost Town in time for the 1979 season. Called the Desperado Plunge, the flume was just one element of a $2.5 million improvement program that season. Other new attractions included a Sky Diver ride, a circus, and the Cinema 180 movie theater.

Also that year, Arto Monaco, who had become one of Wood's best friends, closed his Land of Make Believe theme park in nearby Upper Jay. One of its most popular attractions was a collection of quarter-scale small-town America buildings that kids could play in. Wood bought the buildings and erected them between the Ghost Town and storybook areas in 1981. They immediately became as popular as they had been at Land of Make Believe. In 1983, they were joined by a collection of Old West buildings also constructed by Monaco.

Escaping Storytown

By now Storytown had grown into a full-fledged theme park that offered much more than its name implied. As long as it kept its original name, it would be associated with the storybook displays that appealed to small children. Wood realized that he had to change the park's name to better reflect its new identity, so he held a contest at the end of the 1981 sea-

Steamin' Demon was part of The Great Escape's transition from a kiddie park to a full-blown theme park.

son. Out of twenty thousand entries, two submitted a name that the park felt best identified what it had become: The Great Escape.

The transition to the new name began in 1982, with the park advertising itself as Storytown–The Great Escape. The Ranger, a looping thrill ride, was erected by front entrance in place of the relocated Astrowheel to show the public that the park offered more than kiddie rides. By the next year, the transition was complete, and the Storytown name was officially retired. That year also saw the addition of two spinning rides: the Rotor and Spider.

With the park now appealing to a broader audience, Wood realized that The Great Escape needed a new high-profile thrill ride. In 1983, Pontchartrain Beach in New Orleans shut down, and The Great Escape purchased the park's looping roller coaster. Renamed Steamin' Demon, the 55-foot-tall, 1,430-foot-long ride features a vertical loop and a corkscrew that flips riders upside down three times. It was erected on a hillside at the front of the park, again demonstrating to the world that the renamed park was not just for kids.

Throughout the 1980s, The Great Escape expanded its ride lineup. A bumper car ride and the Cannonball Express opened in 1985. Raging River, a large river rapids ride, debuted in 1986. In 1987, the Balloon Ferris wheel opened and the Rainbow replaced the Ranger.

The year 1989 was one of change for The Great Escape. Three new rides were added, including the Balloon Race, 95-foot-tall Giant Wheel, and Condor, a 112-foot-tall spinning ride. Unfortunately, the 1989 season also marked the last year for The Great Escape's antique carousel. With prices in the collectors' market skyrocketing, the park sold the animals off for $1.3 million. The carousel was replaced by a modern fiberglass model the next year.

The biggest change in 1989 was a new owner. That April, Charley Wood sold The Great Escape and Fantasy Island, an amusement park near Buffalo that he also owned, to International Broadcasting Corporation (IBC) for $36 million. IBC owned the Harlem Globetrotters and Ice Capades and thought theme parks would be a natural extension of its business. The sale did not mark the end of Wood's involvement with a park he thought of as "his baby," however. He was appointed head of IBC's new theme park division.

The first major addition under the new owners was Noah's Sprayground, a large water play area for children filled with fountains, pools, climbing structures, and slides. The play area was intended to be the first phase of a complete water park, but, by the time Noah's Sprayground opened in 1992, IBC was in bankruptcy because of high debt levels and a sluggish economy. Wood could not bear to see his beloved park caught up in IBC's problems, so in late 1992, he reached a deal to reacquire The Great Escape and Fantasy Island for $14 million. As Wood said at the time, "I wanted to get my baby back."

Wood soon sold Fantasy Island, but he never looked back with The Great Escape. The ride lineup saw a major upgrade in 1993, with the addition of seven new rides. The Astrowheel gave way to the Flying Trapeze swing ride, and the turnpike was renovated. Other new rides included a swinging Pirate ship and the Black Cobra, an enclosed "dry" water slide.

Charley's Comet

The 1993 season was tremendous, but it paled in comparison to the addition the following year of the Comet, a huge wooden roller coaster. Five years earlier, Crystal Beach, located just over the Canadian border near Buffalo, closed after 101 years of operation. Its signature attraction had been the Comet, a 95-foot-tall, 4,197-foot-long roller coaster created in 1948 by Herbert Schmeck, one of history's great designers. It was renowned for its fourteen hills, sustained speed, and "airtime"— that delightful sensation of floating out of your seat.

Wood fondly recalled riding the Comet in his youth and knew that it would round out the ride lineup at The Great Escape. He succeeded in

The Comet was a particular favorite of park founder Charley Wood.

purchasing the ride at Crystal Beach's liquidation auction for $210,000, then quickly dismantled it and placed it in storage. Given the size of the massive ride, getting the necessary approvals was a slow process that took until September 1993.

Once the approvals were finalized, construction began the next day. More than a thousand concrete footers were installed, and by December, the ride's structure started going up. Forty-nine tractor trailers hauled the ride from storage in Buffalo, and a special workshop was erected on-site to sandblast and paint the steel supports. Work progressed rapidly through the frigid winter, and by May, the $3.5 million project was complete. The reconstruction of the Comet generated national publicity for The Great Escape, helping to bring a 10 percent increase in attendance.

With the Comet filling out the ride lineup, Wood now turned his attention to completing the water park. The 1995 season saw the opening of the $2 million Splashwater Kingdom, which complemented the existing Noah's Sprayground with two water slides and the 1,100-foot-long Capt'n Hook's Adventure River. An additional water slide debuted in 1996.

Another Expansion Premiers

As the 1990s were winding down, the amusement industry was changing. Several operators were buying up amusement parks in hopes of building national chains. One of those companies was Premier Parks (now Six Flags), which got its start in 1981 when the company, then known as Tierco, purchased Frontier City, a run-down amusement park in Oklahoma City. It originally intended to redevelop Frontier City, but when those plans fell through, it renovated the park instead. The turn-around was successful, and the company sought out other amusement parks to acquire. By the time Premier Parks approached Charley Wood, it had grown to nine amusement parks across the country. The company saw The Great Escape & Splashwater Kingdom as just the type of park it was looking for and bought it from Wood for $33 million.

A key part of Premier's strategy was to invest heavily in new attractions to spark interest in the park and broaden its market. The company's approach to The Great Escape & Splashwater Kingdom was no different and resulted in a $6 million expansion in 1997, the largest in park history. The highest-profile addition was the Boomerang roller coaster, which replaced Danny the Dragon. The ride has just 935 feet of track but maximizes thrills by hauling riders backward up a 125-foot-high incline. The train is released, and it travels back through the station into a twisting "boomerang" that flips riders upside down twice, passes through a vertical loop before climbing up another 125-foot-high incline, then reverses and goes through everything again backward. In all, riders are turned upside down six times.

Two new attractions were added to Splashwater Kingdom: Lumber-jack Splash, a 500,000-gallon, 25,000-square-foot wave pool, and Paul Bunyan's Bucket Brigade, a large water play area dominated by a five-story treehouse tower with geysers, showers, water cannons, and a huge

Expansion of the waterpark was a key component of The Great Escape's renovation under Premier Parks (now Six Flags).

overhead water barrel that tips over to drench those below. The new management also extended the park's operating hours past 6 P.M. for the first time. The changes were a huge success, and attendance increased by 22 percent.

Investment in the park continued in 1998 with $3 million in improvements, anchored by the Alpine Bobsled, a 65-foot-high, 1,650-foot-long roller coaster purchased from Six Flags Great America in Gurnee, Illinois. Unlike traditional roller coasters, this one has a steel trough in which eight passenger cars careen like bobsleds.

In 1999, for the third year in a row, The Great Escape debuted a new roller coaster: Nightmare at Crack Axle Canyon, a 45-foot-tall, 1,772-foot-long steel-track roller coaster completely enclosed in a 16,000-square-foot building. The ride was relocated to The Great Escape from one of its sister parks, Darien Lake near Buffalo, and had previously operated at Kentucky Kingdom in Louisville, another theme park that Premier Parks had acquired and reinvigorated. Other features of the $3 million improvement program included a 900-foot-long go-cart track and Fright Fest, a Halloween festival complete with a special Haunted House, pumpkin carving and painting, and trick or treating. Attendance jumped again by 17 percent, to a record nine hundred thousand.

In 2003, Canyon Blaster debuted in the Ghost Town. Replacing the Tornado dark ride and Ghost Town train, the 2,036-foot-long steel-track roller coaster stands 56 feet high and features lift hills of 46 and 31 feet and a top speed of 45 miles per hour. The ride was acquired by the parent company in 1997 when Opryland in Nashville closed.

Most recently, The Great Escape redeveloped the area around Jungleland into Looney Tunes National Park, a 2-acre kiddie area that introduced the famous cartoon characters to the park. Eight new family rides include Road Runner Express, a roller coaster; Taz's Twister, a swing ride; Speedy Gonzales Camptown Racers; Elmer Fudd Scenic Railway; and Daffy Duck Wilderness Bus Tours.

The Great Escape & Splashwater Kingdom Today

From a simple 5-acre storybook attraction, The Great Escape & Splashwater Kingdom has grown into one of the leading theme parks in the Northeast. Today the park features more than forty rides spread out over 140 acres, including a dozen kiddie rides, seven roller coasters, a full-scale water park, two walk-throughs, and a full lineup of live shows.

Visitors enter through the International Village shopping area, which leads to Storytown, the park's original section. In addition to many of the original storybook attractions, Storytown features classics such as Arto's Miniature World, the Cinderella Coach, and swan boats; family favorites, including the Storytown train, Grand Carousel, and Thunder Alley Turnpike; and thrill rides, including the Rainbow and Boomerang.

To the left of the entrance, Storytown leads to Ghost Town. Here visitors will find the Canyon Blaster, Nightmare at Crack Axle Canyon, and Steamin' Demon roller coasters; Desperado log flume; and Condor.

Behind Storytown, along the banks of the River Dee, is Looney Tunes National Park, home to most of the kiddie rides and the Jungleland walk-through. Crossing the River Dee leads to the Fest Area home of the Alice in Wonderland walk-through. Many of the park's spinning rides, such as the Mystery Tour indoor scrambler and Flying Trapeze swings, are located here as well. Visitors will also enjoy the Sky Ride, Giant Wheel, Raging River, Alpine Bobsleds, and Comet roller coaster.

Beyond the Fest Area is the Splashwater Kingdom water park, with four water slides, the Bucket Brigade play area, Lumberjack Splash wave pool, and Noah's Sprayground kiddie area.

NEW YORK

Enchanted Forest/ Water Safari

OPENED 1956

IN THIS SLEEPY ADIRONDACK MOUNTAIN RESORT COMMUNITY, ENCHANTED Forest/Water Safari leaps out at you. Perched on the edge of town, the sky blue roof of the entrance building with towering letters announcing the park's name beckons passersby to come inside and enjoy the attractions. Enchanted Forest/Water Safari is unique in that its growth followed three key trends in the industry's development: the growth of roadside storybook parks in the 1950s, the rollout of water parks in the 1980s, and the spread of family entertainment centers in the 1990s.

The Adirondack's Enchanted Forest

During the 1950s, America was seeing a construction boom of roadside attractions. The two dominant themes for these facilities were the Wild West and storybook tales. In the mountain town of Old Forge, three businessmen, A. Richard Cohen, Joseph Uzdavinis, and Donald Rice, thought that the resort area surrounding the community might be a great location for just such a project. They hired Russell Patterson, who had designed similar facilities in New Jersey and Texas, to develop the concept, and purchased 80 acres of swampland at the north end of town. In April 1956, construction began on the $500,000 project.

Enchanted Forest/ Water Safari

3183 State Route 28
Old Forge, NY 13420

315-369-6145

info@watersafari.com
www.watersafari.com

After almost three months of round-the-clock work, Enchanted Forest of the Adirondacks opened for business on July 7, 1956, on 35 wooded acres. The heart of the park was the storybook area. A huge statue of Paul Bunyan greeted visitors and beckoned them down through the Story Book Lane

Little Houses, which featured Sleeping Beauty, Peter Pumpkin Eater, Ali Baba, Cinderella, Goldilocks and the Three Bears, Little Red Riding Hood, and the Seven Dwarfs, as well as the Crooked House. Captain Kidd's Pirate Ship was converted from a 50-foot former sightseeing boat that dated back to 1917.

Other attractions included Dawson City, a replica of a Yukon mining community complete with gunfights and covered wagon and burro rides; a petting zoo; an Eskimo Village; a replica of the Alamo; the Bowl Mill, where guests could watch woodenware being produced from logs to the finished products; and a train that wound through the woods, the only mechanical ride.

Enchanted Forest quickly became a popular attraction, and new features were added. In 1958, Chief Maurice Dennis and his family opened an Indian Village where guests could learn about Adirondack Indian life and lore. Around this time, the park also brought in a number of mechanical kiddie rides, including the Little Dipper roller coaster and Ferris wheel.

But a disastrous season was looming for the park in 1962, when a major highway project hampered access to the park. To attract attention, Enchanted Forest booked the famed Wallendas high-wire act for twenty-seven shows as part of a Circus Days promotion. The act drew several television shows to the park, and the increased attention offset the traffic lost to the construction project. The success of the Wallendas

Storybook displays remain the heart of Enchanted Forest, as they were in 1956.

prompted the park to book them for a sixty-four-day run in 1963. Both NBC and Canadian Broadcasting featured the act in documentaries filmed at Enchanted Forest. The park decided to make circus acts a key part of its entertainment offerings, a tradition that continues to this day.

The kiddie ride lineup continued to grow, with the debut of the Flivver Cars in 1964 and the kiddie boats, handcars, and helicopters in 1965.

By the time Enchanted Forest celebrated its tenth anniversary in 1966 with a 200-pound birthday cake and a new whale boat ride, more than 1.25 million visitors had walked through its gates. Enchanted Forest's landmark entrance arch, acquired from the 1964 New York World's Fair, was hoisted into place in 1968, and a $100,000 Sky Ride manufactured by Halls Ski Lift Company opened the following season. In 1970, the Sky Ride cars were themed to resemble hot-air balloons by the famed theme park designer Arto Monaco.

By the 1970s, Enchanted Forest was a well-established attraction. For the 1972 season, the park added a carousel manufactured in 1920 and acquired from Suburban Park in Manlius, which was shutting down. It also introduced a new live entertainment offering that year: the Enchanted Forest Parade in the Sky, in which characters from the forest all rode the Sky Ride at a special time, and then met and greeted guests for photos.

The ride lineup continued to be expanded the next couple seasons, with the addition of the Ferris wheel in 1975 and Tilt-A-Whirl in 1976. But then Joseph Uzdavinis died, and the other two partners, who were not involved with the park on a day-to-day basis, put the facility up for sale.

The park's ride line-up expanded throughout the 1970s. ENCHANTED FOREST/WATER SAFARI

VISITING

ENCHANTED FOREST/WATER SAFARI

LOCATION

Enchanted Forest/Water Safari is located less than an hour north of Utica. From I-90 (New York State Thruway), take Exit 31. Follow NY Route 12 North to NY Route 28 North to Old Forge.

From I-87, take Exit 23 (Warrensburg) to U.S. Route 9 to NY Route 28 through Blue Mountain Lake to Old Forge.

OPERATING SCHEDULE

The park is open daily from mid-June through Labor Day. On weekdays in June, it is open from 10 A.M. to 4 P.M. The remainder of the season, it opens at 9:30 A.M. with closing time varying between 6 and 7 P.M.

ADMISSION

Pay-one-price admission of about $25 entitles visitors to all rides and attractions. Children ages three to eleven receive a discount.

FOOD

The park has seven food outlets. The major facilities include Klondike Kates, which has indoor seating and serves pizza and wings; the Oasis Café, featuring burgers, chicken and fish sandwiches, hot dogs, and clam rolls; the Carousel Café in A Step Beyond, which offers wraps, hot dogs, nachos, and pretzels. Other stands sell french fries, ice cream, popcorn, and funnel cakes.

Outside food and beverages are permitted in the park and picnic pavilions. Tables and grills are available on a first-come, first-served basis. Glass containers are prohibited.

FOR CHILDREN

Enchanted Forest/Water Safari offers a full variety of attractions for children. Kids love going through Story Book Lane and exploring the displays. Most of the mechanical rides in A Step Beyond can be enjoyed by the entire family. There are also several kiddie attractions in the water park. Clustered together in the front of the park are Tadpole Hole, Pygmy Pond and Slides, and Kiddie Car Wash. The Sawmill in the back of the park is another favorite water attraction for kids.

SPECIAL FEATURES

The park's Story Book Lane area is one of the largest and best-preserved story-book attractions in the country. Once common in the 1950s, only a few are left. It still has most of its original displays.

Water Safari is one of the largest water parks in the country, with more than thirty attractions, and has one of the most complete assortments of water slides around.

(continued on page 152)

VISITING (continued from page 151)

ENCHANTED FOREST/WATER SAFARI

TIME REQUIRED

Enchanted Forest/Water Safari can easily occupy an entire day, with its water park, amusement rides, circus, and storybook displays. If you are pressed for time, the major attractions can be enjoyed in about three hours.

TOURING TIPS

Visit on weekdays or early or late in the season for the lightest crowds.

If you plan to visit more than once a season, consider joining the Paul Bunyan Club. For a small service charge, you can return as often as you like for half price.

If you arrive after 3 P.M., you will receive a Siesta Pass valid for reentry at any time during the season.

Arrive early and hit the water slides first. The water is heated, and crowds will be at their lightest.

A second changing area is located at the back of the park, between A Step Beyond and Adirondack Expedition.

Don't miss the circus. There are two performances at noon and 4 P.M.

A Noonan Perspective

Around this time, Timothy Noonan, a liquor store owner in nearby Utica, was looking for a seasonal business to invest in. He wanted to acquire a hotel, but when he had trouble reaching an agreement on the one he was interested in, his broker mentioned that Enchanted Forest was for sale. Noonan took a look at the park and was intrigued with its potential. On April 18, 1977, the deal was closed, and he and his family found themselves in the amusement park business.

Noonan brought a fresh perspective to the operation, which was just what it needed. It had a very limited market at the time, as older children were not interested in the storybook attractions and kiddie rides. He knew that broadening the park's appeal was key to growing the business.

As a result, his first major addition was A Step Beyond in 1978, a new area at the back of the park that featured several larger rides, including bumper cars, a Round Up, the Bullet, and the Rock O Plane. The new rides were joined by a relocated helicopter and boat rides, while some older attractions, such as the whale boats, Covered Wagon, and ponies, operated for the final time.

The new rides revitalized the operation. A Giant Slide was purchased from Lagoon Park in Farmington, Utah, and by the time Noonan celebrated his fifth season as owner in 1982, attendance had increased by 70 percent from 1977.

A Step Beyond is where the park's amusement rides are located today.

On Safari

By the early 1980s, the amusement industry was being changed by a new type of attraction, the water park, which emphasized participatory water attractions rather than mechanical rides. A number of new water parks had been built from the ground up, but adding water slides to an existing amusement park was a new concept. Noonan knew, however, that this would be the perfect way to distinguish his park from the competition.

In 1984, the kiddie handcar ride was removed, and Wild Waters was constructed in its place. It consisted of two 350-foot-long flumes built by Dick Croul, one of the originators of the water slide. The impact of Wild Waters on the park was profound. Located at the front of the park, the slides attracted people who previously had never thought of going to Enchanted Forest, and business doubled.

Other changes also took place at the park. In the storybook area, an elaborate new Hansel and Gretel gingerbread house opened in 1985, the Little Dipper's last season. Created by Jack Molesky, the house had taken four years to complete. But Noonan knew his future lay in the water slides and set about building a full-blown water park.

In 1986, the carousel and Tilt-A-Whirl were moved to A Step Beyond to make room for Raging Rapids, a 700-foot-long tube ride, and the Tadpole Hole, a kiddie slide and pool. But construction really took off the next fall, when fourteen new water rides and attractions were added for the 1988 season, making Enchanted Forest the largest water park in the state. More than 200,000 yards of fill were trucked in to create a large hill on which most of the slides were built, and the park's size increased to 50 acres. To clear the way for the new slides, the giant slide was removed, the Ferris wheel relocated to A Step Beyond, and the Flivver Cars and kiddie Ferris wheel moved near the petting zoo, where the deteriorating Alamo had been demolished a few years earlier.

Many of the rides added were the first of their kind in New York. These included the Congo River Rapids, Bombay Blasters, Nairobi Narrows, Killermanjaro Speed Slide, Serengeti Surf Hill, Lake Nakura activity pool, and Safari River Expedition. For kids, the Pygmy Pond and Kid Wash premiered. With the addition of all of the water attractions, the park took on a new name: Enchanted Forest/Water Safari. Water Safari had transformed the park, and in 1989, attendance increased by another 70 percent over the previous year.

In response to the increased crowds, two more water attractions debuted in 1991: the Amazon Family Tube Ride, featuring 7-foot-diameter tubes that could accommodate the entire family down a 1,100-foot-long river, and the quarter-acre Tidal Wave Pool nearby.

Enchanted Forest/Water Safari embraced another industry trend in 1994, with the opening of Calypso Cove. When Noonan purchased the park in 1977, a restaurant at the front of the property was included in the deal. After operating it under several different formats, he decided to develop the area around the restaurant into Calypso's Cove to provide patrons with entertainment in the evening. Calypso's Cove is a family entertainment center, a type of scaled-down amusement park that began spreading throughout the country during the 1990s. Among its attractions are adult and kiddie go-carts, batting cages, miniature golf, bumper boats, and an arcade. The addition of Calypso's Cove brought Noonan's total investment in the park to $18 million since he bought it.

While Noonan hit his stride with the park, there were some hiccups. On July 15, 1995, a huge microburst hit Old Forge in the middle of the night and knocked out power to the park. It was closed for two and a half days, including a critical summer Saturday. Vowing never to lose another day because of a lack of electricity, Noonan installed four diesel generators.

Enchanted Forest/Water Safari faced down another challenge in 1996. The park's mountain location meant that the water did not hold its heat during the night, so it was chilly for early-morning visitors. To counteract that, Enchanted Forest became one of the few amusement parks in the country to heat its water, adding two diesel-powered, 6 million BTU water heaters to keep the water at a constant 80 degrees.

An aerial view of Enchanted Forest/Water Safari shows its array of offerings.
ENCHANTED FOREST/WATER SAFARI

The following year, the petting zoo was renovated, but 1998 saw two of the older attractions, the Indian Village and Bowl Mill, taken out in preparation for another major expansion. With the water park enjoying ever-increasing popularity, Noonan decided to expand its capacity by developing a large area in the back of the park into the Adirondack Expedition. Here visitors find five water attractions: three water slides, an action river, and the Sawmill, a water play area complete with a gigantic tipping bucket.

Enchanted Forest/Water Safari has continued to change. The Flivver Cars were relocated to A Step Beyond in 2000, while the kiddie Ferris wheel was removed. In 2002, Wild Waters, the original water slide, was replaced with the Shadow, a completely enclosed water slide.

Enchanted Forest/Water Safari Today

From a 1950s-style roadside kiddie attraction, Enchanted Forest/Water Safari has evolved into a well-rounded entertainment destination featuring a dozen rides; Story Book Lane, with nearly twenty displays; and one of the largest water parks in the state, with thirty-three attractions.

As they were in 1956, visitors are greeted by a giant statue of Paul Bunyan just inside the entrance. This area features a variety of shops and services, the Sky Ride, and a train that provides transportation to and from A Step Beyond, located in the back of the park.

Just beyond the front entrance is Story Book Lane, the oldest area in the park, featuring well-preserved replicas of beloved tales. Don't miss Ali Baba's Cave and Hansel and Gretel. Next to Story Book Lane is Dawson's City, with food, shops, and games. Adjacent to this area is Water Safari, with its wide variety of attractions. Most of the kiddie attractions are located toward the front of the park. At the back are A Step Beyond, home to the park's mechanical rides and circus, and Adirondack Expedition, the newer water area.

Martin's Fantasy Island

OPENED 1961

IN THE LATE 1950S AND EARLY 1960S, THE AMERICAN AMUSEMENT PARK industry experienced a gold rush of sorts as entrepreneurs scrambled to cash in on the success of Disneyland. While major theme parks were proposed for most larger cities, almost every city saw someone trying to develop his or her own version. In Western New York there were several attempts, but only one still remains: Martin's Fantasy Island.

A Real Estate Investment

In 1959, Buffalo area real estate developer Lawrence Grant was standing at a construction site in Grand Island, a suburb of Buffalo completely surrounded by the Niagara River, when the project's architect mentioned to him that the land across the street would make a great location for a theme park. Grant was inspired, and in December of that year, he formed a corporation called Fantasy Island to develop the park. He brought in several partners, including Gerald Birzon, who is credited with developing the park's general concept. The company purchased a 20-acre parcel across from the shopping center and broke ground in October 1960.

On July 1, 1961, Fantasy Island threw open its gates with a ribbon-cutting ceremony for five hundred guests. The park itself occupied 12 acres, with the remaining land used for parking. The front gate opened onto a broad, grassy mall anchored by a Happy Birthday house shaped like a huge cake. Surrounding the mall were five themed areas: Western Town, Indian Village, Garden of Fables, Animal Kingdom, and Action Town.

Martin's Fantasy Island
2400 Grand Island Blvd.
Grand Island, NY 14072-3198
716-773-7591
info@martinsfantasyisland.com
www.martinsfantasyisland.com

Western Town was a replica of an Old West town, complete with a saloon providing live entertainment and gunfights in the street. Indian Village featured Seneca Indians demonstrating their customs. Garden of Fables was filled with re-creations of beloved fairy tales, including Jack and the Beanstalk, Little Bo-Peep, Li'l Red Riding Hood, and Jonah's Whale. Animal Kingdom was anchored by a large petting zoo, and Action Town was where the rides were concentrated. The Allan Herschell Company, based in nearby North Tonawanda, laid out Action Town and filled it with ten rides: a train, merry-go-round, antique autos, and seven kiddie rides. Admission was $1 for adults and 50 cents for kids. Ride tickets, called Whimsies, were sold in books of twenty for $1. Rides required three to seven Whimsies.

Unfortunately, the public was slow to come to Fantasy Island, and the 1961 season did not measure up to expectations. The owners were undaunted and announced a $250,000 expansion beginning in 1962. They switched to a pay-one-price admission, with $1.50 allowing visitors to enjoy all the rides and attractions, and installed new rides including a riverboat and stagecoach. Expansion continued in 1963 with the addition of the Space Whirl, a large outer-space-themed spinning ride acquired from the 1962 Seattle World's Fair, and the Magnetic House, a walk-through illusion attraction. Three years later, a twenty-five-hundred-seat arena was erected for Tarzan Zerbini's circus, which became a favorite attraction for the next ten years. The Blue Goose debuted in

Animal Kingdom was one of Martin's Fantasy Island's original themed areas.

VISITING

MARTIN'S FANTASY ISLAND

LOCATION

Martin's Fantasy Island is located less than ten minutes from Niagara Falls, just north of Buffalo. From I-190, take Exit N-19, Whitehaven Road, to the park.

OPERATING SCHEDULE

The park opens at 11:30 A.M. on weekends starting in mid-May and daily from mid-June through Labor Day, closing between 7:30 and 9 P.M., depending on the day of the week and time of year. The water park opens at noon.

ADMISSION

Pay-one-price admission of less than $25 entitles visitors to all rides and attractions, with the exception of games and miniature golf. Children under 48 inches tall and senior citizens receive a discount.

FOOD

The park has a dozen different food outlets, ranging from sit-down restaurants, many of which are air-conditioned, to portable carts. They include Basghetti's, serving pizza, subs, pasta, and goulash; the BBQ Barn, featuring barbecued roast beef and turkey specialties; and Boppers, with hamburgers, hot dogs, chicken sandwiches, and Italian sausage. Other outlets offer hot dogs, tacos, chicken fingers, nachos, popcorn, ice cream, and cotton candy. Don't miss the Waffle Tower for sugar waffles, a regional favorite.

Outside noncommercially prepared food and beverages are permitted in the park, although alcoholic beverages and glass containers are prohibited.

FOR CHILDREN

The kiddie area, located just to the right of the main entrance, features nine rides, many of which also accommodate adults. Other rides in the park that can be enjoyed by the entire family include the big slide, train, antique autos, and Giant Gondola Wheel.

The water park features several attractions for kids, including their own water slides and pool.

SPECIAL FEATURES

Several of the original storybook displays are clustered in the kiddie area.

The Silver Comet is Martin's Fantasy Island's flagship attraction. This wooden roller coaster gives an action-packed ride with plenty of "airtime."

TIME REQUIRED

With all of its rides and attractions, as well as the water park, Martin's Fantasy Island will easily fill an entire day. If you are pressed for time and visit on a day when crowds are light, the major attractions can be enjoyed in about four hours.

(continued on page 160)

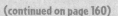

VISITING (continued from page 159)

(continued from page 159)

> **TOURING TIPS**
>
> Try to visit Martin's Fantasy Island on a weekday, when the park tends to be less crowded.
>
> Canadian currency can be exchanged at the Oasis refreshment stand, the General Store, and in the water park.

1971. Dating back to 1930, the unique kiddie ride was a classic attraction that featured fourteen wooden birds on which children sat.

Growing Up

Fantasy Island was moderately successful throughout the 1960s, but the owners knew that their long-term success depended on appealing to a wider variety of visitors. In 1974, the park launched a five-year program to transform the kiddie-oriented park to a full-fledged theme park. In all, $10 million was to be spent. The owners purchased additional land, increasing the park's total holdings to 85 acres, and spent $1.2 million on new attractions for the 1974 season. They built a thirty-five hundred-seat arena for the circus, as well as a game building and shooting gallery, and added six rides: bumper cars, the Paratrooper, Scrambler, Tilt-A-Whirl, Trabant, and Wildcat, a 45-foot-tall, 1,500-foot-long steel-track

Martin's Fantasy Island launched a major expansion in the 1970s, adding several new areas.

roller coaster built by Anton Schwarzkopf, one of the most important roller coaster designers of the era. The new attractions were a huge hit, and Fantasy Island saw revenues double and attendance increase by 65 percent, to 242,000.

The park followed up this successful season with an additional $375,000 in capital improvements for 1975, developing 5 more acres, constructing additional game and merchandise buildings, and installing new rides, including a larger train and Devil's Hole, whose riders defied gravity in a spinning drum. Attendance jumped another 14 percent, to 275,000, and peaked at 300,000 in 1977.

Following the 1975 season, expansion slowed. Only a few more attractions were added during this period, such as the double Sky Wheel in 1979. In the late 1970s, business started to decline along with the economy of western New York. Fantasy Island filed for bankruptcy in May 1982 and failed to open for the season.

A New Beginning

Chemical Bank, the largest creditor, soon took control of the shuttered park and made plans to sell it. The effort caught the attention of Charley Wood, one of the most successful amusement park operators in the country, with his two theme parks in Lake George: the Great Escape opened in 1954, and Gaslight Village, in 1959. He had grown up not far from Grand Island, in Lockport, and had long dreamed of building an amusement park in his hometown area. In fact, he already owned a parcel of land in nearby Niagara Falls, where he had intended to build a park.

On November 23, the deal was finalized, and Wood held a festival in Buffalo's Niagara Square to announce his purchase of Fantasy Island. The celebration came complete with costumed characters and a Space Shuttle ride that he intended to install at the park. "We're going to do everything possible to make Fantasy Island the type of operation to make everyone proud," he announced. "What we make on this park will remain in this area and will be plowed back into the park."

Wood launched a $1 million renovation and expansion program to inject new life into the facility. He hired Arto Monaco, a noted designer of several theme parks in the eastern part of the state, to oversee the renovation. Monaco guided the restoration of the buildings and storybook displays, as well as construction of two new rides: the Arto Train, a trackless train ride, and the Coronation Coach, a horse-drawn carriage that traveled around a miniature castle. The coach ride replaced the birthday pavilion in the park's central mall.

A new front entrance was created from buildings acquired from the 1982 World's Fair in Knoxville, Tennessee. Wood also purchased another

New buildings around the entrance mall anchored the park's 1983 renovation.

26 acres, which allowed him to rearrange the rides for better flow of pedestrian traffic. He was also able to extend the midways to the edge of a nearby highway, increasing Fantasy Island's visibility. In addition to the Space Shuttle and Arto Monaco's two rides, antique autos and a Yo Yo swing ride were added. A new circus and high-dive show also premiered.

Fantasy Island reopened to an appreciative public and was officially on the road back. Wood continued the improvements in 1984 by installing Raging Rapids, twin 400-foot-long water slides that were the first phase in the development of a complete water park. One newspaper at the time of its opening rated Raging Rapids as the best water slide in western New York.

Growth of the water park continued in 1985, with the addition of two attractions: the Water Garden, a series of activity pools purchased from the 1984 New Orleans World's Fair, and the Kids Wash, which came from the 1982 Knoxville World's Fair and sent visitors through car-wash-type elements. Other additions included bumper boats and two kiddie rides. Wood followed that up in 1986 with the construction of the Old Mill Scream, an 1,100-foot-long log flume featuring two splash-down hills of 30 and 40 feet. Built by the Japanese firm Sansei, it was acquired from Petticoat Junction, a theme park in Panama City, Florida, that had gone out of business.

By 1987, Wood had spent more than $8 million improving Fantasy Island, but he was not done yet. Throughout the remainder of the decade, improvements continued on an almost annual basis. Surf Hill, a kiddie water slide complex, opened in the water park in 1987. Paddle boats and kiddie bumper boats debuted in 1988, and kiddie bumper cars and a Balloon Race spinning ride joined the lineup in 1989.

The Owner-Go-Round

In April 1989, Wood sold Fantasy Island along with the Great Escape, one of his two amusement parks in Lake George, to International Broadcasting Corporation (IBC) for $36 million. IBC owned the Ice Capades and Harlem Globetrotters and saw theme parks as the perfect complement to its other businesses. IBC continued Wood's improvement program during the first season with the opening of Splash Creek, a river ride in the water park, and the Flying Bobs, a spinning ride purchased from the nearby Crystal Beach when it closed in 1989. But IBC was soon struggling under the weight of a large debt load and a sluggish economy, even though its park operations were profitable.

Fantasy Island drifted through the next two seasons, as IBC had limited funds to make improvements. By 1992, IBC was in bankruptcy. To protect his investment, Wood reacquired Fantasy Island and the Great Escape late in the year for just $14 million. To give Fantasy Island a new identity, Wood changed the name of the park to Two Flags Over Niagara

Old Mill Scream joined the park's ride line-up in 1986.

Fun Park, reflecting its location close to the Canadian border. He made some improvements for the 1993 season, such as the addition of a Sea Dragon swinging ship and new shows, but Wood, who was now seventy-nine years old, wanted to slow down. He decided to focus on his holdings at the other end of the state and placed this park on the market. By the end of the season, three parties were interested. The winning bidder was Martin DiPietro.

While in high school, DiPietro had decided to turn his expertise at playing midway games into operating his own game booth at weekend festivals. His success led him to purchase a small, portable amusement ride company from the retiring operator of Tony's Amusement Rides. "It was the last thing I thought I'd be doing," he later told the *Buffalo News*. DiPietro grew Tony's Amusement Rides from a five-ride show into a thirty-ride, two-unit midway, earning the reputation of running the cleanest, safest family-oriented show in western New York. Tiring of the grind of constantly moving his business, he sought to bring his reputation to the somewhat tarnished image of Fantasy Island.

The deal to purchase the park was finalized on February 23, 1994. DiPietro changed its name to Martin's Fantasy Island and immediately announced a $5 million upgrade. The grounds and buildings desperately needed attention, as the park had seen few upgrades during the IBC era. DiPietro devoted $500,000 to repairing buildings, replacing fences, and improving utilities, and used most of the remaining funds to replace 75 percent of the park's rides with more modern models. "We're going to improve it, not necessarily number-wise but quality-wise," he told the *Buffalo News*. Almost twenty new rides were installed and some old ones removed, including the Magnetic House, Paratrooper, Devil's Hole, and Trabant. The new rides included the Patriot, which flipped riders head-over-heels; the Super Sizzler; and a $750,000, 90-foot-tall Giant Gondola Wheel, erected right along the highway as a signal that the park was here to stay.

The kiddieland was also completely upgraded, with all but two rides replaced. Rides such as the Blue Goose, removed by its former owner, as well as the Little Dipper roller coaster, Arto Train, and Roto Whip, gave way to the Dragon roller coaster, Rio Grande train, Granny Bug, and Red Baron. In addition, the merry-go-round was overhauled and moved to a prominent location in a lushly landscaped oasis in the center of the park, where it replaced the Coronation Coach. More games were added, a new miniature golf course was installed, the petting zoo was improved, and new shows were launched.

The public responded well to the changes and flocked to Martin's Fantasy Island. By the end of the 1994 season, more than 200,000 people visited the revitalized amusement park, nearly twice the number that had visited the year before. DiPietro sought to keep the positive momentum going in 1995 and spent $1 million to install several more attractions. The Crazy Bus and a large swinging ship, called the Sea Ray, were added in the ride park, and a wave pool was constructed in the water park. Measuring 170 by 112 feet, the 216,000-gallon pool replaced the bumper boats and water garden. Again the public responded positively, and attendance jumped to 275,000. In 1996, DiPietro added two more spinning rides—Chaos and Up, Up and Away—along with a new petting zoo.

Making an Impression

Martin's Fantasy Island had been completely revitalized. With the existing facilities upgraded, DiPietro knew it was time to add the signature attraction that both he and the public desired—a large wooden roller coaster. Through much of 1997, he worked with Custom Coasters, the world's largest manufacturer of wooden roller coasters at that time, to develop a design for the new ride that would appeal to the park's family audience but still be a thriller.

By the end of the 1998 season, the $3 million project was ready to go, and in October, installation of the hundreds of concrete footers began. Work progressed rapidly, and on May 11, 1999, the train rounded the track for the first time. A contest was held to name the ride, and Silver

The Silver Comet is now Martin's Fantasy Island's signature attraction.

Comet emerged as the winner. The name paid homage to the defunct Comet roller coaster, which had operated until 1989 at Crystal Beach, just across the Canadian border. As another tribute, the coaster station was a replica of the original Comet's. The coaster forever changed the park's skyline, standing 95 feet tall with 3,000 feet of track and a top speed of 55 miles per hour.

New attractions have continued to appear. The Daredevil, a 120-foot-tall launch tower, debuted in 2001. Nitro, a multiaxis spinning ride, replaced the Flying Bobs in 2003, and Jack and the Beanstalk, a bouncing tower ride that took the place of the Dragon roller coaster, was added in 2004. By now the Wildcat had seen three decades of faithful service and was getting tired. It was sold to an amusement park in Russia and was replaced for 2005 by the Crazy Mouse, a $2 million spinning coaster from Zamperla, one of the world's largest ride manufacturers.

Martin's Fantasy Island Today

Like the Silver Comet, Martin's Fantasy Island has seen its share of ups and downs, but during the past twelve years under DiPietro's ownership, it has definitely been on a continual upswing. It is now one of the leading amusement parks in the state, featuring more than seventy rides, shows, and attractions, including a full-scale water park.

The park's entrance leads to the central mall, which served as the heart of the park when it opened in 1961. At the center of the mall is the merry-go-round, one of Fantasy Island's original rides, in a lushly landscaped garden. Immediately to the right is the train, which links the front and back of the park. Next comes the entrance to the kiddieland, with nine family and kiddie rides, miniature golf course, petting zoo, and the storybook displays that helped launch the park more than four decades ago. At the back of the mall are the picnic groves.

To the left of the entrance is the Western Town, location of the Wild West shootout and revue shows. From here, visitors pass the canoe ride and entrance to the water park before entering the back area of the park, where the major rides are concentrated.

A long midway leads past the big slide, Silver Comet, Chaos, Patriot, Daredevil, and Midway Theater. At the end of the midway are the antique autos, Giant Gondola Wheel, Crazy Mouse, and Old Mill Scream log flume.

Adventureland

OPENED 1962

IN THIS HECTIC CORNER OF SUBURBIA, WHERE SHOPPING CENTERS AND industrial parks compete for attention along a busy six-lane thoroughfare, Adventureland seems oddly out of place. Its colorful twirling rides seem to call out to passing cars, inviting them into the oasis that lies within its wrought-iron fences.

Growing with Suburbia

In the early 1960s, suburbia was marching down Long Island. Throughout the island, massive housing developments were followed by shopping centers and industrial parks. Entertainment was an important part of this mix, and spurred by the postwar baby boom, entrepreneurs dotted the island with kiddielands, which were small amusement parks with scaled-down rides. Included in this group were Alvin Cohen and Herb Budin. They thought that the central part of the island would make an ideal location for a new kiddieland, so they acquired a 6-acre site along NY Route 110, a major north-south artery on which some eighteen thousand cars drove daily.

After visiting the amusement industry trade show in Chicago during the fall of 1961, the partners set about constructing their new park. At the heart of the new operation, they built a large building housing a restaurant, arcade, and four rides so that the park could be open year-round. One of the rides was an antique carousel featuring a variety of animals carved by William Dentzel. Outdoor operations included a miniature golf course and four addi-

Adventureland
2245 Route 110
Farmingdale, NY 11735
631-694-6868
www.adventureland.us

167

When Adventureland opened in 1962, it featured this antique Dentzel carousel. It was sold in 1979. AMUSEMENT BUSINESS

tional rides: a half-mile-long miniature train, the Little Dipper roller coaster, kiddie cars, and boats. The $1 million facility was ready to open in the spring of 1962 under the name Adventures 110 Playland.

The park, whose name was soon changed to 110 Adventureland, quickly became a popular destination for the residents of Long Island. In 1965, the park added its first major ride, the Skyliner, a 35-foot-tall sky ride that traveled the entire 500-foot length of the park.

Growing Up

By the early 1970s, the kiddieland boom had waned as baby boomers were growing up. The dwindling target market combined with rising property values led to the demise of many of 110 Adventureland's competitors. Cohen, who by now was the primary owner of the facility, knew that he had to expand his operation to keep it viable. In 1972, he was able to purchase an additional 6 acres behind the original park for nearly $1 million.

Over the next few seasons, Cohen doubled the ride count from sixteen to thirty, complementing the existing kiddie-oriented ride lineup with a number of major rides. In 1973, four rides were added, including the Toboggan, a compact roller coaster ride; the Amor Express, a high-speed circular ride; and the Galaxi, a steel-track roller coaster. The following season saw the addition of the Wave Swinger, a large, colorful European-manufactured swing ride that was one of the first of its kind in the United States.

The success of the Wave Swinger prompted Cohen to start bringing in other flashy European rides that had not yet spread throughout the country. In 1976, he leased two large spinning rides, the Enterprise and Troika, from Willy Miller, a German immigrant who came to the United States in 1972 and started a ride-importing business. Miller was impressed by the growing operation, and Cohen asked him if he would be interested in purchasing 110 Adventureland.

The two parties negotiated over the next year, and on September 15, 1977, the sale was finalized. Miller continued Cohen's successful growth

VISITING

ADVENTURELAND

LOCATION

Adventureland is located on NY Route 110 in East Farmingdale. It is easily accessible from I-495 (Long Island Expressway) and the Southern State Parkway. From I-495, take Exit 49S and head south for 2 miles; the park will be on the left. From the Southern State Parkway, take Exit 32N and head north for about 3 miles; the park will be on the right.

OPERATING SCHEDULE

Adventureland opens at noon on weekends, starting in late March. On weekdays from mid-April though late May, only the kiddie rides are open at noon. From Memorial Day weekend through late June, the park is open daily, with hours and the number of rides open varying by the day of the week. From late June through Labor Day, the park opens at 11 A.M. on weekdays and noon on weekends. After Labor Day, the park opens on weekends at noon, and the kiddie rides open at noon on weekdays in September. On weekends from November through mid-March, select kiddie rides operate inside the arcade starting at noon. Closing times vary throughout the year, so call ahead.

ADMISSION

Pay-one-price admission of less than $25 entitles visitors to all rides and attractions except games and the climbing wall. Children under 48 inches tall receive a discount. Adventureland offers two pay-one-price sessions: from opening until 7 P.M. or from 4 P.M. until closing. Ride tickets are also available for about 80 cents each. Rides require three to five tickets.

FOOD

The park has about eight food outlets. The main restaurant, located next to the kiddieland, is air-conditioned and features a wide variety of food, including pizza, hot dogs, hamburgers, deli sandwiches, salads, and wraps. Other outlets offer hot dogs, nachos, popcorn, homemade ice cream, churros, and cotton candy.

Outside food and beverages are not permitted in the park.

FOR CHILDREN

The kiddie area, located at the front of the park, features fourteen kiddie and family rides. Other rides in the park that can be enjoyed by the entire family include the train, antique autos, and Paul Bunyan Express roller coaster.

During the winter, Adventureland moves several of its kiddie rides inside the arcade and operates them on weekends.

SPECIAL FEATURES

Adventureland is one of the most aesthetically pleasing amusement parks around. From its brick walkways to its lush landscaping, the park is a pleasant oasis.

(continued on page 170)

VISITING (continued from page 169)

(continued from page 169)

ADVENTURELAND

The park has a long reputation of adding the latest European-manufactured rides and as a result has several unique attractions, including Crocodile Run, the John Silver Twist Tower, and Surf Dance.

TIME REQUIRED

Adventureland can take several hours to enjoy, and families with small kids will likely want to spend much of the day.

TOURING TIPS

During much of June, Adventureland hosts school groups early in the day, and the park can get quite crowded. Most groups leave in early afternoon, so consider arriving after that.

strategy. For 1978, Miller brought in several new rides, including an antique auto ride that had originally operated at the 1964 New York World's Fair. He also overhauled existing attractions and shortened the park's name to Adventureland. The first season under new ownership was a huge success, with revenues increasing by 50 percent.

Miller sold the antique carousel to collectors in 1979, replacing it with a more modern merry-go-round, and added other new attractions. In 1980, the Black Hole, an indoor spinning ride with an elaborate light and sound show, debuted, along with the Lost Continent, a dark ride featuring twenty different special effects. Miller also continued to bring in the latest in European rides, including the Looping Star at the end of the 1982 sea-

The Toboggan was one of Adventureland's most popular rides in the 1970s.
ADVENTURELAND

The Wave Swinger was the first of numerous flashy European rides added to Adventureland.

son and the UFO in 1983. The UFO was one of six new rides added that season, replacing attractions such as the Enterprise and Troika. Others included a new bumper car ride and Captain Willy's Wild Waters bumper boats in a 100,000-gallon pool. The following year, a Gravitron spinning ride replaced the Black Hole, and a new Bavarian Village area, with food outlets and shops, was erected at the back of the park.

The Bavarian Village kicked off a multiyear program aimed at completely upgrading the park's aesthetics. By this time, Adventureland was competing for increasingly sophisticated customers. Theme parks and their carefully planned environments were becoming ever more dominant, and Miller knew that a park consisting of a bunch of rides set up in an asphalt lot could no longer be competitive. Over the next several seasons, the blacktop gave way to brick paving stones, cyclone fencing was replaced by wrought iron, and the entire facility was transformed into a lushly landscaped oasis. In 1986, the Lost Continent was converted into a new dark ride called 1313 Cemetery Way. In addition, the park received national attention when it was featured in movie *Sweet Liberty* and Chaka Khan's *Love of a Lifetime* video.

The year 1987 was an important one. Willy Miller sold his interest in the business to Tony Gentile, who had become a partner in Adventureland in 1978. The Gentile family was not content with keeping the operation as it was, and they undertook a major expansion. To make room for Pirate's Plaza, a new midway area at the rear of the park, they had to reconfigure the antique auto ride. Pirate's Plaza was anchored by two new rides: the swinging Pirate Ship and multiarmed Scorpion. One of the Scorpion's pieces was so large that it required a special truck and trailer to bring it to Adventureland from the port in New Jersey where it had arrived by ship from the Netherlands. Assembling the ride required the largest hydraulic crane on Long Island. Phase two of Pirate's Plaza opened in 1988, with the addition of Treasure Island, an elaborate miniature golf course that was soon voted the best on Long Island by *Long Island Magazine.*

A Long Island Oasis

As the 1990s dawned, Adventureland had been totally transformed from a bunch of rides in a blacktop lot into an oasis along what was now a busy six-lane highway in a congested commercial area. For years, the park's customers had requested more water rides at Adventureland, but given the constraints of the 12-acre site, installing a water park was not feasible. To remedy this, the Gentiles soon purchased a 30-acre site 30 miles away in Riverhead, Long Island, to develop Splish Splash, a $6 million water park.

The opening of the new water park did not divert the Gentiles' attention from Adventureland, however. After two years of planning, the Galaxi was replaced in 1991 by the Hurricane, a 1,430-foot-long, 59-

Added in 1991, the Hurricane is Adventureland's largest roller coaster.

The Balloon Wheel provides a great view of Adventureland's offerings.

foot-tall steel-track roller coaster distinguished by a series of tight turns banked at angles of up to 80 degrees.

New attractions were a regular occurrence throughout the 1990s. The Super Raiders, a large climbing structure for kids, debuted in 1992. The next year, the antique auto ride was updated with newer models; the Scorpion gave way to the Surf Dance, a large, churning, multiarmed ride that was the first of its kind in the country; and Tubs of Fun and Flying Clowns replaced older kiddie rides. The Balloon Wheel took the place of the ten-year-old Big Wheel in 1995, and the Dragon Wagon, a 12-foot-tall, 300-foot-long kiddie roller coaster, debuted in 1996.

By the end of the decade, family entertainment centers, which were scaled-down amusement parks, began spreading throughout the country. Adventureland saw the potential in this type of facility and, in early 1999, opened Bullwinkle's, 9-acre family entertainment center located in Medford, roughly 25 miles away. Soon after the opening, the Gentiles sold both Bullwinkles and Splish Splash to Palace Entertainment, a company that was building a national chain of family entertainment centers and water parks. "I got an offer you just don't refuse," Gentile told *Newsday.* "It's the greatest thing I've ever done in my business life."

Now the Gentile family concentrated on upgrading Adventureland. An elaborate double-decker Venetian Carousel complete with spinning tubs opened in 1999. In 2000, the Paul Bunyan Express, a 19-foot-tall, 662-foot-long family roller coaster, was purchased from a defunct amusement park in Japan. In 2001, Adventure Falls, manufactured by FAB of Luxembourg, replaced Treasure Island. This 920-foot-long log flume, featuring two drops of 25 and 40 feet, was the first ride of its type to operate on Long Island. That year also saw three kiddie rides take the place of the Dragon Wagon.

Replacing older rides with newer ones has been a consistent strategy at this space-constrained facility that continues to this day. The Looping Star gave way to the first Top Scan spinning ride in America in 2002. The Viking Voyage boat ride took the place of the kiddie boats, the park's last original ride, in 2003. Adventureland debuted two first-of-their-kind rides in 2004. After twenty years, the bumper boats were replaced by Crocodile Run, a circular water ride featuring rider-controlled, two-person boats. Also added was the John Silver Twist Tower, 37-foot-tall ride from ABC Engineering of Switzerland, on which an eight-person gondola drops down the tower as it sways from side to side. Originally intended to be a kiddie ride, the tower quickly became popular with teens and adults, and the park ended up increasing the speed to boost the thrill factor.

Adventureland Today

From a small, simple, eight-ride kiddieland, Adventureland has grown into the largest amusement park on Long Island, with twenty-six rides, including two roller coasters and ten kiddie rides. The park is laid out roughly in the shape of a long, narrow rectangle leading back from NY Route 110. It has three entrances: one through the restaurant, another toward the front of the park, and a third in the back.

The front entrance leads to the park's kiddie area, featuring fourteen kiddie and family rides, including the double-deck carousel, Balloon Ferris wheel, Wave Swinger, and Balloon Tower. Adjacent are the park's restaurant, arcade, and bumper car ride.

A long midway extends to the back of the park and is surrounded by most of the larger rides, including the Top Scan, Crocodile Run, Music Express, Surf Dance, John Silver Twist Tower, Hurricane and Paul Bunyan Express roller coasters, and 1313 Cemetery Way dark ride. At the back of the park are the Bavarian Square area and rear entrance, along with the antique autos, Pirate Ship, and Adventure Falls flume.

Magic Forest

OPENED 1963

MAGIC FOREST IS PROBABLY THE ONLY AMUSEMENT PARK IN THE WORLD that has Uncle Sam as an official greeter. But this is no ordinary Uncle Sam. This one stands 38 feet tall and is part of a group of large fiberglass sculptures known as Muffler Men. Originally created as a restaurant promotional tool, they achieved their greatest recognition for being used to market autombile mufflers and copies soon became popular commercial icons in the 1960s. They remain scattered throughout the country in new identities, such as Paul Bunyan, Cowboys, Indians, Vikings, and the infamous Happy Half Wit. Magic Forest has become a bastion of Muffler Men. Joining Uncle Sam are a Clown, an Amish Farmer, and Paul Bunyan. These are just a few of the hundreds of fiberglass figures that adorn this unique amusement park.

Settling Down

Arthur Gillette was a showman. Starting in 1944, he traveled throughout the Northeast with his carnival, Gillette Shows. By 1956, however, he was tiring of being on the road and sought to use his experience at an amusement park. That year, he leased a parcel of land in Lake George and opened Lake George Amusement Park. But leasing costs in the growing resort area increased too rapidly, and the park closed in 1957 when the land was sold for hotel development.

Not wanting to walk away from the amusement park industry, Gillette opened Carson City, a Western theme park in the Catskills in 1958. Though he enjoyed operating it, and owned it until 1979,

Magic Forest
P.O. Box 71
Lake George, NY 12845
518-668-2448
www.magicforestpark.com

he missed the atmosphere of Lake George and sought to return there with a new amusement park on land he actually owned.

He located a parcel just south of town. Now the challenge was coming up with a concept. Back in his carnival days, Gillette had been part of a Christmas Park promotion in Albany, and he thought that a Christmas-themed amusement park would be a great addition to Lake George.

But there was much work to do. The land he acquired was a former junkyard full of old cars that had to be disposed of, a large hole had to be filled for the parking lot, and paths had to be carved through the thickly wooded property. But Gillette worked hard to make his dream a reality, and by the spring of 1963, Christmas City USA was ready to open. The new park was a pleasant diversion in the resort area. Spread out among the trees were log buildings housing attractions, including a tilt house, Santa's House, a museum, gift shop, entrance building, and refreshment stand, as well as a chapel that had been reconstructed from parts of a church from Rensselaer that had been removed by the state for a highway project. Apart from Santa, the primary attraction was animals—in particular, several large pens of deer.

Soon after the park opened, Gillette realized something was missing. Customers kept asking where the rides were located. As a result, halfway through the season, he leased three rides from a carnival: a merry-go-round, Chair-O-Plane, and kiddie airplane.

After the first season, Gillette saw that the park had to broaden its perspective beyond Christmas to grow over the long term. He changed the park's name to Christmas City Featuring Magic Forest, adding an Indian Village and expanding the ride lineup. The leased rides were replaced with several purchased from a defunct amusement park in Burlington, Vermont, including a merry-go-round and five kiddie rides: a Sky Fighter, Caterpillar, whip, pony carts, and boats. With the exception of the pony carts, all of the rides remain in operation at the park.

The changes that second season transformed the park, and the Christmas City moniker no longer adequately described it. For the 1965 season, the name was changed to Magic Forest and Indian Village, and it soon became just Magic Forest. With the business now firmly established, Gillette's seventeen-year-old son, Jack, joined the operation as manager in 1969.

The park undertook a major expansion in 1972, with the addition of a train and the first dolphin show in New York State. The train is one of only seven built by Arrow Development, the leading manufacturer of amusement park rides in the 1960s and 1970s. The dolphin show lasted only until 1975, but its replacement has become a longtime tradition. In 1977, Rex the Diving Horse took up residence at the old dolphin pool.

MAGIC FOREST

LOCATION

Magic Forest is located just south of Lake George on U.S. Route 9 between Exits 20 and 21 off I-87, which runs parallel to Route 9.

OPERATING SCHEDULE

Beginning in late May, Magic Forest opens on weekends at 9:30 A.M. From late June through Labor Day, the park is open daily from 9:30 A.M. until 6 P.M.

ADMISSION

Pay-one-price admission of about $15 entitles visitors to all rides and attractions. Children two to ten years old and seniors over fifty-five receive a discount.

FOOD

Peppermint Lounge Snack Bar serves burgers, hot dogs, grilled cheese sandwiches, popcorn, french fries, onion rings, and ice cream.

Customers are permitted to bring their own food into the park.

FOR CHILDREN

The park was built with kids in mind, and they can enjoy all of the rides and attractions. In fact, Magic Forest has one of the largest collections of kiddie rides in the country.

SPECIAL FEATURES

Magic Forest is one of the most densely wooded amusement parks around. All of the rides and buildings are carefully tucked among trees, and the temperature in the park is often several degrees cooler than in the parking lot.

The park has one of the largest collections of fiberglass sculptures in the world. Hundreds are scattered throughout the property, including Santa Claus, Pecos Bill, Paul Bunyan, Smokey Bear, and the Statue of Liberty. This makes the park a destination for enthusiasts of roadside architecture and fiberglass sculpture.

The park's large collection of kiddie rides has several lovingly restored vintage models that are rare in today's amusement parks. Among the classics are the Blue Goose, Roto Whip, Caterpillar, Turtle, Tanks, merry-go-round, cars, and Sky Fighter.

Don't miss the Snow White walk-through. Built for Walt Disney for the 1939 New York World's Fair and installed at Magic Forest in the early 1970s, it tells the story through several faithfully re-created dioramas.

TIME REQUIRED

If you have small children with you, a visit to Magic Forest can occupy most of the day. If you just want to experience the major attractions, the park can be enjoyed in about two hours.

TOURING TIPS

Visit during the week or early in the season, when the crowds are lighter.

As it has since the beginning, Magic Forest beckons to passersby on Route 9.
MAGIC FOREST

The original Rex is long since retired, but a new generation of Rexes has taken his place.

While attractions continued to be added, such as the Ferris wheel in 1978, the park was struggling, and by 1979, traffic was at an all-time low. The Gillette family briefly considered closing the facility, but Jack could not bear to see his father's work lost.

Bouncing Back

In 1980, Jack Gillette took over control of Magic Forest from his father. He worked hard to reinvigorate the operation and bring in new attractions. In 1981, his first season, he constructed several displays of beloved storybook characters in one corner of the park. The park's identity changed in 1982, when the Danbury, Connecticut, fairgrounds was sold for real estate development. One of the largest and oldest fairs in the United States, it was a treasure trove of equipment. Over a six-day period, more than twelve thousand items were sold to the highest bidder, and Gillette was an aggressive purchaser, filling a trailer each day and hauling it back to Magic Forest in the evening. Of particular interest to Gillette were the hundreds of fiberglass statues that filled the fairgrounds, including several Muffler Men, such as the park's now famous Uncle Sam. They were a perfect fit for Gillette, who restored Corvettes as a hobby and was skilled in working with fiberglass.

Around this time, he traveled to Knoxville, Tennessee, to a fiberglass junkyard to get spare Corvette parts. When he arrived, he discovered the junkyard had hundreds of old figures. He started going twice a year to bring some back. Combined with the Danbury acquisitions and later purchases, there are now more than a thousand fiberglass figures of every description throughout the park, including Santa Claus, Spacemen, Smokey Bear, the Statue of Liberty, and the hysterical hot dog and french fry figures in front of the refreshment stand.

The introduction of the first of the fiberglass figures was not the only addition that year. Magic Forest also installed a walk-through attraction telling the story of Cinderella, purchased from Fairyland in Gettysburg, Pennsylvania, after that park closed. That season also marked the debut of one of Magic Forest's most popular attractions, the Safari Trail. Gillette acquired a used tram ride from the Catskill Game Farm and laid a path through a wooded ravine. Throughout the trees, he placed dozens of fiberglass animal statues of every description, from dinosaurs to zebras. The abundance of improvements changed the look of Magic Forest and brought in new customers, leading to its most successful season ever.

Following a record 1982 season, Magic Forest followed up in 1983 by replacing the Indian Village with a kiddie roller coaster that the Gillette family had originally operated at Lake George Amusement Park and had in storage. Two years later, a larger kiddie coaster was purchased from Canobie Lake Amusement Park in Salem, New Hampshire.

Installing the new roller coaster posed a unique challenge. Jack Gillette holds the thick tree cover at the park in special esteem and will purchase only those rides that can fit within them. If he has to chose between moving a ride and cutting a tree, he will move the ride. When Gillette installed the new roller coaster, he had it three-fourths of the way up before discovering it would not fit. He wound up having to set it up three times before finding an alignment that would work among the trees.

While there was sadness in 1988 with the passing of Arthur Gillette, Jack was now-firmly in control and expanding the now-thriving operation. Before that season, Kaydeross Park in nearby Saratoga Springs had closed after seventy-five years of operation. Magic Forest was an aggressive purchaser at the auction, acquiring four rides: a Paratrooper, Tilt-A-Whirl, kiddie cars, and a replacement Ferris wheel.

The rides acquired from Kaydeross proved to be so popular with the customers that Jack started searching for more rides at other amusement parks that were closing. He was able to purchase used rides at a fraction of the cost of new ones and employ his skills to restore them. Today Magic Forest is full of classic family and kiddie rides that look as good as new.

Magic Forest grew rapidly over the next several years as it added attractions acquired from other facilities that were liquidating. The Chaser, on which cars travel over an undulating track at a high rate of speed, was acquired from Lincoln Park in North Dartmouth, Massachusetts, in 1988. In 1990, a Scrambler and kiddie merry-go-round were purchased from Nay Aug Park in Scranton, Pennsylvania. The Spiral Slide arrived in 1991 from Angela Park in Drums, Pennsylvania, followed by the kiddie turtles from Maple Leaf Village in Niagara Falls, Canada, in 1993.

With all of the ride purchases, Magic Forest was outgrowing its original boundaries. In 1995, the park developed an all-new midway area, with four recently acquired and relocated kiddie rides and a new boarding station for the Safari Trail.

Jack Gillette acquired one of the park's most unusual rides in 1998. Among the items being offered at an auction of surplus carnival equipment near Buffalo was the Blue Goose. Dating back to the 1930s, the ride features eight wooden birds on which children sit. Gillette knew that the ride was the perfect fit for Magic Forest's family audience and purchased it. Now completely restored, it holds a place of honor at the park.

Magic Forest is renowned for its extensive collection of kiddie rides.

The lovingly restored Blue Goose is one of Magic Forest's most unique rides.

Magic Forest Today

From a small, narrowly focused roadside attraction, Magic Forest has grown into a well-rounded family amusement park featuring two dozen rides, twenty storybook dioramas, three walk-throughs, and Rex the Diving Horse.

The park is easy to spot along U.S. Route 9, with a 38-foot-tall statue of Uncle Sam inviting you inside. From the entrance on a hill overlooking the parking lot, the park is roughly laid out in a large oval. To the right, the trail leads past the diving horse pool, Ferris wheel, Tilt-A-Whirl, and tilt house to the animal displays in the back of the park, where the chapel is also located.

The trail then leads past the Scrambler and train rides to the main ride area. Behind this area are the Little Dipper roller coaster and storybook displays. From here, a path heads down the hill past four kiddie rides to the Safari Trail. Heading back to the entrance, the path goes past the Cinderella and Show White walk-throughs, Santa's House, Blue Goose, merry-go-round, and slide.

Nellie Bly
Amusement Park

OPENED 1967

WITH ITS LOW-KEY RIDES, PETTING ZOO, AND RIDE OPERATORS THAT greet you as you board, Nellie Bly feels like a small-town amusement park. But just a short distance away, the heavy traffic of the Belt Parkway and high-rise apartment buildings serve as a reminder that you are in actually in the heart of one of the most densely populated areas in the country.

A Park Grows in Brooklyn

Following his service in the infantry during World War II, Gene Romano moved to Brooklyn and went to work in real estate. In 1951, he became an investor in a snack bar his brothers, Alfred and Henry, were opening at a new kiddie amusement park. In the postwar era, kiddielands were opening throughout the country to cash in on the burgeoning postwar baby boom. On a whim, the facility had been named Nellie Bly Kiddieland, after the pioneering female journalist who gained international fame in 1890 by traveling around the world in less than eighty days.

For the next fifteen years, the Romano brothers were able to make a nice living from the snack bar to support their growing families. All along, Gene was becoming increasingly enamored with the industry. But in 1966, the land on which the park stood was sold for development.

Although they had no say in the sale, the Romanos hated the prospect of leaving the business that had served them so well and decided to open their own park. Gene, who had fallen in love

**Nellie Bly
Amusement Park**

1824 Shore Parkway
Brooklyn, NY 11214

718-996-4002

www.nellieblypark.com

with the amusement industry, became involved on a full-time basis. "I slowly shed my suit for work coveralls," he was fond of saying about his career change.

When Nellie Bly's eleven rides went up for auction in March 1966, the Romano brothers purchased four. They located a city-owned junkyard with an adjacent driving range just down the street from the old park and were able to work out a lease with the city for the property.

The new Nellie Bly Amusement Park opened in the spring of 1967. Occupying a 3-acre site, the park featured a snack bar, miniature golf, batting cages, and five rides: a merry-go-round, kiddie roller coaster, kiddie fire engine, and kiddie boats from the old park, along with a helicopter ride. All but the helicopter ride remain in operation today. The neighborhood appreciated the new operation and flocked to it, prompting the brothers to quickly add a Tilt-A-Whirl, giant slide, Ferris wheel, and train. In 1969, they took over operation of the adjacent driving range, but it was later developed by the city as a maintenance garage.

Throughout the 1970s, Nellie Bly relied on temporary concessionaires to bring in new rides, as the park's year-to-year lease with the city discouraged the brothers from making many permanent improvements. They did make some, however, including a new bumper car ride in the mid-1970s. In 1977, despite the year-to-year lease, they launched a

Nellie Bly has always offered a well-rounded line-up of family rides. NELLIE BLY AMUSEMENT PARK

three-year improvement program, erecting new food and game stands, constructing a new miniature golf course in 1977, and adding a kiddie motorcycle jump ride in 1978.

Growing Up

In 1982, the Romanos were able to finally obtain a ten-year lease from the city. The lease restricted the park's use of outside concessionaires, ending the era of booked-in rides, but it meant that the brothers could make long-term plans and permanent upgrades. They celebrated the new lease by adding the Flash, a 43-foot-tall wheel roller coaster with a unique box-shaped configuration. The following year saw $100,000 in improvements, including a 65-foot-long fun house themed as Around the World in 80 Days with Nellie Bly. A go-cart track soon followed.

Gene Romano loved coming to work and once said that it was like "going to a party every day." In 1986, he bought out his brothers. Now, in sole control of the park along with his family, Gene Romano led the park to its greatest era of growth in the 1990s.

The decade kicked off with the addition of a Red Baron airplane ride, followed by a Scrambler around 1992. The next year saw $200,000 in improvements, anchored by the Big Blue Water Ride, a large water slide that can be ridden in street clothes. That was followed by a new front entrance and the Panda-Go-Round kiddie ride in 1994. A larger train

The Flash was a unique roller coaster that operated at the park from 1982 until 1996.

 **VISITING**

NELLIE BLY AMUSEMENT PARK

LOCATION

Nellie Bly Amusement Park is located just east of the Bay Parkway exit off the Belt Parkway. Shore Parkway intersects with Bay Parkway just south of the interchange and runs parallel to the Belt Parkway.

OPERATING SCHEDULE

The park opens at 11 A.M. on weekends starting in late March and weekdays starting in late May. Weekday hours continue through mid-September, and weekend operations continue through the end of October. Closing times vary by season.

ADMISSION

Admission to Nellie Bly is free, with rides available on a pay-as-you-go basis. Tickets are available for about $1 each, with rides requiring two to four tickets. Discounted ticket books are available. The park has pay-one-price sessions every Tuesday and Thursday from 11 A.M. until 2 P.M. and Wednesday evenings starting in late June from 7:30 P.M. until 10:30 P.M. for about $20, or slightly less for kiddie rides only.

FOOD

The park features three food stands. The main stand in the middle of the park offers a wide variety of items, including pizza, hot dogs, burgers, Italian sausage, cheese steaks, grilled cheese sandwiches, french fires, and knishes. The others focus on snacks such as popcorn and cotton candy.

FOR CHILDREN

Since the beginning, Nellie Bly Amusement Park has been for and about kids. Almost all the rides can be enjoyed by most members of the family.

SPECIAL FEATURES

Nellie Bly has a number of classic kiddie rides that are rare in today's amusement parks, including the fire engines and boats.

TIME REQUIRED

The park can be enjoyed in about two hours, although if you have smaller kids along, you should allow more time.

TOURING TIPS

If you intend to ride a lot, plan to visit on Tuesday or Thursday afternoon or Wednesday evening, when pay-one-price admission is available.

ride replaced the older one in 1996, and the Crazy Bus replaced the helicopter ride in 1998. The decade closed with the opening of the Haunted Hotel, a walk-through attraction that was built by the park over the course of two years to replace an earlier Haunted House.

This was a good decade for Nellie Bly Amusement Park, but it ended on a sad note when Gene Romano died in October 1999. But he left the park in good hands—those of his wife, Antoinette, and daughter Gena, who had served as general manager since 1983 and got her start at the park at age twelve working as a "cotton candy specialist."

Gena continued the same policies that had made the park a success by focusing on the family market. Her first major addition was the Frog Hopper, a bouncing tower ride. Jungle Jammin', a unique kiddie ride, replaced the Crazy Bus in 2003. The Whirl Wind, a family swing ride, debuted in 2004 on the site of the Flash, which operated for the final time in 1996.

Nellie Bly Amusement Park Today

From a small, five-ride kiddieland, Nellie Bly Amusement Park has grown into a full-blown amusement park without losing its focus as a family-oriented facility. Today the park features twenty rides, including ten kiddie rides, along with a miniature golf course, petting zoo, Haunted Hotel, and fun house.

Nellie Bly Amusement Park is an oasis in the heart of Brooklyn.

The park's main entrance is on Shore Parkway and leads into the heart of the park, home to most of the food and game concessions. To the right are the miniature golf course and bumper car ride. Behind the bumper cars are several larger rides, including the Scrambler, Whirl Wind, and go-carts. To the left of the entrance are most of the kiddie rides, along with the petting zoo, train, Big Blue Water Ride, and fun house. The back corner of the park is home to the slide and Haunted Hotel.

Six Flags Darien Lake

OPENED 1977

TRAVELING THROUGH THE FARMLANDS OF WESTERN NEW YORK, YOU SEE
the agrarian landscape interrupted by seemingly out-of-place landmarks:
roller coasters, a giant Ferris wheel, and a sky coaster. Putting a major
theme park in such an out-of-the-way location is no accident, but a key
factor in the founding of what is now known as Six Flags Darien Lake.

The park's history dates back over four decades, when entrepreneur
Paul Snyder purchased 164 acres of farmland for $115,000. At that time,
Snyder was already an accomplished businessman. His first job out of
college was as an assistant to a food broker, but he soon grew restless
and, in 1957, founded Freezer Queen Foods, a company he ended up
selling to Nabisco in 1970 for more than $40 million.

An Ever-Expanding Dream

Snyder initially had modest plans when he acquired the 164-acre parcel
in 1964. He thought it would be a great place for his family to get away
from it all, but his entrepreneurial zeal soon took over. He added twenty-
three campsites to the park, and in 1968, he hired Cornell University to
study the land's potential. They recommended developing the property
into a major camping facility, stocking its seven
lakes with fish and adding picnic areas.

Six Flags Darien Lake
9993 Allegheny Rd.
P.O. Box 91
Darien Center
NY 14040-0091
908-928-1821
www.sixflags.com/darienlake

With that, Snyder set out to build his resort. He
acquired more land, eventually increasing his
holdings to nearly 1,000 acres. On it, he added
more campsites and resort activities, such as a petting zoo, horseback and pony rides, skateboard-

ing, paddle boats, tennis, and miniature golf. One of the resort's most popular features debuted in 1975, when Snyder acquired several recreational vehicles and installed them permanently at the campground. Now totaling over four hundred, these RVs are continually booked throughout the summer.

By 1975, Darien Lake had grown into one of the largest camping resorts in the country, with nearly two thousand sites and a full array of resort activities. Always looking for novel attractions for his guests, Snyder discovered a new sensation that was just starting to spread across the country: water slides. In 1977, he created a hill, dubbed Rainbow Mountain, and constructed four water slides down the slopes.

The next year, he hired Economics Research Associates, a major theme park consulting company, to analyze the ultimate potential of the resort. It identified western New York as the second-largest region in the country (after New England) not served by a major theme park, with a potential market of 50 million people living within a day's drive, and recommended that Darien Lake add a theme park to its resort offerings.

Snyder sought to create a unique facility, sticking to the resort's roots as an escape in the country. The campground remained a focal point, and all the new activities were integrated into the camping experience. He also wanted to use the theme park as only one part of a much broader range of activities, telling *Amusement Business* magazine, "We believe very strongly that major theme parks of the future must include a wide

Paddle boats were one of the original attractions at Six Flags Darien Lake.

Six Flags Darien Lake shown during its 1980 expansion. SIX FLAGS DARIEN LAKE

range of participation activities that will insure customers' involvement in the entertainment/recreation program."

The 1979 season welcomed a few new features, including a bumper car ride. But the transformation really began in 1980, with the addition of $8 million in rides and attractions, including the Silver Bullet, Hay Baler, Lasso flying swings, merry-go-round, four kiddie rides, and a miniature golf course. Most of the rides were purchased from International Amusement Devices, one of the industry's most experienced ride manufacturers, but the Lasso swing ride was supplied by Huss Trading Corporation, a major Swiss provider of rides. When delivering the swings, Huss was impressed with Snyder's vision and approached him about becoming more involved with his operation.

Entering the Big Leagues

Huss's interest proved serendipitous, as Snyder was seeking capital to launch the next phase of his expansion. In the fall of 1980, Snyder signed an agreement with Huss allowing him to begin a $22 million expansion of the fledgling theme park. Huss agreed to provide $16 million in equipment, including seventeen major rides and a water slide complex, as part of a seven-year agreement in which Huss would receive a percentage of the park's admission revenues.

Phase one of the expansion was ready for the summer of 1981, with eleven new rides, including a 1,370-foot log flume that traveled through a tunnel in Rainbow Mountain, antique auto ride, riverboat ride on Darien Lake, swinging Pirate ship, several spinning rides, and the park's first roller coaster, now known as the Brain Teaser, a 200-foot-long, 10-foot-tall kiddie model built by the German firm Zierer. Rounding out the expansion was a 67-acre nature area, with elevated walkways through herds of deer and other animals, a 1-acre roller-skating arena, and two

 **VISITING**

SIX FLAGS DARIEN LAKE

LOCATION

Six Flags Darien Lake is located midway between Buffalo and Rochester on NY Route 77, 6 miles south of I-90 (New York State Thruway) off Exit 48A.

OPERATING SCHEDULE

The park is open weekends in May and early June, daily from mid-June through Labor Day, and weekends through October. During most of the season, the park is open from 10:30 A.M. to 10 P.M., though hours can vary by season.

ADMISSION

Pay-one-price admission of less than $35 entitles visitors to all rides and attractions except games, miniature golf, paddle boats, the Sky Coaster, Slingshot, and Turbobungy. Parking costs extra. Discounted tickets can be purchased from the park's website.

FOOD

Six Flags Darien Lake has some sixty different food outlets, ranging from air-conditioned sit-down restaurants to portable carts. Beaver Brothers Lakeside Café, in Darien Square, serves a variety of breakfast, lunch, and dinner items; Chicken Ranch Café, near the Giant Wheel, has fried chicken; Maria's Spaghetti House features Italian items; the Daily Planet, near Superman Ride of Steel, offers burgers and tacos; and Trappers, in Darien Square, has a late-night menu of pizza, subs, and ice cream. Several outlets, including Porky's in Looney Tunes Seaport, Waterfront Boardwalk, and Scalywags in the water park, serve kid's meals as well as standard fare.

Outside food and beverages are not permitted in the park. A public picnic area is available near the front gate.

FOR CHILDREN

Looney Tunes Seaport has ten rides, most of which can be enjoyed by the entire family, and a special play area. A second kiddie area is located near Grizzly Run and is home to the Brain Teaser kiddie roller coaster and kiddie bumper cars.

Hook's Lagoon in the water park is a great place for kids to splash around. It has three wading pools, ranging in depth from 8 to 18 inches, and dozens of fountains, geysers, and places to climb.

The park also has a number of other rides and attractions for the entire family, including the Giant Wheel and Tin Lizzys.

SPECIAL FEATURES

A complete resort, Six Flags Darien Lake makes a perfect one-stop vacation. On any given night, up to six thousand people will be staying at the campground and hotel. Both are located within the resort complex and are closely integrated with the theme park, allowing visitors easy access to all attractions.

(continued on page 192)

VISITING (continued from page 191)

SIX FLAGS DARIEN LAKE

Superman Ride of Steel anchors New York's biggest roller coaster lineup and is the largest and fastest roller coaster in the state, standing 208 feet tall with a top speed of 75 miles per hour.

The Giant Wheel, at 165 feet tall, is the third-largest Ferris wheel in North America. It's a great way to see both the park and the surrounding countryside.

TIME REQUIRED

To enjoy all the rides and attractions, plus the water park, you should plan to spend at least one full day, with a second day being optimal. If you are pressed for time and visit on a day when crowds are light, the major attractions can be enjoyed in about six hours.

TOURING TIPS

Take advantage of the resort accommodations. It is the best way to fully experience Six Flags Darien Lake. Whether you stay in the hotel, bring your own camping accommodations, or rent a recreational vehicle, admission to the theme park is included for the length of your stay.

Try to visit Six Flags Darien Lake on a weekday, when the park tends to be less crowded.

Arrive just before the park opens, and try to hit the big attractions such as Superman Ride of Steel first, before the crowds arrive.

The Giant Wheel provides a panoramic view of the entire resort and is a great way to get the lay of the land to plan your visit.

---

theaters, the indoor Jubilee Theater and an 8,500-seat outdoor amphitheater called the Lakeside Theater. The expansion also included a new front gate and 25 acres of parking. To oversee the design of this massive project, Snyder hired Randall Duell and Associates, the country's leading designer of theme parks.

The new theme park was named Darien Lake Fun Country, combining the rural location and resort attractions to promote a day-in-the-country theme. "If you were to walk through the park at night, it would remind you of how the country used to be," Snyder said in explaining his vision to *Amusement Business* magazine. "People are roasting hot dogs over quiet campfires at one side of the park, while on the other the rides are at full capacity."

The new additions were hugely popular, and attendance more than doubled to 1.1 million in 1981 despite a late opening as a result of construction delays.

Phase two of the theme park began in 1982, with another $10 million in improvements, including four more water slides and a river raft ride on Rainbow Mountain, creating the world's largest water slide complex, as well as two more spinning rides. One of these, called the Ranger, was a $1.1 million ride that flipped riders head-over-heels, the first of its kind in North America. But the big addition was the Viper, a $6.5 million steel-track roller coaster.

The Viper was just the type of signature attraction Darien Lake Fun Country needed to put itself on the national map. It was one of the largest steel-track roller coasters in the world when it opened, standing 121 feet tall with 3,100 feet of track. Viper was the first roller coaster to flip riders upside down five times, with a vertical loop, a double-inversion corkscrew, and a boomerang that turned riders upside down twice. The ride brought national attention to Darien Lake and helped increase attendance by 20 percent and revenues by 51 percent.

By now Snyder had spent more than $72 million building Darien Lake Fun Country into the largest theme park in the state. The phenomenal success of the park had caught the attention of numerous people in the industry. One interested party was Funtime, an Ohio-based amusement park operator. Funtime was founded in 1968, when three industry veterans from Cedar Point in Sandusky, Ohio, acquired Geauga Lake, a run-down amusement park in Aurora, Ohio. Within ten years, they totally transformed the facility, expanding the developed acreage from 40 to 120, grew ride count from thirty-one to fifty, and increased revenues from $795,000 to $10.4 million. By the early 1980s, they were looking to acquire additional properties. Darien Lake was the perfect fit, and they agreed to acquire a 50 percent interest in 1982.

Darien Lake had just undergone two years of tremendous growth, so the first season under the new ownership arrangement was less ambitious, though still significant. In 1983, the park's skyline was changed with the addition of the Giant Wheel, the largest Ferris wheel in North America at that time. Standing 165 feet tall with forty six-passenger gondolas, the 220-ton ride, manufactured by Vekoma of the Netherlands, initially operated at the 1982 World's Fair in Knoxville, Tennessee. Its journey to America for the World's Fair was not smooth. Three large containers holding the wheel's 67-foot spokes were washed overboard off the ship transporting the ride. Vekoma had to quickly fabricate replacements and fly them to Knoxville in a specially outfitted 747 to get the ride in operation in time for the fair. The journey to Darien Lake was not as eventful, taking place in twenty-six tractor trailers. To install the massive ride, 8 million gallons of water had to be temporarily drained from Fun Lake, where the Giant Wheel now sits. Fifteen thousand computer-controlled lights rounded out the installation.

That same year, Kids World was installed next to the front gate. This was a large participatory play area, with climbing areas and a ball crawl.

Six Flags Darien Lake shown in the mid-1980s, following its development into a major theme park. SIX FLAGS DARIEN LAKE

Expansion work was moderate over the next several seasons, while the park focused on finishing touches. In 1984, $1 million in improvements were made, including a new petting zoo and the 35-foot-tall Hydroforce, which sent riders into Darien Lake on one-person toboggans. By now the Fun Country part of the name had been phased out in favor of Darien Lake, and Paul Snyder sold his remaining interest in the resort to Funtime.

The park attracted nationwide attention in 1986, when it hired professional iceberg builder Bob Horan to create a 20-foot-high iceberg in Trout Lake, one of several in the park. Horan championed the idea of creating icebergs in the Arctic and towing them to drought-stricken countries. He struck an agreement to make his first iceberg at Darien Lake to demonstrate the feasibility of his system. To build his iceberg, Horan inflated a large industrial-gauge plastic balloon in the lake and, throughout the winter, pumped water over the top. By spring, the iceberg measured 200 by 200 feet and filled half the lake. People from throughout the region came to Darien Lake to see the iceberg and have their photo taken next to it. The iceberg remained well into the summer season, but Horan's dream soon melted.

Moving to the Next Level

After running Darien Lake on its own for a full season, Funtime knew that it was time to take the park to the next level. In 1987, the company announced a five-year capital expansion program. The first season focused on more live entertainment offerings, anchored by Circustown USA, an old-fashioned big-top event presented by the Royal Hannaford Circus, and Splashmania, a water-ski show in the 47-acre Darien Lake. Another part of that year's $1 million improvement program was the addition of the Grand Prix Speedway go-cart ride.

Darien Lake's youngest visitors were the recipients of the bulk of the $3.8 million spent in 1988, with the opening of Adventureland for Kids, a 2-acre mini amusement park. Darien Lake's three kiddie areas were consolidated into a new area near the main entrance. The eight existing kiddie rides were supplemented by the Critter Chase, along with the Kid's World play area, Circustown, and the petting zoo.

The space freed by relocating one of the kiddie areas made room for the anchor attraction of the 1989 season: Grizzly Run, a $2.5 million, 1,422-foot-long river rapids ride that simulated white-water rafting in round, twelve-person boats.

Despite all the recent expansion, Darien Lake's guests were still requesting a wooden roller coaster. Once almost given up for dead during the theme-park era, the wooden roller coaster was in the midst of a renaissance in the late 1980s. Leading the charge was the Dinn Corporation, which had introduced the wooden roller coaster to a new generation of riders. The roller coaster that Darien Lake had in mind was a moderate-size ride that would pack plenty of thrills into a small space. The result was the Predator. Standing 95 feet tall, the $2.5 million ride was reminiscent of a roller coaster from the 1920s, with an abundance of drops and fast turns along its 3,400 feet of track.

But this was just one part of the park's ambitious $4.5 million expansion in 1990. After thirteen seasons, Rainbow Mountain had been surpassed by newer water slide complexes around the country. To compete, most of the park's existing water slides were replaced by Barracuda Bay, an all-new $1.5 million water park featuring fourteen water slides and a raft ride.

Darien Lake rounded out its five-year program in 1991 with a $1 million, 2-acre expansion of Adventureland for Kids, including a miniature train ride, junior bumper cars, and Tad Pole Island, a children's wading pool.

What is now a longtime Darien Lake tradition debuted in 1992, when the Lakeside Amphitheater was renovated to accommodate the Laserlight Reality show. The show has been continually updated since and remains the perfect way to complete a visit at the end of the day.

With the Laserlight show drawing throngs to the Lakeside Amphitheater and Darien Lake's concert series pulling in increasingly larger crowds, the park kicked off the 1993 season with the first phase of a new Performing Arts Center. The $8 million facility accommodates twenty thousand, allowing the park to invite the most popular acts of the day.

The success of Barracuda Bay prompted the addition of Cuda Falls in 1994, a $1.3 million complex of four water slides standing six stories high. The following season saw the introduction of the 180-foot Skycoaster, a giant A-frame under which riders are suspended by a cable. The cable is hauled back to a second tower, where the riders pull a rip cord and free-fall at speeds of up to 70 miles per hour in a giant swinging motion over Fun Lake.

Building a Premier Attraction

By 1995, Darien Lake had established itself as western New York's leading entertainment destination, with its campground, theme park, water park, and amphitheater. But the industry was changing. The mid-1990s were a period of consolidation, with amusement park companies merging to achieve greater economies of scale in marketing, purchasing, and capital improvements. Funtime, Darien Lake's parent company, was no different. In August 1995, it was acquired by Premier Parks of Oklahoma City for $60 million.

Premier Parks had gotten its start in 1981, when the company, then known as Tierco, purchased Frontier City, a run-down amusement park in Oklahoma City. The original intent was to redevelop the park for other uses, but when the economy in Oklahoma took a downturn, Tierco found itself in the amusement park business. It renovated Frontier City and, after seeing the increase in business that resulted, decided to expand the company, purchasing a water park in Oklahoma City. In 1992, the company bought Wild World in Largo, Maryland. Tierco then changed its name to Premier Parks and went public with the intent of acquiring midsize amusement parks around the country. Funtime was the perfect fit, and acquiring it allowed Premier to double its size.

A crucial part of Premier Park's strategy was to invest heavily in new attractions to generate renewed interest in its facilities. At Darien Lake, it invested more than $8.6 million in 1996, the largest expansion there since the early 1980s. No part of the operation was untouched. The water park was supplemented with Hook's Lagoon, a $2.1 million aquatic playground located next to Adventureland and connected to Barracuda Bay by a bridge over the main midway. Hook's Lagoon covered 36,000 square feet and included more than seventy-five water play features, spread among three wading pools, and a 40-foot-tall "tree house" topped by a 1,000-gallon barrel that drenched people below it every five minutes.

Darien Lake's youngest guests received an all-new kiddieland, Popeye's Seaport, which replaced the Treasure Island miniature golf course. The $2 million Popeye's Seaport, themed after the cartoon show characters, featured ten kiddie rides, many of which could accommodate the entire family, and a play area. Among the more popular rides were monster trucks, spinning tubs, a miniature Ferris wheel, and a small train.

Thrill seekers were not forgotten. Another $2 million was spent to add Nightmare at Phantom Cave, a 45-foot-tall, 1,772-foot-long steel-track roller coaster completely enclosed in a building. The ride was relocated to Darien Lake from one of its sister parks, Kentucky Kingdom in Louisville, another theme park that Premier Parks had acquired and reinvigorated with heavy investments in new attractions.

In addition to the theme park expansion, $3 million was spent to improve the Darien Lake Performing Arts Center, and another $1 million to upgrade the campground. "If you haven't visited Darien Lake lately, you haven't visited it at all," remarked the park's general manager, Bradley Paul. The public agreed, and attendance increased by 23 percent.

Hoping to continue the momentum of a very successful 1996 season, the park spent an additional $12 million on new attractions the next year. Topping the list was the Mind Eraser, an $8.5 million steel-track roller coaster. Standing 109 feet tall with 2,261 feet of track, Mind Eraser represented a new generation of roller coasters in which riders negotiated drops, turns, and five inversions in trains suspended underneath the track. Hook's Lagoon also gained a new neighbor that year when Adventureland for Kids was replaced by Crocodile Isle, anchored by a 25,000-square-foot, million-gallon wave pool. Several of the Adventureland rides, including the Brain Teaser, were relocated elsewhere in the park. Families were not forgotten, with the addition of the Scrambler, a classic spinning ride.

Premier Parks was not yet done and invested another $12 million for 1998. The bulk of the funds, $8.5 million, went into building the Lodge on the Lake, a 161-room hotel. The hotel has a north woods theme and sits along the shores of Darien Lake, on the former site of the nature preserve, which had been closed for several years.

As if two new roller coasters in two years were not enough, the park added its third consecutive roller coaster: Boomerang Coaster to Coaster. This compact ride had just 935 feet of track but maximized thrills by

Serial Thriller was one of the highlights of the mid-1990s expansion by Premier Parks (now Six Flags).

hauling riders backward up a 117-foot-tall incline. The train was then released, and it traveled back through the station into a twisting boomerang that flipped riders upside down two times and then passed through a vertical loop before traveling up another 125-foot tall incline. The train then reversed and went through everything again backward. In all, riders were turned upside down six times.

Next to the Boomerang, a new 454-seat restaurant, Beaver Brothers Café, was added to Darien Square, an area of shops and restaurants that serve not only the theme park, but also the campground and hotel.

Raising the Flags

By the end of 1998, Premier Parks had spent more than $30 million improving Darien Lake. Attendance had increased by 44 percent, and the park was now a leading resort destination. But an event that had occurred earlier in the year would have a profound effect on its future. Following the 1995 acquisition of Darien Lake's parent company, Premier Parks had continued to make acquisitions and emerged as the third-largest amusement park chain in the United States. In February 1998, Premier Parks stunned the industry by announcing that it would acquire the nation's second-largest amusement park operator, Six Flags Theme Parks.

Six Flags' origins dated back to 1961, when a Texas real estate developer, Angus Wynne, opened a theme park to anchor the Great Southwest

Industrial District, a 5,000-acre development in Arlington, Texas. During this period, developers throughout the United States were trying to duplicate the success of Disneyland, which changed the industry when it opened in 1955. All previous attempts had failed.

The park had six areas themed after the countries of which Texas had once been a part—France, Mexico, Spain, Texas, the Confederacy, and the United States—leading to the name Six Flags Over Texas. By pioneering the pay-one-price admission and introducing new rides such as the Runaway Mine Train and Log Flume, Six Flags Over Texas succeeded where others had failed. Soon the concept was expanded to new Six Flags theme parks in Atlanta and St. Louis. Throughout the 1970s and 1980s, Six Flags acquired more parks throughout the United States. In 1985, the Looney Tunes characters, including Bugs Bunny and Daffy Duck, became the chain's official ambassadors.

By the time Six Flags was acquired by Premier Parks, it had established itself as an operator of cutting-edge thrill rides. Premier, which would soon be renamed Six Flags Inc., knew that several of its existing parks had grown enough under its management to warrant conversion to the better-known Six Flags format. In October 1998, the company announced that Darien Lake, along with sister parks in California, Colorado, Kentucky, and Maryland, would become Six Flags theme parks, joining seventeen others in the chain. The switch would involve infrastructure improvements, thrill-ride additions, and the introduction of the famous Looney Tunes characters, a Six Flags staple.

Converting Darien Lake into Six Flags Darien Lake cost $20 million. The front gate was rebuilt into an elaborate $6 million entrance plaza with a north woods theme. In keeping with company tradition, the entrance plaza was adorned with six flags reflecting the history of the area—those of Six Flags Inc., the Iroquois Confederacy, United Kingdom, United States, New York State, and Genesee County.

Popeye's Seaport became the Looney Tunes Seaport, home to the beloved Looney Tunes cartoon characters. At the heart of the park was the Looney Tunes Emporium, a giant new gift shop set among a garden devoted to Looney Tunes and Six Flags. The Nightmare at Phantom Cave ride was relocated to Great Escape in Lake George, and the building that remained was converted into a 1,200-seat theater featuring the Batman Thrill Spectacular, an action-packed stunt show.

But what really signaled the change of Darien Lake to a member of the Six Flags family was the parks new signature ride: Superman Ride of Steel. Towering over the local landscape, the $12 million, 4-million-pound, steel-track roller coaster was nearly a mile long, with 5,350 feet of track. It topped out at 208 feet, after which riders dropped 205 feet at a 70-degree angle and negotiated a 90-degree turn over the Trout Pond at 75 miles per hour. Superman Ride of Steel also featured several hills where riders floated out of their seats and two high-speed spirals. Built by Intamin, a leading Swiss ride manufacturer, it was the tallest roller coaster east of the Mississippi River when it opened.

The new Six Flags name attracted attention to the park from throughout the region, and attendance for the season increased by nearly two hundred thousand, almost twice park projections.

Six Flags Darien Lake has continued to add new attractions. In 2000, the Twister, a $2 million flipping spinning ride, joined the lineup. The 2002 season saw the addition of the Slingshot, a reverse bungee thrill ride that catapults riders up to 300 feet in the air, and the replacement of several older water slides by Shipwreck Falls, a shoot-the-chutes water attraction that soaks riders and spectators alike with its huge splash. The Tornado, a vortex-shaped water slide, joined the water park for the 2005 season.

Six Flags Darien Lake Today

Occupying nearly 1,000 acres, Six Flags Darien Lake is one of the most well-rounded resorts in the country. At its heart is the largest theme park in New York, with a full-scale water park and thirty-nine rides, including six roller coasters, the most in the state. Six Flags Darien Lake

Superman Ride of Steel anchored the Six Flags conversion and towers over the smaller Predator roller coaster.

Six Flags Darien Lake features a full assortment of water rides.

also has one of the largest campgrounds in the country, with 2,000 sites including 430 rental RVs, as well as a 163-room on-site hotel and a twenty thousand-seat concert amphitheater.

Visitors enter the park through the rustic-themed main entry. The area beyond the main gate contains an array of shops and is flanked on either side by the water park, with the water slides on the right and Hook's Lagoon and Crocodile Isle on the left. A bridge over the midway connects the two sections.

Traveling down the midway past the Looney Tunes Emporium, visitors come across the Predator roller coaster. To the left, through the Predator's lift hill, is Superman Ride of Steel. Traveling right from the Predator, visitors pass many of the park's spinning rides and the back entrance, which leads to Darien Square, home of Beaver Brothers Lakeside Café, the Lakeside theater, campground, and hotel, all of which surround Darien Lake.

Near Darien Lake is the smaller Fun Lake, which is surrounded by attractions such as Boomerang Coast to Coaster, the Skycoaster, Giant Wheel, Pirate, and Tin Lizzys.

Walking away from the Giant Wheel, visitors come across Looney Tunes Seaport, Viper, Grizzly Run, Mind Eraser, and the Poland Springs Plunge log flume, the last two of which are located along Willows Lake.

New York's Smaller Parks

ONE OF THE WONDERFUL CHARACTERISTICS OF NEW YORK'S AMUSEMENT park industry is that in addition to the wealth of larger parks, the state also has a variety of smaller ones. Though these parks may not be large enough for a full day's outing, they are well worth a stop if you are in the area. Following are profiles of some of New York's most interesting smaller amusement parks.

CATSKILL

Catskill Game Farm
OPENED 1933

Roland Lindemann had a natural affinity for animals. The son of a zoology and botany teacher, he immigrated to the United States at age seventeen and set up a loan business, all along dreaming of opening a zoo. In 1933, he was able to realize that dream when he purchased a 1,060-acre site in the Catskill Mountains.

The operation initially was a hobby he pursued on weekends while maintaining his job in New York. It featured caged birds; pens with elk, llama, and sheep; and a large feeding ground where people could interact with more than two hundred deer. By 1941, he started charging admission to help offset the costs of the

Catskill Game Farm
400 Game Farm Rd.
Catskill, NY 12414
518-678-9595
www.catskillgamefarm.com

growing operation, and two years later, he quit his job in New York to devote his full energies to Catskill Game Farm.

Although World War II delayed growth, things really took off in the 1950s. Lindemann started the decade by erecting a new animal contact area where people could interact with English fallow deer, donkeys, and baby llamas. That was soon followed by the Animal Nursery section, filled with a variety of barnyard animals. Like many attractions at the time, the Game Farm adorned the grounds of the Animal Nursery with several storybook attractions, such as Jack and Jill, the Old Woman in the Shoe, and Cinderella's Pumpkin Coach, which a Lindemann family friend made in the basement of his house. They remained a popular attraction through the 1960s.

Catskill Game Farm expanded in a new direction in 1951, when it rented a merry-go-round to keep the children entertained. It proved to be so popular that the next year Lindemann purchased several more rides, including a new merry-go-round, fire truck, stagecoach, and airplane ride. The ride area has since grown to feature eight mechanical rides.

In 1958, the park became the first privately owned establishment to be recognized as a zoo by the U.S. Department of Agriculture. This enabled Catskill Game Farm to import animals from around the world, leading to a new era of growth.

By now Lindemann's reputation for breeding and caring for animals had spread throughout the country. He started supplying animals to other zoos and was able to purchase some thirty llamas from William Randolph Hearst's San Simeon estate following Hearst's death in 1951. In 1958, he worked with August Busch to stock Anheuser Busch's new bird gardens in St. Louis and Tampa. The Tampa facility eventually grew into the Busch Gardens theme park. In exchange for the birds, Lindemann received several of Busch's famous Clydesdale horses.

 **VISITING**

CATSKILL GAME FARM

Catskill Game Farm is located on Game Farm Road just off NY Route 32 in Catskill. Starting with a few animal pens operated as a hobby, Catskill Game Farm is now one of the largest private zoos in the country, featuring nearly two thousand animals representing more than 150 species from all over the world. It has eight food outlets, including a cafeteria and deli stand that serve a wide variety of items such as pizza, sandwiches, hot dogs, chicken nuggets, grilled cheese, popcorn, and other snack items. Admission of less than $20 entitles visitors to all shows, animal displays, and the Splash Pad. Rides, animal food, and miniature golf are an extra charge.

Catskill Game Farm's ride area features an array of attractions.

While collecting birds for Busch in Australia, Lindemann also assembled a collection for Catskill Game Farm to open a new bird gardens area in 1958. He linked this hilltop location to the Animal Nursery with a train ride. By now, his daughter Kathie was becoming increasingly involved in the operation and celebrated her eighteenth birthday in 1959 with the opening of a cafeteria next to the bird gardens. The family traveled to Africa in 1960 to collect animals for a new African section that was developed over the next couple years. A reptile house followed in 1962.

Catskill Game Farm started offering live entertainment in 1976, when Lindemann left on an animal-collecting trip. He left his daughter, now Kathie Schulz, with $20,000 and told her to "do something" in the park. She decided that an elephant show would be the perfect addition and, although pregnant, went to work installing it. To offset the costs of the show, elephant rides were offered. When her father returned, he was not happy. "You're turning my zoo into a circus!" he exclaimed. But upon discovering that customer revenues increased, he warmed to the idea and the next season expanded the show ring, adding permanent seating, a roof, and additional acts.

In 1989, control of Catskill Game Farm passed to Kathie Schulz and her children, Serena and Christopher. Roland remained close to the operation until his death in 1998 at age ninety-one. Catskill Game Farm has continued to grow, most recently opening the Splash Pad in 2001, a series of pools and fountains where families can cool off on hot summer days.

Harris Hill Amusement Park

OPENED 1949

High on a hilltop outside Elmira sits Harris Hill County Park, a large park popular with the local residents, who fill the picnic groves and other facilities. Adjacent to one picnic area is Harris Hill Amusement Park. The two facilities both largely owe their existence to one family. For many years, Kenneth and Frances Merrill operated a Shetland pony farm on top of the hill. Although they sold 100 acres of their land to the county so that it could expand the park and turn it into a true destination, the Merrills continued to raise ponies, selling them throughout the country and operating a pony ride concession at Eldridge Park, an amusement park in Elmira.

> **Harris Hill Amusement Park**
> 557 Harris Hill Rd.
> Elmira, NY 14903
> 607-732-1210
> www.harrishill
> amusements.com

In 1949, as the county park became more popular, the Merrills decided to cater to the growing throngs by opening a pony ride on a part of their property next to the park. At first the operation consisted of little more than eight Shetland ponies forming a live merry-go-round and ten more used for trail riding. But it was a success and grew rapidly over the next decade.

With the postwar baby boom in full force, the addition of kiddie rides was a natural, and by 1951, the park had installed a jeep ride, train ride, and Ferris wheel. A petting zoo opened in 1952, followed by the miniature golf course in 1955. Two more kiddie rides, the Roto Whip and choo-choo boats, opened in 1956, followed the next year by a driving range across

 **VISITING**

Harris Hill Amusement Park is located in the heart of Harris Hill County Park on Harris Hill Road, off NY Route 352. The park features seven rides, along with a miniature golf course, batting cages, and a driving range. Admission is free, with attractions available on a pay-as-you-go basis. Tickets cost about 85 cents for kiddie rides and $3.25 for go-carts. A food stand sells pizza, hot dogs, fries, sugar waffles, nachos, pretzels, popcorn, and snow cones.

Harris Hill Park is a classic postwar kiddieland.

the street from the main park. As the park evolved, some attractions, such as the jeeps, Ferris wheel, train, and petting zoo, were replaced with other rides, including two—the airplanes and fire engines—that were built by the Merrills. A hay shortage coupled with a declining demand for ponies prompted the Merrills to exit the pony market in 1965, resulting in the removal of the amusement park's original attraction, the pony ride. Replacing it in 1966 was a merry-go-round built by Theel Manufacturing.

In 1972, Hurricane Agnes struck the region. The heavy rains flooded many amusement parks in the area, but Harris Hill Amusement Park on its hilltop location was spared. The flood-stricken populace of Elmira found the amusement park and adjacent county park a much-needed escape, leading Harris Hill Amusement Park to its most successful season ever.

By 1976, Kenneth Merrill was looking to retire, so his son Scott, who was working in education, stepped in and took over. He was no stranger to the park, having started his career as a kid turning the crank on the popcorn machine. Under his guidance, the amusement park held its own through the 1980s, even though the economy of Elmira was hit hard by factory closings. The park expanded during the next decade, adding batting cages next to the driving range in 1990, a Sky Fighter kiddie ride in 1992, and a go-cart track adjacent to the batting cages in 1993.

By 2001, Scott Merrill and his wife, Nancy, were tiring of the grind and looking to move on. But the park had become too much a part of the family to sell to just anyone. Late that year, he crossed paths with Jay

Goodwin, a longtime family friend who had worked in the park for six years starting in 1982, when he was twelve years old. Merrill mentioned that he was looking for a new owner for the park. By the beginning of the 2002 season, Goodwin had reached an agreement to purchase the facility. He spent the 2002 season managing the park under the guidance of Scott Merrill and in October 2002 formally took over ownership.

While new attractions such as a bumper boats are planned, Goodwin and his wife, Theresa, have continued to run the park in the same manner that was successful for Merrills, as a family park catering to the people of Elmira.

MANORVILLE

NEW YORK

Long Island Game Farm

OPENED 1970

Throughout his life, Stanley Novak loved zoos and was a frequent visitor. In 1958, he came across a picture in the *Saturday Evening Post* of a game farm in which animals roamed freely. He was enthralled by the picture and promised himself that one day he would build a similar facility. Even today that picture has a place of honor in the office of Long Island Game Farm. Over the next several decades, while working in construction and operating go-cart tracks, Novak continued to pursue his dream, learning as much about animals as he could during his free time. By 1969, he was tiring of the rat race and knew it was time to make his move.

The Long Island Expressway had just opened to the farthest reaches of the island, and at the end of the highway, Novak found a 30-acre hay and cattle farm. He knew it was the perfect place for his dream, and in the fall of 1969, he moved his family into the farmhouse and went to work creating Long Island Game Farm.

Throughout the winter, the Novaks worked hard to construct animal barns and pens, build paths through the property, and acquire animals. Areas included Bambiland, a deer enclosure; the Nursery, for baby animals; Storyland; and Old Mac-Donald's Farm. By spring, Long Island Game Farm, the first zoo on Long Island, was ready. On opening day, nine-year-old Melinda climbed on top of the ticket booth to look for the first car. By the end of the day, the new operation had taken in $1,000.

Long Island Game Farm
Wildlife Park & Children's Zoo
P.O. Box 97
Chapman Boulevard
Manorville, NY 11949
631-878-6670
www.longislandgame
farm.com

VISITING

Long Island Game Farm is located on Chapman Boulevard, between Exit 70 off I-495 (Long Island Expressway) and Exit 62 off NY Route 27 (Sunrise Highway). The park features a wide array of animal displays, including Gerry the Giraffe, the Big Cat Encounter show, and four rides. Two refreshment stands serve pizza, hot dogs, chicken tenders, fries, pretzels, popcorn, and other snack items. Admission of less than $20 entitles visitors to all attractions except the merry-go-round and pony rides, which require an additional fee.

The receipts were a harbinger of a successful debut season, but the winter proved to be a challenge. Long Island Game Farm had 125 animals that needed constant attention, and Novak spent his days caring for the animals and nights reading veterinary books. In the end, he lost only one animal that first winter.

The park expanded its holdings to three hundred animals the second season, adding a chimpanzee, camel, Himalayan snow bears, two buffalo, and forty baby lambs and goats. Throughout the 1970s, the park continued to add new attractions. Llamaland opened in 1973, followed by a sea lion show in 1975. The Animal Wonderland Theater opened in 1978, followed by the park's first mechanical ride, a merry-go-round, in 1980. Additional rides continued to appear, including adult and kiddie swing rides and in 1983 a train that circled the grounds. By 1988, the sea lion show had been replaced by a tiger show, which remains one of Long Island Game Farm's most popular attractions. The park continued

Gerry the Giraffe is a favorite attraction at Long Island Game Farm.

to evolve throughout the 1990s, with the addition of new animal displays and attractions. The Sky Slide replaced the adult swings in 1991.

May 1999 was a sad time at Long Island Game Farm, as Stanley Novak passed away. But his family came together, and his wife, Diane, and daughter Susan took over. Melinda, who had never strayed too far from the park, returned on a full-time basis in 2002.

There have been other changes since then. Some rides, such as the train, Sky Slide, and kiddie swings, have been retired, with others, such as the Teacups and Rio Grande train, taking their place. But the heart of the park remains its animals, much as Stanley Novak wanted.

FARMINGDALE

NEW YORK

Fun Zone

OPENED 1993

One of the more fascinating aspects of Long Island is the wide array of amusement facilities tucked away in unexpected places. Fun Zone is just such a place. Along a busy commercial strip, the bright yellow building with amusement rides in its front yard jumps out at you. Besides the four rides in front, much more awaits inside the building.

Fun Zone got its start when a group of Long Island businessmen teamed up in 1993. They knew there was always a shortage of family-oriented entertainment on the densely populated island and thought it needed an indoor entertainment facility. They found the perfect site in a 35,000-square-foot former furniture store.

At the heart of the new operation was a large arcade that had the latest in electronic games. Rides included an electric go-cart track and whirlyball, in which riders steered their bumper cars around while playing a game of basketball.

Fun Zone was successful for the first couple years, but it was not realizing its full potential, because the lineup limited its market. As a result, Fun Zone undertook a major renovation in 1995. Out went the go-carts and whirlyball, which had never been very popular. In their place were added a large laser tag arena and a number of attractions to appeal to smaller children, including a merry-go-round, kiddie train, and play area. A Red Baron airplane ride soon followed.

In 1997, bumper cars and a kiddie Himalaya opened. The following year, a spinning tub ride was added. Fun Zone had now established itself

Fun Zone
229 Route 110
Farmingdale, NY 11735
631-847-0100

VISITING

Fun Zone is located on NY Route 110 in Farmingdale, less than a mile north of Exit 32N off the Southern State Parkway. The park features about ten rides, along with a laser tag arena, kids' play area, and restaurant. Admission is free. Attractions are available on a pay-as-you-go basis, with tickets costing about $2.50. Pay-one-price admission is available for about $20.

as a well-rounded facility for the entire family. But the owners saw an opportunity to grow even further. In 2000, they placed three spinning rides—the Flying Dragon, Tornado, and Sizzler—in a small area in front of the building. A Balloon Ferris wheel followed in 2001.

By now all the park lacked was a flashy, high-speed thrill ride. In 2003, the tubs were replaced with the Disco Star, with cars that traveled around an undulating track at a high rate of speed. The new ride was significantly larger than any of the other indoor rides. Installing the ride inside the building was a unique challenge that required six months of intricate work to put it into operation. With the Disco Star in place, Fun Zone now had something to appeal to everyone and had become an institution in this corner of Long Island.

Long Island's Fun Zone offers indoor and outdoor attractions.

MEDFORD

Boomers!

OPENED 1999

Family entertainment centers come in many shapes and sizes. Some are little more than large game arcades. At the other end of the spectrum are mini amusement parks complete with concession stands, games, and a broad complement of rides. One such place is Boomers!

In the late 1990s, family entertainment centers were quickly spreading throughout the country, and entrepreneurs were seeking to cash in. This included the Gentile family, who had already built Long Island's largest amusement park, Adventureland, and water park, Splish Splash. Seeing a family entertainment center as the next logical step in growing their business, they located a 9-acre site along the Long Island Expressway and signed a franchise agreement with the Bullwinkle's family entertainment center chain of California to theme their center after the well-known cartoon moose.

> **Boomers!**
> 655 Long Island Ave.
> Medford, NY 11763
> 631-475-1771
> www.boomersparks.com/
> parks/medford/

At the heart of the operation was a 16,000-square-foot building that housed an arcade, Bullwinkle's restaurant, a merry-go-round, and kiddie swing ride. In front of the building were an elaborate miniature golf course and bumper boat ride. The back of the property featured batting cages, a go-cart track, and seven family rides, including a train that circled the property, a second merry-go-round, and a 15-foot-tall, 300-foot-long roller coaster.

The new facility was a huge hit when it opened in May 1999, so much so that it soon attracted the attention of Palace Entertainment, a company that had been formed a year earlier to build a national chain of

 **VISITING**

Boomers! is located just off Exit 64 of I-495 (Long Island Expressway), on the South Service Road. The park features about eleven rides, along with a miniature golf course, batting cages, and restaurant. Admission is free. Attractions are available on a pay-as-you-go basis, with tickets costing about $2.50 for kiddie and family rides and $5 for go-carts and bumper boats. Pay-one-price admission is available on weekdays for about $25, less for kiddie rides only.

Boomers! sprang out of the family entertainment center boom of the 1990s.

family entertainment centers by purchasing other operations. By the end of the summer, it had made an agreement to purchase Bullwinkle's, along with the Gentiles' Splish Splash water park.

As part of its plan to build a national chain, Palace Entertainment changed the name of Bullwinkle's, along with most of their other family entertainment centers, to Boomers! in 2002. By then it had become a favorite Long Island destination.

OLCOTT BEACH

NEW YORK

Olcott Beach Carousel Park
OPENED 2003

As far back as 1858, the town of Olcott Beach, on the southern shore of Lake Ontario, was a popular summer resort in western New York. In 1875, the railroad linked the town to larger cities, and by 1879, steamboat service was provided to Canada, Buffalo, and Rochester, followed by trolley service in 1900. In 1902, the Olcott Beach Hotel opened along the lake, providing first-class lodging. Amusements were also developed to cater to the throngs, anchored by Luna Amusement Park, which opened in 1898, followed by the Rialto in 1902.

Unfortunately, Olcott Beach went into a decline following World War I. Luna Amusement Park closed in 1926, the Rialto was demolished in 1928, and the hotel met the wrecker's ball in 1937, when railroad service ceased. The town enjoyed resurgence in the 1940s, with two new amusement parks—New Rialto Park and Olcott Amusement Park—opening in 1940 and 1942 to replace the other long-departed amusement parks.

> **Olcott Beach Carousel Park**
> P.O. Box 308
> Olcott, NY 14126
> 716-778-7066

But the resort once again went into a decline as interstate highways drew vacationers elsewhere. Olcott Amusement Park slowly removed rides and closed for good in 1986, and New Rialto Park faded away in 1992. The small village was struggling, with many of the storefronts along Main Street standing vacant and Olcott Amusement Park's abandoned carousel and bumper car buildings deteriorating.

In 2001, Project Pride was launched by the Eastern Niagara Chamber of Commerce, an initiative intended to revitalize the region's economy. It identified Olcott Amusement Park's abandoned carousel building, which was now owned by the city, as a potential anchor to revitalize the depressed community. A nonprofit corporation called Olcott Beach Carousel Park was formed to take on the project. It developed a multiyear plan that involved restoring the building and acquiring a carousel to place inside it, developing a small amusement park around it with classic kiddie rides, purchasing a band organ, and erecting an amphitheater to present vintage movies and plays.

Fund-raising began in 2001, and within a few months, more than $3,000 had been amassed to restore the carousel building. The group also placed an ad in *Merry-Go-Roundup*, a carousel publication, looking for pictures of the area's old amusement parks. As restoration work started on the carousel building in 2002, Jack Campbell of Culver, Indiana, came across the ad. Though he did not have any photos, he did own

 **VISITING**

OLCOTT BEACH

Olcott Beach Carousel Park is located on Main Street in the heart of Olcott Beach, just north of the intersection of NY Route 18 and NY Route 78. The park features five rides. A separately-owned museum, gift shop, and refreshment stand are adjacent. It is open weekends from Memorial Day through June, Thursday through Sunday from the last weekend in June through Labor Day, and weekends in September. Admission to the park is free, and all rides are just 25 cents each.

Olcott Carousel Park anchors the village's business district.

a kiddie car ride that had operated at New Rialto Park until 1986. He also owned three other kiddie rides—the Sky Fighter, Rocket, and a ride with wooden boats he had built by hand. But most important, he had an antique carousel that he had restored just a few years earlier. It had been manufactured in 1928 by the Herschell Spillman Company of nearby North Tonowanda, New York, and was purchased by Campbell from Buck Lake Ranch in Angola, Indiana, when it closed in 1978.

Campbell offered all the rides, along with a 1934 Wurlitzer band organ, to Olcott, and fund-raising kicked into high gear. Community members stepped forward to "adopt" the twenty-three horses for prices ranging from $1,000 to $2,500 each, brick pavers were sold, and sponsorships were solicited for the kiddie rides. The response was so positive that the carousel was placed into operation Memorial Day weekend 2003 and gave 17,500 rides before the season ended on Labor Day.

Two new pavilions were erected on either side of the carousel to provide covered places for the kiddie rides to operate, and all four opened in August 2004. The amphitheater was finished by 2005, completing the dream of reviving Olcott Beach.

Victorian Gardens
OPENED 2003

Central Park is the crown jewel of Manhattan. Set amid the towering sky-scrapers, the beautifully landscaped park offers an oasis from the hustle and bustle of the city. A stroll through the park can bring unexpected surprises, such as the famous Central Park Carousel, charming little buildings, statues, and amazing rock formations. In 2003, another surprise emerged: Victorian Gardens, a family amusement park nestled among the trees and tall buildings. The location of Victorian Gardens might be better known to people as the Wollman Ice Skating Rink. Managed by the Trump Organization, the rink has been one of Central Park's most popular wintertime destinations since 1950, attracting four thousand people a day. But during the summer, the rink had long sat idle.

> **Victorian Gardens**
> 830 Fifth Ave.
> New York City, NY 10021
> 212-982-2229
> info@vistoriangardensnyc.com
> www.vistoriangardensnyc.com

The city tried designating the site for other uses, such as roller blading, but the City Parks Department wanted to find a more family-oriented activity, given the rink's close proximity to the carousel and zoo. It issued a request for proposals, which attracted the attention of Zamperla, the world's leading manufacturer of family amusement rides. Zamperla suggested using the rink as an amusement park, which was just the kind of thing the city had in mind.

Zamperla formed a new company called Central Amusements International LLC to operate the amusement park and formalized a lease with the Trump Organization. Considering the amusement park's location, Central Amusements knew that it had to build a quality operation. As a result, each of the rides was custom built with its own Victorian touches.

 **VISITING**

Victorian Gardens is located in the southeastern corner of Central Park in the heart of Manhattan. The park features about ten rides, along with games and a concession stand. Many of Central Park's most popular attractions, including the carousel and zoo, are close by. General admission of less than $8 includes two ride tickets, with additional tickets available for $1 each. Pay-one-price admission is available on weekdays for about $12.

Victorian Gardens offers a striking contrast to the soaring skyscrapers of Manhattan.

The park's location presented some unique challenges. The rink's cooling system was located just an inch below the concrete surface and could not be penetrated, which necessitated specially built ride supports, fencing, and landscaping. In addition, an ice-skating rink is designed to hold water, not drain it, which meant that water had to be vacuumed up even after light rains.

Victorian Gardens opened in May 2003, with nine rides targeted at kids and their parents. Almost all the rides can be enjoyed by the entire family, including the Family Swinger, Crazy Bus, Samba Balloon, and Mini Mouse, the first roller coaster to operate in Manhattan since Fort George Park burned down in 1913.

Zamperla saw the park not only as a good business opportunity, but also as a way to show off its lineup of rides to potential customers. As a result, each season, some of the existing rides are swapped for Zamperla's latest offerings. In 2004, the Red Baron airplane ride and Jumpin' Star gave way to the Kite Flyer, Baja Buggy, and Aero Max, a large airplane ride that resembles the classic circle swings of old.

In just a few short years, Victorian Gardens has become another beloved Central Park institution.

Other Amusement Facilities

- *Adventure Racing and Family Fun Center*, Lake George Road (U.S. Route 9), Queensbury. Adult and kiddie go-carts, paintball range, and laser tag. 518-798-7860.

- *The Animal Farm Petting Zoo*, 291 Wading River Road, Manorville. Animal park with train ride and two kiddie rides. 631-878-1785. www.afpz.org.

- *Atlantis Marine World*, 431 Main Street, Riverhead. Marine life park with aquarium, sea lion show, observation tower, and boat rides. 631-208-9200. www.atlantismarineworld.com.

- *Bayville Amusement Park*, 8 Bayville Avenue, Bayville. Waterfront amusement park with bumper cars, a kiddie ride, outdoor play area with several inflatable attractions, miniature golf, and batting cages. 516-628-9000.

- *Calypso's Cove*, 3183 State Route 28, Old Forge. Adjacent to Enchanted Forest/Water Safari. Adult and kiddie go-carts, bumper boats, miniature golf, and batting cages. 315-369-6145. www.watersafari.com.

- *Cooperstown Fun Park*, State Route 28, Cooperstown. Go-carts, bumper boats, batting cages, and miniature golf. 607-547-2767. www.cooperstownfunpark.com.

- *Coney Island Batting Range and Go Cart City*, 3049 Stillwell Avenue, Brooklyn. Two go-cart tracks, bumper boats, miniature golf, and batting cages. 718-449-1200. www.coneyislandbattingrange.com.

- *Eagle Mills Cider Company*, Eagle Mills Road, Broadalbin. Train, kiddie play area, gem mine, cider mill, and petting zoo. 518-883-8700. www.eaglemillsfun.com.

- *Family Fun Park at Colonial Village*, 578 State Highway 11B, Potsdam. Go-carts, two kiddie rides, simulator, miniature golf, nature trail, and indoor fun center. 315-265-PARK (7275). www.colonialvillagefunpark.com.

- *The Fun House at New Roc City*, 33 LeCount Place, New Rochelle. Indoor park with six rides, including go-carts and a 185-foot-tall Space Shot tower ride on the roof, arcade, kiddie play area, and laser tag. 914-637-7575. www.newroccity.com.

- *The Fun Park*, 11233 East Corning Road, Corning. Bumper boats, miniature golf, kiddie play area, and arcade. 607-936-1888.

- *Fun Spot*, 1035 U.S. Route 9, Queensbury. Adult and kiddie go-carts, water slides, kids' water area, laser tag, and roller skating. 518-792-8989. www.lakegeorgefun.com.

- *Fun Station USA*, 40 Rocklyn Avenue, Lynbrook. Indoor family entertainment center with four rides, laser tag, and a kiddie play area. 516-599-7757.

- *Fun Station USA*, 3555 Victory Boulevard, Staten Island. Indoor family entertainment center with six rides, kiddie play area, laser tag, bowling, and indoor batting cages. 718-370-0077.

- *Funtime USA*, 2461 Knapp Street, Brooklyn. Multistory indoor entertainment center with four rides, kiddie play area, and large arcade. 718-368-0500. www.funtimeusa.net.

- *The Gravel Pit*, 5158 East Main Road, Batavia. Go-carts, bumper cars, miniature golf, paintball, and driving range. 585-343-4445. www.5a.com/gravelpit/.

- *Jeepers!*, 161 Washington Avenue Extension in Crossgate Commons, Albany. Indoor kiddie park with five rides, play area, and an arcade. 518-452-0103. www.jeepers.com.

- *Jeepers!*, Palisades Center Mall, 4662 Palisades Center Drive, West Nyack. Indoor kiddie park with five rides, play area, and an arcade. 845-353-5700. www.jeepers.com.

- *Jeto's Ballpark*, 180 Sawkill Road, Yorktown Heights. Go-carts, batting cages, and miniature golf. 845-331-2545. www.wdst.com/get/jetosballpark.

- *Junior Speedway*, 7399 State Route 32, Cairo. Adult and kiddie go-cart tracks, kiddie bumper boats, and miniature golf. 518-622-4050.

- *Magic Castle*, 273 Canada Street, Lake George. Indoor arcade with simulators, merry-go-round, and indoor miniature golf. 518-668-3777.

- *McCullough's Kiddie Park*, Bowery and West Twelfth Street, Brooklyn. Located in the heart of Coney Island, this park has a dozen rides. Phone number not listed.

- *Page's Kiddyland*, 7001 Packard Road, Niagara Falls. Five-ride kiddie park. Adjacent Page's Restaurant is renowned for its Whistle Pig hot dogs. 716-297-0131.

- *Roseland Waterpark*, 250 Eastern Boulevard, Canandaigua. Water park with six water slides, river ride, wave pool, and play area. 585-396-2000. www.roselandwaterpark.com.

- *Safari Amusement Park*, 855 Arthur Kill Road, Staten Island. Three rides, including go-carts and bumper cars, as well as batting cages and miniature golf. 718-984-4400.

- *Seneca Grand Prix Family Fun Center*, 2374 State Route 414, Watkins Glen. Two go-cart tracks, bumper boats, and miniature golf. 607-535-7981. www.sgpfun.com.

- *Splash Down Park*, 2200 U.S. Route 9, Fishkill. Water slides, bumper boats, and miniature golf. 914-896-5468.

- *Splish Splash Waterpark*, 2549 Splish Splash Drive, Riverhead. Largest water park in New York State, with nearly two dozen water slides, river ride, wave pool, play areas, and kiddie attractions. 631-727-3600. www.splishsplashlongisland.com.

- *Sports Connection*, P.O. Box 333, Washington Avenue Extension, Saugerties. Go-carts, batting cages, and miniature golf. 845-246-4501.

- *Sports Plus!*, 110 New Moriches Road, Lake Grove. Large indoor entertainment center with seven rides, including the Thriller roller coaster, kiddie play area, ice-skating rink, laser tag, and bowling alley. 631-737-2100. www.sportsplusny.com.

- *Supersonic Speedway*, State Route 145, Durham. Four rides, including go-carts, plus batting cages and miniature golf. 518-634-7200.

- *Thunder Island*, 21 Wilcox Road, Fulton. Water park, go-carts, miniature golf, and Ferris wheel. 315-598-8016. www.thunder-island.com.

- *Water Slide World*, U.S. Route 9 at L, Lake George. Water park with more than a dozen water slides, wave pool, river rides, and two kids' water areas. 518-668-4407. www.adirondack.net/tour/waterslideworld.

- *Wild West Ranch*, Bloody Pond Road at U.S. Route 9, Lake George. Old West themed attraction with horseback, pony, and stagecoach rides, plus petting zoo and Wild West show. 518-668-2121. www.wildwest ranch.com.

- *Zoom Flume Water Park*, Shacky Glen Road, East Durham. Water park with more than a dozen water slides, pool, and river ride. 518-239-4559. www.zoomflume.com.

INDEX OF MAJOR RIDES
IN OPERATION
IN NEW YORK

Roller Coasters
WOOD TRACK

Cyclone, Astroland, opened 1927.
Comet, The Great Escape & Splashwater Kingdom, opened 1994.
Silver Comet, Martin's Fantasy Island, opened 1999.
Dragon Coaster, Playland, opened 1929.
Kiddy Coaster, Playland, opened 1928.
Jack Rabbit, Seabreeze, opened 1920.
Predator, Six Flags Darien Lake, opened 1990.

STEEL TRACK

Hurricane, Adventureland, opened 1991.
Paul Bunyan Express, Adventureland, opened 2000.
Big Apple, Astroland, opened 1980s.
Roller Coaster, Boomers!, opened 1999.
Sea Serpent, Deno's Wonder Wheel Park, opened 1998.
Alpine Bobsleds, The Great Escape & Splashwater Kingdom,
    opened 1998.
Boomerang Coast to Coaster, The Great Escape & Splashwater
    Kingdom, opened 1997.
Canyon Blaster, The Great Escape & Splashwater Kingdom,
    opened 2003.
Nightmare at Crackaxle Canyon, The Great Escape & Splashwater
    Kingdom, opened 1999.

Road Runner Express, The Great Escape & Splashwater Kingdom, opened 2005.
Steamin' Demon, The Great Escape & Splashwater Kingdom, opened 1984.
Little Dipper, Hoffman's Playland, opened 1960.
Python Pit, Jeepers! (Albany), opened 1997.
Python Pit, Jeepers! (West Nyack), opened 1998.
Little Dipper, Magic Forest, opened 1985.
Crazy Mouse, Martin's Fantasy Island, opened 2005.
Dragon, McCullough's Kiddie Park, opening date not known.
Little Dipper, Midway Park, opened 1955.
Kiddie Coaster, Nellie Bly Amusement Park, opened 1967.
Crazy Mouse, Playland, opened 2003.
Family Flyer, Playland, opened 2001.
Super Flight, Playland, opened 2004.
Roller Coaster, Santa's Workshop, opened 2003.
Bear Trax, Seabreeze, opened 1997.
Bobsleds, Seabreeze, opened 1968.
Whirlwind, Seabreeze, opened 2004.
Boomerang Coast to Coaster, Six Flags Darien Lake, opened 1998.
Brain Teaser, Six Flags Darien Lake, opened 1981.
Mind Eraser, Six Flags Darien Lake, opened 1997.
Superman Ride of Steel, Six Flags Darien Lake, opened 1999.
Viper, Six Flags Darien Lake, opened 1982.
Thriller, Sports Plus, opened 2004.
Galaxi, Sylvan Beach Amusement Park, opened 1993.
Mini Mouse, Victorian Gardens, opened 2003.

Wooden Carousels

Only California has more wooden carousels in operation than New York State, which features more than two dozen. It is interesting to note that most of these treasures are not located at amusement parks, but at municipal parks and similar facilities. Broome County has the heaviest concentration of wooden carousels in the country, with six at municipal parks in Binghamton, Endicott, Endwell, and Johnson City. For a complete listing, visit the website of the National Carousel Association, www.nca-usa.org. Wooden carousels at amusement parks include the following:

Coney Island, Coney Island Carousel, manufactured by Mangels/Carmel (date unknown), installed 1932 (currently undergoing restoration).

Enchanted Forest/Water Safari, manufactured in 1920s by Herschell
   Spillman, installed 1972.
Olcott Carousel Park, manufactured in 1928 by Herschell Spillman,
   installed 2003.
Playland (Carousel), manufactured 1915 by Mangels/Carmel,
   installed 1928.
Playland (Derby Racer), manufactured 1928 by Prior and Church,
   installed 1928.
Seabreeze, manufactured in 1996 by Ed Roth using a Philadelphia
   Toboggan Company frame, installed 1996.

Dark Rides

1313 Cemetery Way, Adventureland, opened 1986.
Dante's Inferno, Astroland, opened 1971.
Ghost Hole, Coney Island, opened late 1990s.
Spook A Rama, Deno's Wonder Wheel Park, opened 1955.
Flying Witch, Playland, opened 1971.
Old Mill, Playland, opened 1929.
Zombie Castle, Playland, opened 1930s.
Laffland, Sylvan Beach Amusement Park, opened 1954.

Walk-Throughs and Fun Houses

Alice in Wonderland Walk Thru, The Great Escape & Splashwater
   Kingdom, opened 1965.
Jungleland Walk Thru, The Great Escape & Splashwater Kingdom,
   opened 1962.
Cinderella Walk Thru, Magic Forest, opened 1982.
Around the World in 80 Days Fun House, Nellie Bly Amusement Park,
   opened 1983.
Haunted Hotel, Nellie Bly Amusement Park, opened 1998.
Mirror Maze, Playland, opened 1928.

Log Flumes

Adventure Falls Flume, Adventureland, opened 2001.
Log Flume, Astroland, opened 1964.
Desperado Plunge, The Great Escape & Splashwater Kingdom,
   opened 1979.
Old Mill Scream, Martin's Fantasy Island, opened 1986.
Flume, Playland, opened 1994.
Log Flume, Seabreeze, opened 1984.

River Rapid Rides

Raging River, The Great Escape & Splashwater Kingdom, opened 1986.
Grizzly Run, Six Flags Darien Lake, opened 1989.

Splash-Water Rides

Playland Plunge, Playland, opened 2001.
Shipwreck Falls, Six Flags Darien Lake, opened 2002.

Giant Ferris Wheels

Wonder Wheel, Deno's Wonder Wheel Park, 150 feet tall, opened 1920.
Giant Wheel, The Great Escape & Splashwater Kingdom, 90 feet tall,
    opened 1989.
Giant Wheel, Martin's Fantasy Island, 90 feet tall, opened 1994.
Giant Wheel, Playland, 90 feet tall, opened 1992.
Giant Wheel, Six Flags Darien Lake, 165 feet tall, opened 1983.

BIBLIOGRAPHY

Books

Adams, Judith A. *The American Amusement Park Industry: A History of Technology and Thrills.* Boston: Twayne Publishers, 1991.

Anderson, Norman. *Ferris Wheels: An Illustrated History.* Bowling Green, OH: Bowling Green State University Popular Press, 1992.

Berman, John. *Coney Island.* New York: Barnes & Noble Publishing, 2003.

Cartmell, Robert. *The Incredible Scream Machine: A History of the Roller Coaster.* Fairview Park, OH: Amusement Park Books; Bowling Green, OH: Bowling Green State University Popular Press, 1987.

Denson, Charles. *Coney Island: Lost and Found.* Berkeley, CA: Ten Speed Press, 2002.

Fried, Frederick. *A Pictorial History of the Carousel.* Vestal, NY: Vestal Press, 1964.

Griffin, Al. *Step Right Up Folks.* Chicago: Henry Regnery Company, 1974.

Kasson, John F. *Amusing the Million.* New York: Hill & Wang, 1978.

Kyrazi, Gary. *The Great American Amusement Parks.* Secaucus, NJ: Citadel Press, 1976.

Mangels, William F. *The Outdoor Amusement Industry.* New York: Vantage Press, 1952.

Manns, William. *Painted Ponies: American Carousel Art.* Millwood, NY: Zon International Publishing Co., 1986.

McCullough, Edo. *Good Old Coney Island.* New York: Charles Scribner's Sons, 1957.

O'Brien, Tim. *The Amusement Park Guide.* Old Saybrook, CT: Globe Pequot Press, 2003.

Onorato, Michael P. *Another Time, Another World: Coney Island Memories.* Bellingham, WA: Pacific Rim Books, 1998, 2000.

———. *Steeplechase Park and the Decline of Coney Island: An Oral History.* Bellingham, WA: Pacific Rim Books, 2002.

———. *Steeplechase Park, Sale and Closure, 1965–1966: Diary and Papers of James J. Onorato.* Bellingham, WA: Pacific Rim Books, 1998.

Reed, James. *Amusement Park Guidebook.* New Holland, PA: Reed Publishing, 1978, 1982, 1987.

Register, Woody. *The Kid of Coney Island.* New York: Oxford University Press, 2001.

Schilling, Donovan. *Rochester's Lakeside Resorts and Amusement Parks.* Charleston, SC: Arcadia Publishing, 1999.

Snow, Richard. *Coney Island: A Postcard Journey to the City of Fire.* New York: Brightwaters Press, 1984.

Thompson, Donald. *The Golden Age of Onondaga Lake Resorts.* Fleischmanns, New York: Purple Mountain Press, 2002.

Magazines and Newspapers

Amusement Business. 1961 to 2004. Billboard Music Group, P.O. Box 24970, Nashville, TN 37203.

Amusement Park Journal. 1979 to 1987. Amusement Park Journal, P.O. Box 478, Jefferson, OH 44047-0478.

Carousel News and Trader. 1986 to present. Carousel News and Trader, 87 Park Ave. West, Suite 206, Mansfield, OH 44902-1657.

Merry-Go-Roundup. 1975 to present. National Carousel Association, 128 Courtshire Lane, Penfield, NY 14526.

NAPHA News. 1978 to present. National Amusement Park Historical Association, P.O. Box 83, Mount Prospect, IL 60056.

Roller Coaster. 1978 to present. American Coaster Enthusiasts, 3560 Annapolis Ln., Suite 107, Minneapolis, MN 55447.

Selections from 1908 *Street Railway Journal*, in *Traction Heritage* 9, no. 4 (July 1976), Indianapolis.

INDEX

ABOUT THE AUTHOR

JIM FUTRELL BECAME FASCINATED WITH THE AMUSEMENT PARK INDUSTRY at a young age as he followed the development of the Great America theme park near his boyhood home of Northbrook, Illinois. Since then, he has visited over 300 amusement parks around the world and ridden nearly 400 different roller coasters. Through the years, Jim has worked as a consultant for several Pennsylvania amusement parks (Kennywood in West Mifflin, Idlewild in Ligonier, Conneaut Lake Park in Conneaut Lake Park, and Bushkill Park in Easton). He has authored numerous

articles on the industry, is an avid collector of amusement park memorabilia, serves as historian for the National Amusement Park Historical Association, and is on the Hall of Fame Committees of the International Association of Amusement Parks and Attractions. His first book, *Amusement Parks of Pennsylvania*, was released in 2002, followed by *Amusement Parks of New Jersey* in 2004. Jim lives with his wife Marlowe and three sons, Jimmy, Christopher, and Matthew, near Pittsburgh, where he works as a market research director for a regional economic development agency.